GENTRIFICATION
AND THE ENTERPRISE CULTURE

Gentrification and the Enterprise Culture

Britain 1780–1980

F. M. L. THOMPSON

THE FORD LECTURES
DELIVERED IN THE UNIVERSITY OF OXFORD
IN HILARY TERM 1994

OXFORD

UNIVERSITY PRESS

OXFORD
UNIVERSITY PRESS

Great Clarendon Street, Oxford OX2 6DP

Oxford University Press is a department of the University of Oxford.
It furthers the University's objective of excellence in research, scholarship,
and education by publishing worldwide in

Oxford New York

Athens Auckland Bangkok Bogotá Buenos Aires Calcutta
Cape Town Chennai Dar es Salaam Delhi Florence Hong Kong Istanbul
Karachi Kuala Lumpur Madrid Melbourne Mexico City Mumbai
Nairobi Paris São Paulo Shanghai Singapore Taipei Tokyo Toronto Warsaw
with associated companies in Berlin Ibadan

Oxford is a registered trade mark of Oxford University Press
in the UK and in certain other countries

Published in the United States
by Oxford University Press Inc., New York

British Library Cataloguing in Publication Data

Data available

Library of Congress Cataloging in Publication Data

Data available

ISBN 0-19-924330-1

1 3 5 7 9 10 8 6 4 2

Typeset by J&L Composition Ltd, Filey, North Yorkshire
Printed in Great Britain
on acid-free paper by
T.J. International Ltd, Padstow, Cornwall

Preface

I was greatly honoured by the invitation from my old university to give the 1994 Ford Lectures, and after the customary delay I am pleased to offer this book as a more permanent version of those lectures. The subject grew out of a long-standing interest in the history of landownership and its social and economic significance, fired and nourished by my former supervisor, Sir John Habbakuk. This interest has been redefined and refocused in the most recent couple of decades by the attention which other scholars, most notably the late Professor Lawrence Stone, Professor Martin Wiener, and Professor Bill Rubinstein, have paid to the relationship between 'new men of wealth' and the acquisition of land, and also by the arrival of cultural history as a distinctive branch of social history, although perhaps those who associate cultural history with the linguistic turn and deconstructionism may not recognize its influence on this offering. It would have been perfectly possible to use the lectures simply as a core for a wide-ranging treatment of the social and economic history of landownership in Britain in the last couple of centuries. It seemed more sensible, however, and less of an imposition on the reader, to restrict myself to some direct reinforcement of the lectures by way of strengthening the evidence supporting the main arguments. Other important aspects of the wider story have been pursued in the works of my mentors, friends, and colleagues, as well as in my own earlier writings. Sir John Habakkuk, Professor David Spring and Eileen Spring, Professor Bill Rubinstein, Professor Richard Wilson, Professor John Beckett, Professor Martin Daunton, Professor David Cannadine, Professor Mordaunt Crook, Dr Tony Howe, and Dr Roland Quinault have all helped me, usually without being aware of it, through their ideas and publications, although none has any responsibility for what I have written.

F. M. L. T.

February 2000

Contents

List of Tables

Abbreviations

BPP	British Parliamentary Papers
DBB	*Dictionary of Business Biography*, 5 vols. (1984–6)
DL	Deputy Lieutenant
DNB	*Dictionary of National Biography*
EIC	East India Company
HC	House of Commons
HL	House of Lords
ICS	Indian Civil Service
IR	Inland Revenue
TRHS	*Royal Historical Society Transactions*
VCH	*Victoria History of the Counties of England*

I
Posing the Problem

A future Prime Minister once remarked: 'A desire for wealth is the source of all progress. Civilization comes from what men call greed. Let your mercenary tendencies be combined with honesty and they cannot take you astray.' Here is an affirmation of the creed of the profit motive, and the doctrine that unrestrained pursuit of self-interest is the way to promote the general welfare, which is as succinct and as modern as one could hope to find. Yet these are not the words of the Leader of the Opposition in the 1970s looking forward to unleashing greed in the 1980s as the engine of an economic miracle, but the views of a fictional future premier, Plantagenet Palliser, nephew of the Whig grandee, the Duke of Omnium, lecturing his cousin Jeffrey, an idle aristocratic youth, on the basics of self-help and political economy.[1] Nothing might seem farther apart and more antithetical than the gentry culture of duty, consideration, and fair play, and the counting-house culture of sanctified rapacity. Yet Anthony Trollope attributed this praise of the economic virtue of self-interest to the quintessentially aristocratic Palliser in the mid-1860s in a novel, *Can You Forgive Her?*, that is all about the traditional aristocratic culture and the traditional code of conduct of gentlemen and gentlewomen. The politics and economics of Palliser, who 'though a Radical in public life, would not for worlds transgress the social laws of his ancestors',[2] are indeed peripheral to the story of Alice Vavasor and her double jilting of the men to whom she became engaged, one a spendthrift scoundrel who rides supremely well, and the other a blameless minor country gentleman who never does anything reckless or interesting, while the manners, morals, and ethics of the gentry culture are central to it. Nevertheless, while a blue-blooded aristocrat who simultaneously upholds unquestioningly all the hierarchical, patriarchal, and patronizing values and prejudices of the old order, and champions economic individualism and the central tenets of the enterprise culture, may be no more than a figment of creative literature, his position is a faithful reflection of the dilemma facing all historians who attempt to explain the course of social and economic history in terms of the clash of cultures and the struggle for ascendancy between competing value systems.

[1] Anthony Trollope, *Can You Forgive Her?* (1864–5; Penguin edn., 1986), 283.
[2] Ibid., 815.

The dilemma arises not so much from the fact that group or class cultures so frequently turn out not to be confrontational and mutually exclusive, but to share much common ground, although that is certainly part of the problem. It arises more directly from the contrast between the ideal and the actual or historical, and from the inherently elusive and subjective character of the concept of a group culture. The ideal type of an aristocratic or a business culture can be constructed from selective observations of contemporary comment and behaviour, and then when it is found that the actual behaviour of particular individuals departed from this ideal or contradicted it, either it can be asserted that the deviants were unrepresentative and should be ignored, or it has to be admitted that the foundations of a cultural interpretation of developments are insecure and that its explanatory power is limited. Alternatively, when an empirical approach through the study of specific groups of aristocrats or businessmen shows that they did not conform to any single homogeneous group cultural model, then the theoretical possibility of a cultural interpretation is fatally damaged. Such was the fate of the ancestor of all cultural explanations, the Weber thesis of *The Protestant Ethic and the Spirit of Capitalism* and its English adaptation in R. H. Tawney's *Religion and the Rise of Capitalism*. The powerful simplicity of the theory that Protestantism, especially its Calvinist and Puritan manifestations, provided the doctrinal structure and motivation which liberated and legitimated the individual pursuit of profit, and hence capitalist enterprise, captivated generations of historians after it was first enunciated in the early 1900s; but it was not powerful enough to survive the onslaughts of doggedly persistent empirical research. No amount of intellectual ingenuity has ever succeeded in demonstrating a clear and necessary connection between a particular doctrinal position and capitalism rampant; and the counting of heads has finally banished the idea of any obvious relationship between entrepreneurial success and denominational persuasion among the early industrialists and businessmen of Britain's classic Industrial Revolution period. The most comprehensive analysis, by W. D. Rubinstein, concludes that 'entrepreneurial success has little or nothing to do with religion'.[3]

For Weber or Tawney, growing up in the late nineteenth century, it was natural to suppose that religious beliefs and religious teachings were dominant, even paramount, influences on human behaviour, since religion was

[3] W. D. Rubinstein, *Men of Property* (1981), 145–63, analyses the religion of all successful British businessmen born between 1720 and 1879. The earlier work by E. E. Hagen, *On the Theory of Social Change* (Homewood, Ill., 1962), apparently validated the Weber thesis by showing that a disproportionate percentage of entrepreneurs were Dissenters, but his definitions and methodology were questionable. The thesis was stated by Max Weber, *The Protestant Ethic and the Spirit of Capitalism* (first published in German, 1904–5; English tr., 1930), and in R. H. Tawney, *Religion and the Rise of Capitalism* (1922). For criticism of the Weber thesis see K. Samuelsson, *Religion and Economic Action* (English tr., New York, 1961) and R. W. Green (ed.), *Protestantism, Capitalism, and Social Science: The Weber Thesis Controversy* (Lexington, Mass., 1973).

central to the values and conventions of contemporary society and provided the measure of conformist and rebel alike. It may well be that the general Weber thesis today lies discarded or discredited because religion has been intellectually and morally marginalized, as well as because it has been exposed as too imprecise and too inaccurate. Some of the bricks from which the edifice was constructed remain intact, however, even if the building itself has collapsed. Features like the work ethic and the virtue of thrift were not imaginary: they existed, they shaped conduct, and they had moral qualities backed by religious sanctions. More generally, religion was a staple of discourse, private as well as public, in the eighteenth and nineteenth centuries (and of course in earlier centuries), and was the language in which the great issues of the day were expressed: from relations with the American colonies to resistance to Napoleon, from parliamentary reform to the proper basis of poor relief, from the imposition of income tax to the treatment of Ireland, the reference to Christian moral principles and precepts was never missing. One would expect, therefore, that merchants, manufacturers, or moneymen would tend to use a religious terminology when reflecting on their business activities, and to invoke a religious justification for their successes or failures.

Where the whole moral and mental environment was permeated with religion and the importance of salvation it is natural to assume, but difficult to prove, that most actions were religiously motivated. By the 1960s religion had patently long ceased to be the dominant active ingredient in the environment, and scholars looked for alternative, secular, vocabularies and sets of concepts which could more satisfactorily describe and explain the motivations of entrepreneurs. In an environment now comparably dominated by sex and the importance of gratification it would be easy to assume, and hard to prove, that most actions are sexually motivated. Historians have, of course, taken to sex with marked enthusiasm, but more with the aim of showing that there is a history of sex than with any intention of producing a general theory linking economic performance to sexuality and changing attitudes to it. Lawrence Stone, for example, explicitly excludes any connection between his long swings in attitudes to sex and economic factors.[4] This periodization, positing a time of toleration towards sexual behaviour until the late sixteenth century, a phase of repression from 1570 to 1670, followed by a time of permissiveness verging on licence from 1670 to 1810, a new wave of repression getting under way from 1770 and reaching a mid-Victorian peak, and finally renewed permissiveness gathering weakness (or strength) from 1870 onwards, could, with a bit of juggling with the dates, be made to fit long swings in economic performance, although whether permissiveness accompanied vigorous economic growth or prolonged economic

---

[4] Lawrence Stone, *The Family, Sex, and Marriage* (Pelican edn., 1979), 339.

decline would appear to be a matter of choice, while both economic stagnation and unparalleled economic expansion have attracted stern sexual repression. Arthur Marwick, on the other hand, has devoted a whole chapter to 'Beauty and the Growth of Entrepreneurial Society, c.1800–c.1905', but that is about the effects of economic change on ideas of beauty, sex appeal, and the 'beauty industry' of magazines, manuals, and cosmetics, and does not examine the effects of beauty on entrepreneurial performance or on economic growth.[5]

Psycho-history might have filled the gap left by the absence of any articulated sexual interpretation of economic development, insofar as its psychological analysis is Freudian or neo-Freudian, but it has gone nowhere fast, chiefly because its reading of what meagre scraps of usable evidence there are is widely perceived to be inherently subjective and predetermined. Marxist historians, who never believed in the independent character of a religious variable, regarding religious beliefs and structures as part of the social superstructure determined by the prevailing mode of production, and who have made few pronouncements about sex, had for decades a secular terminology and a powerful theory ready to hand to explain the whole course of human history. Dialectical materialism, however, while good at doing what it was designed to do, namely chart the collisions and convergences of great impersonal forces and their consequences for economic and social relations, was awkward and unconvincing in handling individuals. The individual, in straight Marxist analysis, was no more than an agent thrown up by the economic and social forces that had produced him or her, and hence could be of only secondary importance in determining the course of events. The best that could be done with the question of entrepreneurs and economic growth, therefore, was to take as given the existence of a pool of potential entrepreneurs, from which some responded successfully to new opportunities for making profits created by war and the conquest of markets (the beggar-my-neighbour theory of initial growth), and to a lesser extent by the expanding prosperity of existing export and domestic markets. Any particular entrepreneurs, as individuals, were in such a scheme dispensable and virtually irrelevant, since the existence of an adequate reserve army of essentially similar individuals was simply taken for granted. In this view it was indeed flesh and blood businessmen who revolutionized methods of production in the Industrial Revolution, but they acted as impersonal factors, instruments of destiny responding to conditions in the markets, whose motives of profit-seeking were so obvious and so universally felt as to require no special notice.[6]

[5] Arthur Marwick, *Beauty in History* (1988), 182–222.
[6] This is a simplified, but essentially faithful, version of the explanation of the origins of industrialization given in such a standard account as E. J. Hobsbawm, *Industry and Empire* (1968), 26–38.

This notion that no individual is indispensable, that it would not have made much difference if Richard Arkwright or Matthew Boulton had never existed, because some unknown near-clone was waiting in the wings of history to take their places, has proved congenial to historians of many different persuasions. It has provided an escape route from thinking of economic history as the product of a handful of key men and women, a conclusion long dreaded as leading into the intellectual cul-de-sac of biography, where lurks the 'Cleopatra's nose' theory of history. It has also freed historians to concentrate on the apparently more objective task of investigating and explaining the preconditions of economic growth in terms of markets, the supply of capital and labour, and the availability of technology, without the need to incorporate the awkward imponderables of unusual or extraordinary human talents into their theories.[7] More recently, the most nimble quantifiers have constructed and reconstructed sets of not very reliable figures to project the national accounts back into the seventeenth century, on the strength of which it has been decided that in the long run there have never been any specially sharp upturns or downturns in rates of economic growth, that is of national income per capita, thus at a stroke smoothing the Industrial Revolution out of existence and abolishing any need for either an entrepreneurial explanation of growth spurts or an explanation of entrepreneurs.[8]

Those who have been less impressed by the aggregative analysis of the econometric historians, however, have been reluctant to accept either the depersonalization of economic history or the disappearance of the Industrial Revolution as its most momentous set of changes, and have persisted in regarding the people who carried out those changes as central to the action and its interpretation. The result has been that the entrepreneur has continued to lurk in the wings of history, and periodically to return to centre stage. He (and, occasionally, she) consequently remains an indistinctly defined actor in the economic performance. In the seventeenth century the English cast called for an 'undertaker' to devise, contrive, promote, launch, and manage a business undertaking or enterprise. By the end of the eighteenth century an 'undertaker' was becoming confined to disposing of the dead, and the French 'entrepreneur' was increasingly used to denote the business variety. Etymology, however, is an uncertain guide to definition, and the entrepreneur remains somewhat hazily and elusively defined in the economic and business vocabulary as some kind of innovator, profit-seeker, and risk-taker who in some measure is more than just a routine manager of an

---

[7] For a recent, and sharply critical, discussion of this position see P. K. O'Brien, 'Entrepreneurs in Economics, History and Psychology', in Paul Klep and Eddy Van Cauwenberghe (eds.), *Entrepreneurship and the Transformation of the Economy (10th–20th Centuries)* (Leuven, 1994), 83–9.

[8] For example, N. F. R. Crafts, *British Economic Growth during the Industrial Revolution* (Oxford, 1985), esp. pp. 81–7, advances the gradualist view of economic change over the period 1760–1860.

established business, a definition that embraces an extremely wide spectrum of businessmen (and women) from robber barons to highly respectable and conservative managing directors, and at times implies that 'businessman' and 'entrepreneur' are interchangeable terms.

The entrepreneur has been relegated to a minor place in the action by technical economic historians, who explain significant developments in terms of factor endowments and growth rates over which businessmen had no control, but has been accorded a key role by business historians and social historians, who insist that the kind of businessmen performing in different periods and in different countries had profound effects on the pace and direction of innovation and growth, and hence on the whole structure of society. The literature of business history is replete with accounts of the achievements, and sometimes the shortcomings, of individual entrepreneurs in creating whole new industries and finding needs and desires which were previously unknown and unsuspected by the consumers, and many business historians are in effect engaged in writing modern and methodologically sophisticated versions of Smiles's *Industrial Biography*. This kind of history is very good at telling us what individual entrepreneurs have done, and how they did it, but is less informative or forthcoming in explaining why they did it or, indeed, what made them into entrepreneurs in the first place. The best that a leading business historian can do when reflecting on 'Businessmen and their motives' is to conclude of the giants who founded modern British businesses—Lever of Sunlight soap, Robert Barlow of Metal Box, Julius Drewe of Home & Colonial Stores and Castle Drogo, Alfred Mond of ICI, James Weir of Clydeside engineering, Eric Bowater of paper—that they were autocrats, in love with their businesses, pursuing power and control and not profit and riches simply for their own sake. 'Every great man', one of Bowater's successors is quoted as saying, 'wants to own either a newspaper or a shipping line', adult toys for tycoons.[9] Theorizing about what makes entrepreneurs tick has, indeed, been largely left to the social or cultural historians, who have illuminated the subject with paradoxical effect.

---

[9] W. J. Reader, 'Businessmen and their Motives', in D. C. Coleman and Peter Mathias (eds.), *Enterprise and History* (Cambridge, 1984), 42–51, quot. on p. 48. The introduction to R. H. Campbell and R. G. Wilson, (eds.), *Entrepreneurship in Britain, 1750–1939* (1975), 1–31, gives a good summary of the literature. P. L. Payne's chapter, 'Industrial Entrepreneurship and Management in Great Britain', in Peter Mathias and M. M. Postan, (eds.), *The Cambridge Economic History of Europe*, vii, *The Industrial Economies: Capital, Labour, and Enterprise*, Part I (Cambridge, 1978), 180–230, is a masterful survey of the state of knowledge for the whole period 1760–1970, while the same author's *British Entrepreneurship in the Nineteenth Century* (1982) covers that century in greater depth. Alfred D. Chandler, Jr., 'Managerial Enterprise and the Entrepreneurial Function', in Klep and Van Cauwenberghe (eds.), *Entrepreneurship*, 541–52, provides a suggestive essay on the post-1945 eclipse of the individual by the corporate manager as the effective entrepreneur in multinational firms.

The explanations on offer fall broadly into two camps, depending on whether attention is focused on the period of Britain's advance to industrial and commercial pre-eminence, or on the period of Britain's supposed economic decline since the 1870s. In the first period, it is argued, entrepreneurs were spurred on to their unremitting efforts by the desire to emulate the style and status of the aristocratic-gentry elite, an ambition which required first the accumulation of considerable wealth and then the acquisition of suitable possessions and of the manners appropriate for achieving social recognition. Harold Perkin is the leading exponent of this thesis, observing that 'the limitless pursuit of wealth for its own sake is a rare phenomenon', and maintaining that the ambition of founding a family which would become part of the country's ruling elite was the mainspring of entrepreneurial acquisitiveness. Adam Smith supports this view, asking: 'To what purpose is all the toil and bustle of the world? . . . It is our vanity which urges us on. . . . It is not wealth that men desire, but the consideration and good opinion that wait upon riches.' 'The pursuit of wealth *was* the pursuit of social status, not merely for oneself but for one's family', Perkin concludes.[10] In the second period, however, admiration of the dominant aristocratic-gentry culture and the adoption of gentlemanly values and attributes are said to have had pernicious effects on the virility and competence of businessmen, producing generations of flabby and lacklustre entrepreneurship which have the major responsibility for Britain's long slide into the second division. Martin Wiener is the best-known advocate of this view, arguing, with a fluency which many politicians and civil servants found convincing, that the gentrification of the industrialist was at the root of Britain's economic decline. From the middle years of the nineteenth century, he said, 'Businessmen increasingly shunned the role of industrial entrepreneur for the more socially rewarding role of gentleman (landed, if possible). The upshot was a dampening of industrial energies, the most striking single consequence of the gentrification of the English middle class.'[11] Here is the nub of the problem to be explored and, perhaps, solved. A gentry culture which in one phase is claimed as the hero of expansion and in the next as the villain of stagnation and contraction; and a relationship of businessmen to gentlemanly values which veers from being stimulating and productive to being stultifying and destructive.

There are as many possible ways of resolving this paradox as there are of skinning a cat. Either the gentry-emulation or the gentry-debilitation hypotheses could be mistaken, mis-specified, or misapplied. The gentry culture may not have remained constant over time. Indeed, it would be surprising if it had

[10] Harold Perkin, *The Origins of Modern English Society, 1780–1880* (1969), 83, 85.
[11] Martin Wiener, *English Culture and the Decline of the Industrial Spirit, 1850–1980* (Cambridge, 1981), 97.

not changed its spots and recast its values under the influences of evangeli-calism, moral reform, and, somewhat later, muscular Christianity; and it is conceivable that any such changes in the content of gentry culture might have converted a stimulant for businessmen into a tranquillizer. Similarly, businessmen were not some impersonal factor of production, predictably responding to signals transmitted from the marketplace, and they might as well have held different and changing attitudes to gentlemanly values as they did to risks and profits. These might not only change over time as economic opportunities and social conventions altered, but also might change with the life cycle, for a businessman on the make did not necessarily have the same aims and ambitions as a businessman who had arrived. That is but a short step away from the intriguing possibility that there is no such thing as an enterprise culture, and never has been, either in the narrow sense of a set of values, habits, assumptions, and aspirations held in common by most businessmen, or in the wider sense of a general social, political, and insti-tutional environment particularly conducive to business enterprise. But before allowing the paradox of a gentry culture—if indeed there was such a thing—which could produce entirely contrary effects to vanish into a quag-mire of multiple varieties of businessmen and enterprise cultures, it is nec-essary to look at the evidence of how different types of aristocrat, gentry, professional men, and businessmen have behaved in the last two hundred years, and of how they have both shaped and been shaped by the great insti-tutions of church and state, of property and education. This exercise will clear the ground for an approach to the possible cultural explanations of the nation's changing economic fortunes which may be more securely based on the evidence of what happened than earlier interpretations with their ten-dency to mistake opinion for fact.

The source of political economy is a reasonable starting point. Adam Smith certainly took it for granted that there was a clear distinction between the economic behaviour of the landed gentry and that of the business com-munity which was so patent that it scarcely required any demonstration. 'A merchant', he remarked, 'is accustomed to employ his money chiefly in prof-itable projects, whereas a mere country gentleman is accustomed to employ it chiefly in expense. The one often sees his money go from him and return to him again with a profit; the other, when once he parts with it, very sel-dom expects to see any more of it.'[12] The implication that landowners were interested in money and income solely in order to support their immediate gratification and to sustain their consumption will be taken up later.[13] The immediate point is that just as the purpose of all production is consump-tion, so the object of making profits is also consumption, albeit con-

---

[12] Adam Smith, *The Wealth of Nations* (Everyman edn., 1947), Bk. III, ch. 4, p. 362.
[13] Notably in ch. 2.

sumption deferred. For it was in the same passage that Adam Smith made the well-known statement that 'merchants are commonly ambitious of becoming country gentlemen,' thus linking the pursuit of profit firmly to one specific kind of future expenditure, the purchase of a country estate. He was simply repeating, and confirming, the conventional wisdom that fortunes made in trade tended to end up in land, an observation about English society with a tradition running from the sixteenth century or earlier, through Daniel Defoe, and on to Richard Cobden and John Bright. It is this tradition which formed the foundation both of Harold Perkin's theory of emulation of the gentry as the motive power of industrialization, and of the monumental criticism of what is termed the 'myth' of the open elite by Lawrence Stone and his wife. Before considering the credentials of those positions some enquiry into what, precisely, the exponents of the conventional wisdom were asserting might be helpful.

On the face of it Adam Smith claimed no more than that it was normal for wealthy merchants to harbour the ambition of becoming country gentlemen. The existence of the ambition was inferred from the evidence of those who had succeeded in fulfilling it, not from any presumed direct knowledge of the motives and aspirations of merchants in general; and in the context in the *Wealth of Nations* the evidence of those who had succeeded was that of mercantile landowners who proved themselves to be greater agricultural improvers than long-established squires. His statement can, however, be read as referring to intentions, only some of which were fully implemented, rather than as an assertion that merchants did commonly succeed in setting themselves up as country gentlemen. It is perhaps fanciful to pretend to knowledge of the motives of a large body of men on the basis of the observed behaviour of a few, and it is certainly unverifiable. All the same, most of Adam Smith's other *obiter dicta* have generally been readily accepted, on the grounds that he had considerable knowledge and understanding of contemporary business practices. In particular, some of his other observations about merchants, that they try to establish monopolies, or that they habitually conspire together to rig prices and markets, have enjoyed wide currency even though they, too, were unverifiable statements.[14]

Half a century earlier Daniel Defoe seems to have been in no doubt that it was a matter of fact that wealthy merchants and tradesmen swarmed out into the country, bought estates, and made themselves into gentlemen. 'The rising tradesman swells into the gentry, and the declining gentry sinks into trade,' he proclaimed; and, warming to his theme, he elaborated 'the declining gentry in the ebb of their fortunes frequently push their sons into trade and they . . . often restore the fortunes of their families. Thus tradesmen

---

[14] Smith, *Wealth of Nations*, Bk. I, ch. 10, p. 117, Bk. IV, ch. 2, p. 406, Bk. IV, ch. 3, p. 436.

become gentlemen, by gentlemen becoming tradesmen.'[15] Some of the specific observations on which he based these generalizations, however, suggest that he was in two minds about their meaning. His examples of 'very considerable estates purchased, and now enjoyed by citizens of London, merchants and tradesmen' are restricted to the home counties, particularly to Essex and Surrey. That was understandable, since the overwhelming concentration of wealthy merchants was to be found in London, and when any of them sought country retreats or gentry status they had for centuries looked chiefly in the immediate environs. It should be remarked, however, that although he was eloquent about the wealth of the trade, and the merchants, of Norwich, Bristol, and above all the fast-growing Liverpool—'one of the wonders of Britain . . . there is no town in England, London excepted, that can equal Liverpoole for the fineness of the streets, and the beauty of the buildings'—Defoe made no claim that these provincial merchants gentrified themselves with estates. Indeed, one of his pertinent comments on the attractions of Yarmouth refers to 'some merchants' houses, which look like little palaces rather than the dwelling houses of private men', implying that they preferred to live in style as urban, mercantile grandees rather than move out into the country.[16]

Moreover, even on the narrower canvas of the home counties there is room for more than one view about what Defoe was claiming for the motives and ambitions of rich merchants. Certainly, there were on the one hand clear statements about the 'considerable estates purchased' by new men, and half a dozen were named in Essex and another half dozen in Surrey. On the other hand, there were references to the much more numerous, but anonymous, group of wealthy merchants who kept one foot in the city and possibly no more than a toe in the country, where they kept a fine house with a large garden or tiny park for use as a summer retreat. In Essex, in villages including Stratford, Walthamstow, West Ham, and Woodford, for example, Defoe spoke of hundreds of newly built 'handsome large houses . . . chiefly for the habitations of the richest citizens, such as either are able to keep two houses, one in the country and one in the city; or for such citizens as being rich, and having left off trade, live altogether in these neighbouring villages, for the pleasure and health of the latter part of their days.'[17] When he claimed that 'the ten miles from Guildford to Leatherhead make one continued line of gentlemen's houses . . . their parks or gardens almost touching one another', the same type of country residence was probably in mind, as it was in describing the neighbourhood of Carshalton as

---

[15] Daniel Defoe, *A Plan of the English Commerce* (1728), quoted in Lawrence Stone and Jeanne C. Fawtier Stone, *An Open Elite? England, 1540–1880* (Oxford, 1984), 19–20.

[16] Daniel Defoe, *A Tour through the Whole Island of Great Britain* [1724–6] (Penguin edn., 1971), 57 (Essex), 86–9 (Norwich and Yarmouth), 361–3 (Bristol), 540–3 (Liverpool), 544–6 (Manchester).   [17] Ibid., 48.

'being, as it were, crowded with fine houses of the citizens of London; some of which are built with such profusion of expense, that they look rather like seats of the nobility, than the country houses of citizens and merchants.'[18] Rounding off his account of Surrey with an evocation of the beauties of Clapham, Peckham, and Camberwell, Defoe offered this conclusion on these rural villas of the new rich:

These fine houses . . . are not, at least very few of them, the mansion houses of families, the ancient residences of ancestors, the capital messuages of the estates; nor have the rich possessors any lands to a considerable value about them; but these are all houses of retreat . . . gentlemen's mere summer-houses, or citizen's country-houses; whither they retire from the hurries of business, and from getting money, to draw their breath in a clear air, and to divert themselves and families in the hot weather; and they that are shut up, and as it were stripped of their inhabitants in the winter, who return to smoke and dirt, sin and seacoal . . . in the busy city; so that in short all this . . . glorious show of wealth and plenty, is really a view of the luxuriant age which we live in, and of the over-flowing riches of the citizens, who in their abundance make these gay excursions, and live thus deliciously all the summer, retiring within themselves in the winter, the better to lay up for the next summer's expense.[19]

It thus appears that Defoe held two distinct, although connected, views about the relationship of the new rich of London to the countryside. Some purchased considerable landed estates, acquired country seats, and in their own persons or those of their successors were accepted into the usual offices and dignities of county society and into the social position of landed gentry. How large this group was was not specified, but it was clearly envisaged as a minority of the new wealthy, and as a minority of that section of the new wealthy which had out-of-town residences of any sort. This second group, which acquired houses in the country but no surrounding estates to support them, was depicted as decidedly more numerous than the first. Whether this group was to be classified as semi-gentrified, since in building style at least there was said to be a conscious attempt to ape the nobility and gentry, or as an independent subspecies of the merchant class with no links even to the coat-tails of the landed gentry, was left unclear. What is clear is that the rich merchant who may have possessed no more than a 'mere summer-house' in the country felt himself to be socially as well as materially superior to those who did not own such a plaything. The class with second homes or holiday houses has been a conspicuous feature of wealthy society in every century. Its trademark may in some sense have been derived from the country houses of the aristocracy and gentry, but that did not necessarily make the desire to possess a summer house into evidence of a desire to imitate or emulate the gentry. It could equally well be taken as evidence of

[18] Ibid., 159, 167.   [19] Ibid., 177.

the ability of rich citizens to borrow agreeable and attractive features from other classes and incorporate them into their own culture, just as aristocratic culture itself incorporated borrowings from courtly conventions or foreign customs.

Nearly 150 years later Cobden gained his place alongside Defoe and Adam Smith in the canon of the conventional wisdom about the nouveaux riches with his trenchant comments on the fawning, ingratiating, and imitative habits of the great industrialists of his day. 'See how every successful trader buys an estate, and tries to perpetuate his name in connexion with "that ilk" by creating an eldest son', he wrote to John Bright in 1851.[20] Taken out of context this was an unqualified assertion that all, or nearly all, wealthy men did not merely aspire to become country landowners, but did in fact do so; although since Cobden did not define what he understood by 'success' nor, by derivation, how much amounted to sufficiently great wealth for the purpose, the truth or falsehood of his statement would be hard to demonstrate, and semantically it could be reduced to the tautology that only those traders who bought landed estate were successful. In the context of the actual letter to Bright, however, the opinion looks less like a statement of purported fact than an exaggerated expression of exasperation at what seemed to him the otherwise inexplicable failure of the mass of influential mercantile opinion to get excited about one of his pet causes, the abolition of primogeniture. Cobden, the epitome of the old-fashioned seventeenth- and eighteenth-century anti-aristocratic radical as well as the most modern practical political economist, crusaded for the abolition of privilege and the aristocratic monopoly in all their legal and political entrenchments quite as keenly as he fought for free trade, and indeed regarded these as but different elements of an integrated, coherent, institutional reform programme in which it had just happened to be expedient to concentrate on the corn laws as a single issue in the 1840s. He found it hard to accept that merchants and manufacturers who had followed him enthusiastically and generously in the campaigns of the Anti-Corn Law League had become lukewarm, indifferent, or hostile in the 1850s, so he in effect labelled them traitors to their class and explained their apostasy by reference to their supposed gentrification. The curiosity that this reductionist reasoning would have required all those turncoat manufacturers who supported the League in the 1840s but opposed land law reform in the 1850s to have indulged in a huge estate-purchasing spree between 1846 and 1851, was a little difficulty which he did not need to face in his private correspondence.

Cobden's friend and ally, John Bright, had a different analysis of the same political situation. He admitted the snobbishness and fawning attitude of many of the richest of the middle class towards the aristocracy, remarking

---

[20] J. Morley, *The Life of Richard Cobden* (1920 edn.), 561, Cobden to Bright, 1 Oct. 1851.

on the Whiggish element among the Manchester free trade liberals which had preferred 'a son or relation of a peer' as a parliamentary candidate in 1847, but ascribed their radical unreliability to their fundamental social conservatism and fear of a militant Chartist-style working class. For him the remedy for sagging radical fortunes in the 1850s was to cultivate the intelligent workingmen and mobilize them in a movement for far-reaching parliamentary and institutional reform; accordingly, nothing is heard from Bright about any wholesale gentrification as an explanation for backsliding by the manufacturers.[21] In his more reflective moods Cobden, indeed, pretty much agreed with Bright's analysis. After they had both lost their seats in Parliament in the 1857 election Cobden explained Bright's rejection by Manchester in terms of the 'aristocratic snobbery' of the great capitalists of the cotton industry, who themselves 'form an aristocracy'. 'The great capitalist class', he went on, 'formed an excellent basis for the Anti-Corn Law movement, for they had inexhaustible purses, which they opened freely in a contest where not only their pecuniary interests but their pride as an order was at stake', but because of 'the great and impassable gulf [which] separates the workman from his employer' in the cotton towns this class would never be in favour of a democratic political movement.[22] There is a hint here of reprehensible deference to the landed aristocracy, but the emphasis was on tension between the great manufacturers and their workers, and on their self-esteem as an independent social estate, not on their hankering after landed possessions or desiring to join the ranks of the class enemy.

Towards the end of his life Cobden expressed his frustration at having achieved so little of the programme for the radical dismemberment of the aristocratic monopoly in church and state at which he had aimed, and at the failure of those in the manufacturing and commercial classes whom he regarded as natural supporters to fight the good fight, in perhaps the most-quoted and most colourful phrases of the gentrification canon. 'We have the spirit of feudalism rife and rampant in the midst of the antagonistic development of the age of Watt, Arkwright, and Stephenson,' he wrote in 1863.

Nay, feudalism is every day more and more in the ascendant in political and social life. So great is its power and prestige that it draws to it the support and homage even of those who are the natural leaders of the newer and better civilization. Manufacturers and merchants as a rule seem only to desire riches that they may be enabled to prostrate themselves at the feet of feudalism.[23]

This showed his utter disillusionment with his youthful hopes of 1838, that the manufacturers would assert themselves, realize their power, and 'become the De Medicis, and Fuggers, and De Witts of England, instead of

[21] G. M. Trevelyan, *The Life of John Bright* (1913), 180, 197 (replying to Cobden's 1 Oct. 1851 letter).   [22] Morley, *Cobden*, 663 (Cobden to Parkes, 9 Aug. 1857).
[23] Ibid., 945–6 (Cobden to Hargreaves, 10 Apr. 1863).

glorying in being the toadies of a clodpole aristocracy', and it echoed his
middle-aged view that 'we are a servile, aristocracy-loving, lord-ridden people, who regard the land with as much reverence as we still do the peerage
and baronetage.'[24] But the 1863 outburst should be read in conjunction with
his continued faith in the manufacturers, or at least some considerable section of them, as the standard-bearers of anti-aristocratic reform, which he
had reaffirmed only the previous year, in 1862. 'I wish we could inspire the
mercantile manufacturing community with a little more self-respect', he
had written. 'With many faults and shortcomings, our mercantile and manufacturing classes . . . are after all the only power in the State possessed of
wealth and political influence sufficient to counteract in some degree the
feudal governing class of this country. . . . It is true they are often timid and
servile in their conduct towards the aristocracy, and we must wink at their
weaknesses'.[25] Thus in this version the mercantile and manufacturing
classes, provided some means could be found for steeling their resolve, were
still thought to be more likely to bring about the end of the domination of
the feudal governing class than to seek to join it.

This glance at the pronouncements of some of the more prominent exponents of the conventional wisdom on the ambitions and behaviour of the
new wealthy suggests, unsurprisingly, that social climbing was a very common aspiration, but beyond that it reveals, less expectedly, agreement only
that the form which that climbing took was varied and uncertain. Most
commonly, the new wealthy were perceived as being deferential, even obse-
quious, towards the established social and political elites, anxious to please
them and reluctant to offend or challenge them: in other words, they were
seen as lacking in cultural self-confidence, and as accepting a position of
moral and social inferiority. This was a perception of the new wealthy as
subservient, but not necessarily as seeking to copy their superiors, any more
than a deferential servant is seen as trying to emulate his employer, or a deferential tenant is seen as a landlord in the making. Hence it was a somewhat
different perception that some, perhaps many, of the new rich aspired to
assume the manners of the gentry, perhaps to acquire a house in the country either as a second home to the place of business, or as a retirement
home. And it was a very different perception that some of the new rich, perhaps a few, perhaps many, for no clearly quantifiable statements were made,
aspired to acquire considerable estates and found landed families. Possibly
all of these observations were correct, since they shade into each other and

[24] Morley, *Cobden*, 134 (Cobden to Frederick Cobden, 6 Oct. 1838); 518 (Cobden to Bright,
4 Nov. 1849).

[25] Ibid., 860–1 (Cobden to Henry Ashworth, 7 Feb. 1862). G. R. Searle, *Entrepreneurial Politics
in Mid-Victorian Britain* (Oxford, 1993), calls this 'the failure of entrepreneurial Radicalism',
meaning the failure of the post-Repeal Cobdenite programme (p. 291), and points out that 'entrepreneurial values', meaning commitment to the rules and spirit of a market economy, were incorporated into the mid-Victorian state by an aristocratic-dominated regime (p. 321).

are consistent with a view that the merchants and manufacturers did not form a monolithic class, but were socially differentiated, entertaining different social ambitions just as they held different political opinions. There is at least no unambiguous and unequivocal assertion in this set of texts that fortunes made in trade or industry habitually ended up in land. Oddly enough, a more uncompromising and unqualified assertion comes from a contemporary observer of the scene in the 1990s: 'Still,' he claims, 'the first thing the ambitious industrialist does when he makes his fortune is to try to buy a country house.' Jeremy Paxman may not be quite the Defoe or Cobden of our time, but he does claim to be well-informed about the ways of the wealthy and powerful.[26]

It is tempting to conclude from all this that Lawrence Stone was tilting at a windmill when he devoted a large book to the refutation of a myth to which its supposed authors and narrators did not seriously subscribe.[27] That would be unfair. It is true that the main thrust of the large book is to argue that at no time since 1540 did any considerable number of the new rich acquire landed estates (strictly, did not acquire large country houses, the property whose ownership was investigated by the Stones), but a casual aside admits that large numbers of the wealthy and not-so-wealthy bourgeoisie did aspire to gentrify themselves 'by copying the education, manners, and behaviour of the gentry' without actually acquiring land.[28] That is a position entirely consistent with much of what Defoe or Cobden had said, two observers of English society whose perceptions were earmarked for dismissal at the start of the book.[29] While the Stones are attached to the notion of a sharp distinction between 'real' gentrification by acquisition of a landed estate, and pseudo-gentrification by acquisition merely of gentry manners, in the real world there was a continuum of gentrifying types running from the 'well-mannered but landless' to the full-blown 'estate-purchaser' (whose acres may well have been better cultivated than his manners), with a great variety of intermediate models combining differing amounts of property and education. There is abundant support from contemporary perceptions of the behaviour of successful merchants and manufacturers for Harold Perkin's thesis that the pursuit of social ambition was the chief driving force of the men who made the industrial revolution, and that the aim of this ambition was pictured less as a fixed quantity of possessions which would confer a definite status, and more in terms of the next step or two up the social pecking order from the starting point. It is true that in some passages his picture of the *Origins of Modern English Society* employs only bold primary colours which announce that the overriding, or sole, form of this ambition was to acquire land and found a family. 'In every generation',

[26] Jeremy Paxman, *Friends in High Places* (1990), 43.
[27] Stone and Stone, *Open Elite?*, 3–5, 16–29.   [28] Ibid., 408–12.   [29] Ibid., 19–28.

he states, 'the richer citizens and townsmen . . . were themselves transmuted into country gentlemen,' and 'in the last resort the ultimate motivation of the industrialists, as for most rising men before them, was a dynastic one: to found a family, to endow them splendidly enough to last for ever, and to enjoy a vicarious eternal life in the seed of one's loins.'[30] Yet in general the picture he paints is in more subtle shades, and allows that the drive of social emulation found satisfaction in many different forms and grades of social advancement. The vanity which spurred men on, Perkin comments, 'took many forms, and not every industrialist, at least at the height of his career, wished to change places with a lord or squire.'[31] In a multi-layered society social advancement can be visualized as an aspiration to take a step up a rather long social ladder; if the landed elite lies at the top of the ladder, then the final step of reaching it will be taken only by the most successful, energetic, or lucky of those who have been climbing up from below.

A ladder is perhaps a misleading metaphor. It implies that anyone who sets foot on it intends to get to the top if at all possible, since that is the purpose of climbing a ladder. In the world of merchants and manufacturers it is virtually impossible to tell whether someone whose efforts in the event expired on a lowly or intermediate rung had once had a dream of reaching the top, which proved to be out of reach, or had always regarded the intermediate position as a sufficiently rewarding perch in its own right: in fact, as not being intermediate at all. Perkin circumvents this difficulty by portraying eighteenth-century society as a cohesive, multi-layered hierarchy, with the landed aristocracy and gentry at the apex, in which each successive layer (variously termed an order, a degree, even an embryonic class) modelled its aspirations, pretensions, and values on the one above it. In such a society aristocratic values were the master values and all others derived from them in a process of downward percolation, until arrested by an impermeable, if ill-defined, barrier separating gentlemen from the common people who had no social pretensions of any kind. Hence in each successive layer everyone who took their lead from the layer above and strove to imitate, please, or join it was, consciously or not, subscribing to a gentry-derived culture.

Other eighteenth-century historians have not been very happy with this formulation, although there are echoes of it in, for example, Paul Langford's view that: 'Eighteenth-century England was an endlessly snobbish society: as foreign visitors liked to remark, nothing distinguished it more than the unceasing struggle of all ranks to emulate those above them.'[32] In an illuminating phrase he likened the paternalist enterprises of the early captains of industry, such as Arkwright's Cromford, Strutt's Belper, or Greg's Styal, to 'the transfer to a manufacturing environment of concepts taken for

---

[30] Perkin, *Origins*, 61, 85.   [31] Ibid., 86.
[32] Paul Langford, *Public Life and the Propertied Englishman, 1689–1798* (Oxford, 1991), 9.

granted in settled agricultural communities', thus making a direct link between rural landlordism and industrial landlordism.[33] Overall, however, Langford's society turns its back on Perkinesque rigidities, with their insistence on a sole ultimate source of social and moral authority, and celebrates the uses and abuses of property by different ranks for different, rather than interlocking, purposes. By the 1790s what impresses is that a section of the wealthiest and most independent in the middle classes mobilized its property, in philanthropic works, to show that it was more virtuous and public-spirited than 'an aristocracy that was rotten at its core'.[34]

The dominant strain in recent writing stresses the importance of local communities and local elites in eighteenth-century society, within which merchants and manufacturers strove for success, recognition, and respect: a whole series of peer groups, as it were, locally or in some cases occupationally organized, and barely linked to, or aware of, the titular peerage at all. This is the message alike of Pene Corfield, who speaks unequivocally of a 'big bourgeoisie' at the head of urban society and comments that 'urban success was no longer simply a prelude to flight into the countryside', and of Linda Colley, who sees the coexistence of separate landed and commercial spheres articulated into a single coherent society by the vigorous support given to commerce by the landed, because it was the source of the country's wealth and power, and the support given to the landed by the commercial men seeking patronage, because the landed controlled the apparatus of government.[35] If, then, the emulation thesis is stripped of its aristocratic backbone what is left is the proposition that what impelled men into business enterprise was a desire for social advancement, and that the achievement of that advance was to be measured by success in reaching whatever goals were locally available and which seemed to be reasonably attainable, rather than against a scale of landed status that for most was unimaginably remote.

That reformulation does not have a particularly sharp cutting edge, but it does have the merit of recognizing that people do not plot, scheme, and toil to make business fortunes without having some idea of what they hope to do with them. Rampant and ruthless pursuit of unlimited profits and wealth for their own sake, as Max Weber recognized, was virtually unknown much before the 1890s, when it became the hallmark of the great and hugely rapacious American tycoons. Even then, it can be argued, the competitive accumulation of riches had itself become the prime form of social advancement open to the successful entrepreneur in a society whose values had been

[33] Ibid., 487.   [34] Ibid., 500–1, 548.

[35] P. J. Corfield, *The Impact of English Towns, 1700–1800* (Oxford, 1982), 130, 132; Linda Colley, *Britons: Forging the Nation, 1707–1837* (New Haven, Conn., and London, 1992), ch. 2, esp. p. 100.

reduced to a dollar standard, and where conspicuous consumption conferred social power. Moreover, the towering figures of American wealth, then and in the early twentieth century, men like Carnegie, Ford, Frick, Mellon, or Rockefeller, used part of their fortunes to endow a cornucopia of universities, libraries, museums, and research foundations, suggesting that ultimately accumulation was not an end in itself but a means towards gratifying a desire for public esteem and recognition or a philanthropic impulse.[36] In Britain, and probably in Europe generally, the limitless pursuit of wealth was, in the eighteenth century, quite unknown, and it remained quite exceptional. Indeed, the leading student of the super-rich finds but one solitary instance in nearly 200 years of British history of a British businessman whose sole interest was 'in making money and continuing to make money': Sir John Ellerman, secretive, self-effacing, self-made shipowner who left nearly £37 million at his death in 1933, the largest individual British fortune (in real terms) ever recorded.[37] Even Ellerman, however, was not so single-mindedly dedicated to profit and income maximization that he neglected the public rewards of the honours system, being made a baronet in 1905 and a CH in 1921, 'for services to shipping' in the Great War, rather than for simply being extremely rich. All the rest of the wealthy British businessmen, it is implied, behaved differently. In a negative sense they laboured under social constraints and inhibitions which made unbridled greed unacceptable or unthinkable; in a positive sense their sights were set on trying to amass a fortune sufficiently large to pay for their ambitions, but not on one indefinitely larger.

The ambitions of those few who reached the top of the pinnacle of wealth can be examined with a modest degree of confidence, at least insofar as it is legitimate to infer goals from the record of what large fortunes were spent on, once amassed.[38] The great mass of businessmen, however, never made large fortunes, and probably never expected to. At all times, subject to cyclical fluctuations, considerable numbers went bankrupt, and amongst those there were generally a few who crashed through aiming at the moon with lunatic, unsound, or fraudulent projects. Most bankrupts were down to earth, run-of-the-mill, businessmen, small traders, manufacturers, and shopkeepers who failed through some simple miscalculation, mismanagement, or adverse turn of the market, not because they were pursuing misconceived grandiose ambitions of financial or social aggrandisement.[39] The pit into which unsuccessful businessmen fell was lined with

[36] Weber, *Protestant Ethic*, 182; Perkin, *Origins*, 83; W. D. Rubinstein, *Elites and the Wealthy in Modern British History* (Brighton, 1987), 135.

[37] Rubinstein, *Elites and the Wealthy*, 136–8.   [38] See below, Ch. 3.

[39] Julian Hoppit, *Risk and Failure in English Business, 1700–1800* (Cambridge, 1987) is the sole systematic study of bankruptcies. A similar study of the nineteenth century is needed, but his general conclusions relating bankruptcies to risks, incompetence, and mischance, rather than to fraud, dishonesty, extravagance, or luxury are likely to apply to later periods (pp. 176–81).

managerial misfortunes, not with the wreckage of social pretensions. Apart from the failures, the economy was, and still is, dominated numerically by small and medium-sized businesses, and, in the view of many business theories, they are also the leading source of entrepreneurial and innovative promise. Direct evidence on the motivation of small businessmen is scarce, but it can be pictured roughly as the inverse of the common reasons for bankruptcy. That is, the aim was to survive, stay afloat, and gain a decent living by exploiting successfully the risks, opportunities, and chances of an unpredictable commercial world: quite likely the outside chance of making great riches was an extra lure for people to enter business, especially in new and untried industries, but that is still a long way short of making emulation or a desire for social advancement into the chief engine of enterprise.

Social advancement, it may be argued, could only begin to be entertained as a realistic goal once the initial steps in making and securing a fortune had been achieved, and thus was a second order rather than a first order motor of enterprise. For a general explanation of the availability and motivation of the mass of businessmen whose collective efforts, and failures, pushed and nudged the British economy into self-sustained growth by the early 1800s, one is close to falling back on the sociologically supine position that society simply contained a pool of actual or potential businessmen from which some were jerked into gainful activity by fresh and expanding economic opportunities. In the words of the historian of bankruptcy: 'What seems clear is that as opportunities developed in various areas of the economy there was a fund of businessmen available who responded to those opportunities when they had the requisite resources.'[40] If the fund was just out there waiting to be drawn upon, then the explanation of the great changes in the eighteenth-century economy becomes wholly economic, a matter of export markets, transatlantic trade, availability of credit, new consumer products, technology, and so on: no room is left for any important social variable, although as a derivative variable the size of the fund of businessmen presumably expanded not only as a product of demographic changes but also as a result of increasing economic openings.

All is not lost. The trouble with both the fund, or pool, vision, and the emulation theory, is that neither can cope very well with the dynamics of change or the inescapable demands of chronology. On the one hand if this fund of potential businessmen had always been latent in society awaiting the appearance of suitable opportunities before becoming manifest, then its pre-eighteenth-century members must have led extremely frustrating and disappointing lives, with severely restricted openings for bursting out into active business. In fact, however, the detailed study of the *First Industrialists*, by François Crouzet, shows that very few indeed were self-made men of

[40] Ibid., 177.

really humble origins emerging from some pool of non-business families, and that the overwhelming majority were the sons of professional, trading, or manufacturing fathers, starting off in a new industry with some, often fairly small, capital behind them.[41] This certainly confirms that there was a pool from which the early industrialists were drawn, but it was a pool which had been created by some previous social changes which had already produced an earlier pool of banking, trading, and manufacturing fathers, and their sons had presumably been raised in an environment where business, trading, and profit were the normal way of life. The trouble with the emulation theory is more serious. If the drive to emulate one's betters, in status, wealth, style, or display, is considered to be part of human nature, then possible objects of emulation would seem to have been around for centuries without having evoked any great explosions of commercial or industrial enterprise. If, on the other hand, the drive is thought to have become critically stronger in the eighteenth century, thus triggering unprecedented entrepreneurial efforts, some explanation of such a shift of gear is needed. It might be possible to argue that very long-drawn-out and gradual changes in social structure and attitudes, stretching back maybe to the Black Death, had displaced a hereditary caste society and eroded constraints and inhibitions which had previously made emulation virtually inconceivable and social mobility very rare. Such an explanation would need to argue that until the eighteenth century the drive to emulate was adequately satisfied through commercial and financial enterprise, so that the emulators did not find themselves drawn into industrial ventures. A more plausible and straightforward explanation is that it was a widening and multiplying of opportunities which released the effective potential of emulation; and that simply reinstates the primacy of economic factors.

A solution lies to hand in standing the emulation theory on its head, reversing the usual direction of flow from ideal model to imitators as an exclusively top-down process. The critical cultural shift in the eighteenth century might have been in the readiness of aristocracy and gentry to behave commercially, not in the intensity or prevalence of the desire among businessmen to become gentry. That would not sit easily with one of the prevailing views of eighteenth-century political historians, that the *Aristocratic Century*, in John Cannon's words, saw a strengthening of aristocratic control over 'the commanding heights of political and social life'.[42] Moreover,

---

[41] F. Crouzet, *The First Industrialists: The Problem of Origins* (Cambridge, 1985), tables 2, 3, 4, and 5. A clear majority in a sample of 226 (52.2 per cent) of the fathers of the founders of large industrial undertakings, 1750–1850, were bankers, merchants, shopkeepers, manufacturers, or industrialists; one-fifth came from outside the commercial-manufacturing sector (chiefly yeomen and farmers); and only 7 per cent were skilled or unskilled workmen.

[42] John Cannon, *Aristocratic Century: The Peerage of Eighteenth-century England* (Cambridge, 1984), 175.

those who see the history of society primarily through its politics may be inclined to accept J. C. D. Clark's idea that the dominant trend for more than a century after 1688 was for an intellectual and moral reinforcement which 'bolstered the cultural and ideological pre-eminence of the aristocracy and gentry' until the political events of 1828–32 destroyed 'the cultural hegemony of the old elite'.[43] To be sure, such views do not presuppose a static aristocratic culture, but the movement is seen primarily as a strengthening of traditional features of authority, social subordination of inferiors, and attachment to the Anglican ascendancy, not as a weakening of aristocratic antipathy to trade and profit. Nevertheless, there is plentiful evidence of the involvement of aristocracy and gentry in a range of business activities; of keen, even obsessive, aristocratic interest in rates of interest, money, and wealth; and of the active concern of the ruling elite with commercial policies. The commercial face of the aristocracy was not new to the eighteenth century; but there is a strong suspicion that it became more prominent and assertive, and hence of more consequence to the rest of society.[44] It is fortunately not necessary to agree with the extreme view that the landed classes virtually engineered the Industrial Revolution by producing 'an economic, political and social environment which was highly conducive to the development of industry, and highly advantageous to the merchant and industrialist', or accept the triumphalist rhetoric that 'England's landed elite . . . demonstrated their approval of the industrial classes by actually rolling up their sleeves and mucking in with them at the business of making money from industry and commerce', in order to believe that aristocratic and gentry culture was the reverse of anti-industrial.[45]

How far it was actively pro-commercial and pro-industrial remains to be seen. It is reasonably clear that the processes of industrialization and economic growth were not simply the product of great impersonal forces, and that individual entrepreneurs were important in determining their timing, shape, and dimensions. Entrepreneurs in turn were not simply interchangeable bits of economic machinery, but as individual and social beings required motivation as well as opportunity to induce them to take the risks which resulted in new enterprises. There were some who seem to have been inspired by the urge to gentrify themselves, particularly those who had already achieved some initial success and were in a position to redefine their goals at more ambitious levels of social advancement. Real-life examples were known to Defoe, Adam Smith, or Cobden, and for the nineteenth century it may be possible to measure with reasonable accuracy how large a

---

[43] J. C. D. Clark, *English Society, 1688–1832* (Cambridge, 1985), 73, 90.
[44] J. V. Beckett, *The Aristocracy in England, 1660–1914* (Oxford, 1986), 206–37.
[45] J. R. Wordie, 'Introduction', in C. W. Chalklin and J. R. Wordie (eds.), *Town and Countryside: The English Landowner in the National Economy, 1660–1860* (1989), 14–15.

fraction the gentrifiers were of the whole population of successful business-men. Neither the gentrifiers nor the much larger group of 'pseudo-gentrifiers' which sought to emulate some of the values and lifestyles which percolated down from the aristocracy and gentry, however, was necessarily of much consequence in the initial processes of drawing potential entrepreneurs out of the woodwork and galvanizing them into the uncharted risks and ventures which produced economic growth. What induced the 'first industrialists' to step out of the ranks of shopkeepers, small traders, and workshop manufacturers may never be known, but is much more likely to have been an instinct for commercial survival and a desire for a more comfortable life for their families than a drive to become either genteel or gentlemanly. Whether later entrepreneurs, in a mature industrial economy, were more dependent on or susceptible to the charms of gentrification, or were corrupted by gentry values, and whether those values took a nasty anti-industrial turn somewhere in the Victorian classroom or drawing room, are questions which await further investigation.

2

Aristocrats as Entrepreneurs

A common view of the landed class, aristocracy and gentry, in the eighteenth and nineteenth centuries is that they were an idle lot, a leisure class—'who toil not, neither do they spin', in Joe Chamberlain's words[1]—whose defining characteristic was that they neither needed to work nor did they work. From the point of view of the economy, particularly of the agricultural economy, they were seen as parasites feeding on the productive work of farmers and labourers and contributing nothing useful or indispensable in return. The intellectual ancestry of that position stems from Ricardo and his theory of rent; it has lately been vigorously reaffirmed by Avner Offer to explain the comparatively poor performance of British agriculture between 1880 and 1914. 'Since the sod-house settler had no other master,' he writes, referring to the frontier farmers and homesteaders of the United States, Canada, and Australasia, 'he was able to compete with the British farmer, saddled with the pretensions and cost of the hierarchy above him.'[2] Those pretensions were an effortless social and political superiority, coupled with high living, self-indulgence, and pity or disdain for all other forms of life. A Chartist rhyme put it this way in 1842:

> What is a peer? A useless thing:
> A costly toy to please a king;
> What is a peer? A nation's curse
> A pauper on the public purse
> Corruption's own jackal:
> A haughty, domineering blade;
> A cuckold at a masquerade:
> A dandy at a ball.
> Ye butterflies, whom kings create;
> Ye caterpillars of the state.[3]

In a less robust way Hippolyte Taine observed of the English aristocracy, in the early 1870s, that 'In their heart of hearts ... they believe ... that a tradesman, a financier, a man of business, constantly obliged to think of profit and details of profit all day long, is not a gentleman and never can

---

[1] J. Chamberlain, 30 Mar. 1883 speech, quot. in R. C. K. Ensor, *England, 1870–1914* (Oxford, 1936), 87.
[2] A. Offer, *The First World War: An Agrarian Interpretation* (Oxford, 1989), 120.
[3] *Northern Star*, 7 May 1842.

be . . . the tradesman, the business man, is made to keep his distance, and his family cannot be received by the reigning families.'[4] Such views, and many others like them, are the ancestors of Martin Wiener's picture of the aristocracy as essentially unproductive, anti-commercial, and anti-industrial, an appraisal which forms one of the legs supporting the grand theory that gentlemanly values have emasculated the 'industrial spirit' and brought about economic decline. The other leg is the assertion that businessmen and the intelligentsia have been seduced and enthralled by gentlemanly values, making them into a firmly embedded part of national culture.[5]

It may seem like a shallow affectation to place two historians as different and as far apart as Avner Offer and Martin Wiener in the same bed, where both will feel uncomfortable. Where a rigorous economic historian and a widely read cultural historian agree on at least one important characteristic of the landed aristocracy, however, it is unlikely that they are both wrong. Indeed, when the characteristic is put to the test examples can readily be found of aristocrats who were idle, spendthrift, self-indulgent, preoccupied with the social round, and neglectful of the duties of public service which were supposed to justify their existence. Such aristocrats, if not positively anti-industrial, were obviously not profit-minded, and their example did nothing to foster the 'industrial spirit'. Aristocrats were first and foremost landowners, but down on the farm agricultural historians do not now maintain that landowners were ever important innovators in introducing new farming methods, and the image of the landlords as an economically functionless class whose property rights enabled them to top-slice the product of the land in order to pay for their grand style of living is one deeply rooted in agrarian populism.[6] The difficulty is that examples can just as readily be found of aristocrats who were actively involved in the development of estate resources in a thoroughly businesslike way, even if it is hard to say whether they partook of anything so nebulous as the 'industrial spirit' while doing so. And in agriculture, leaving out of consideration any contribution they made to the creation of fixed assets, landlords in theory simply collected rents which arose from the differences in quality, fertility, and location between different pieces of land, and did not arbitrarily dictate any level of rent that chanced to suit them. In other words they performed a useful and necessary economic function in allocating resources and effort to ensure that sufficient land was cultivated to satisfy demand; although it remains true that they did not have to do anything to collect the reward for this func-

---

[4] H. Taine, *Notes on England* (1872, English tr. by E. Hyams, 1957), 142–5; quot. in W. L. Guttsman (ed.), *The English Ruling Class* (1969), 60, 37.

[5] Martin Wiener, *English Culture and the Decline of the Industrial Spirit, 1850–1980* (Cambridge, 1981), 5–10.

[6] J. V. Beckett, 'Economic Functions of Landowners', in G. E. Mingay (ed.), *The Agrarian History of England and Wales*, vi, 1750–1850 (Cambridge, 1981), 569–73.

tion except possess the property rights. There was, then, more than one type of aristocrat, more than one way of conceptualizing the landlord class, and more than one imprint which the aristocracy might have stamped on the national culture.

One way round this problem has been to suggest that aristocratic behaviour moved in a cycle from profligacy and sin, through earnestness and high moral endeavour, and back to hedonism, from the late eighteenth century, through the high Victorian period, and on to Edwardian decadence. How their post-1914 behaviour should be described has scarcely seemed to matter to anyone except gossip columnists. Such a sequence can be illustrated with selected examples and instances, and its plausibility has been turned into certainty by frequent repetition of apposite and trenchant contemporary comments on high society.

Thus, the rascally and randy reputation of the later eighteenth century as an era when the aristocracy was becoming rotten at the core, thoroughly dissolute through indulgence in sundry vices, financial irresponsibility, irreligion, and easy-going sexual morality, rests on many authentic instances of individual behaviour which may be taken, according to choice, as proofs of depravity or of relaxed permissiveness. Charles James Fox was a compulsive gambler and indiscriminate borrower, and in a lifetime was thought to have lost hundreds of thousands of pounds in gaming and curious wagers at Brooks's.[7] This had little effect on his reputation as a liberal statesman, at the time or subsequently. Georgiana, Duchess of Devonshire, was not only another gambling addict, running up debts of some £60,000 in a dozen years and turning Devonshire House into a casino, but also was one of a notorious *ménage à trois* in which her best friend, Lady Elizabeth Foster, was her husband's mistress. Shuttling to and fro between Chatsworth and Devonshire House, with trips together to France, the threesome produced seven surviving children, three legitimate and four not: of the illegitimates two were children of the 5th Duke and Lady Elizabeth, one of the Duke and an earlier mistress, and one the child of Georgiana and the future Lord Grey of the Reform Bill. There were no social difficulties or penalties: through all this Georgiana reigned as the queen of high society, the most brilliant Whig political hostess of all time.[8] The misconduct of her sister Henrietta, married to the 3rd Earl of Bessborough, was equally notorious in the 1780s and 1790s; but casual couplings or multiple relationships were hardly a novelty for the late Georgian upper class. A generation earlier the parentage of the Countess of Oxford's many children had been so diverse that they were always called 'the Harleian Miscellany'. It was not without reason that the

[7] C. Hobhouse, *Fox* (1947 edn.), 7–11.

[8] J. Pearson, *Stags and Serpents: The Story of the House of Cavendish and the Dukes of Devonshire* (1983), 100–13.

3rd Earl of Egremont recalled of the London society which he entered as a young man in 1772 that 'there was hardly a young lady of fashion who did not think it almost a stain on her reputation if she was not known to have cuckolded her husband, and the only doubt was who was to assist her in the operation'. Egremont himself assisted, though not with ladies of fashion: he fathered at least eight illegitimate children, with women from various non-aristocratic backgrounds, the eldest of whom succeeded to the family estates and was created Lord Leconfield in 1859.[9]

In themselves such instances show that sinfulness existed and was tolerated in high society, not necessarily that it was something new or was on the increase. That notion was given colour by the propaganda of the many voluntary associations for the suppression of vice and the reformation of manners which became active in the 1790s, and which particularly targeted the top reaches of society. It is worth recalling, however, that these late eighteenth-century associations were in effect revivals, at the national level, of the local societies for the Reformation of Manners which had sprouted in some profusion at the beginning of the century as a form of voluntary moral policing especially of the behaviour of the middling and lower orders, designed, unsuccessfully, to fill the gap left by the withering of ecclesiastical authority and control over drunkenness, sabbath-breaking, and adultery.[10] In the 1790s members of the Clapham Sect, and their chief publicist Hannah More, were convinced of the urgent need for the leaders of society, the aristocracy, to set a good example of sober, godly, morally upright, and prudent behaviour, in order to save the country from impending moral ruin, disintegration, and possible utter destruction. They were equally convinced that the current tone of high society was the reverse of such an example, and had to be purified as the first step towards saving society from collapse. In other words whereas in 1700 the voluntary societies imagined that the urban middle classes would provide the moral policemen to keep society in order, by 1790 their successors cast a reformed aristocracy that role.[11]

This train of thought and its vigorous advocacy through sermons, tracts, and high-level networking did indeed set in motion a crusade which in time succeeded in establishing a new orthodoxy of public morals and public behaviour, the triumph of evangelicalism in setting the standards of mid-Victorian respectability. The initial impetus, however, came from the threat of revolution abroad and the danger of disaffection and insubordination at home: the moral reform crusade was a response to external threats to the

---

[9] H. A. Wyndham, *A Family History, 1688–1837: The Wyndhams of Somerset, Sussex, and Wiltshire* (Oxford, 1950), 217–18, 222–4.

[10] P. Earle, *The Making of the English Middle Class: Business, Society and Family Life in London, 1660–1730* (1989), 268, 379.

[11] J. C. D. Clark, *English Society, 1688–1832*, 243–7; Boyd Hilton, *The Age of Atonement* (Oxford, 1988), 204–5; Linda Colley, *Britons: Forging the Nation, 1707–1837* (1992), 154.

social and political order rather than to any internal crisis attributable to
increasing aristocratic depravity or frivolity. In fact it is more than likely that
there was nothing particularly remarkable about aristocratic morals and
manners in the 30 or 40 years leading up to the outburst of reproval in the
1790s. Not only can one find amazingly debauched and unpleasant aristocrats aplenty at any time since the Glorious Revolution, and before the Civil
War as well, but also representatives of an entirely different stream of well-
behaved, devout, faithful, and industrious aristocrats are not all that rare.
To come upon 'a great Lord who is not ashamed of praying to God' may
have startled Arthur Young on his travels round the country, since a noble-
man heading regular family prayers was not a normal sight in the 1780s.
Nevertheless, decades earlier, when religious scepticism and quietism were
the height of fashion among the court aristocracy, Selina Countess of
Huntingdon had made headway from the 1740s onwards in her mission to
enthuse aristocratic ladies with fervour and a sense of sin, and through that
connection many grand husbands came to adopt good works and seemly
conduct, even if not Methodism itself. At the individual level, Georgiana,
Countess Spencer, was a model of virtue, religion, and philanthropy
throughout the second half of the eighteenth century, although her two
daughters were the most unprincipled and sinful of the age: Georgiana,
Duchess of Devonshire, and Henrietta, Countess of Bessborough. Maybe
they kicked over the traces in a typical reaction to parental example, just as
much as they adopted the permissive conventions of their social milieu.[12]

Most striking of all, however, is that the second half of the eighteenth
century, the time when aristocratic licentiousness and self-indulgence were
apparently rising to a climax, was also the time when aristocratic involvement with the business of making money moved into a new gear. Most
likely there is no incompatibility between loose morals and managerial
competence, between sexual adventures and business ventures: but it so happened that in practice there was little overlap between those whose private
lives dominated society gossip, and those whose economic enterprises have
most caught the eye of historians. Richard, 1st Baron and 1st Earl Grosvenor,
was an exception, actor in one of the favourite scandals with the press on
both sides of the Atlantic when in 1770 his wife committed adultery with
the royal Duke of Cumberland, and in turn exposed his peculiar tastes when
frequenting prostitutes, while at the time he was closely concerned with the
large-scale building development of his Mayfair estate.[13] It was precisely in
this period of apparent aristocratic degeneracy that those who had previously

[12] Paul Langford, *Public Life and the Propertied Englishman, 1689–1798* (Oxford, 1991),
569–72.
[13] Lawrence Stone, *The Family, Sex, and Marriage* (Pelican edn., 1979), 326; id. *Road to Divorce*
(Oxford, 1990), pl. 26, pp. 214, 224, 270.

languished, by and large, in the second rank in point of wealth, prestige, and influence, were busily engaged in promoting the development of their estate resources which would propel them within the next half century into the top rank of aristocratic wealth, leaving former leaders like the Spencers, Newcastles, Leeds, or Manchesters well behind. Inspired by the example of the Duke of Bridgewater, widely admired as the model of the virtuously enterprising aristocrat whose great ventures in canals and collieries brought profit to himself and prosperity and employment to his country, large numbers of mining and transport enterprises were helped on their way, from the Duke of Hamilton in Lanarkshire to the Marquess of Bute in South Wales, the Earl of Dudley in the Black Country to the Earl of Sefton in Lancashire, or the Earl of Durham on the Durham coalfield to the Earl Fitzwilliam in Yorkshire.

How far these and others like them—among the dukes alone Buccleuch, Cleveland, Devonshire, Portland, and Rutland can be placed alongside Bridgewater and Hamilton—are to be taken as genuine entrepreneurs is another question. Of more immediate concern, it was held at the time that this was the period when it became normal for landowners to adopt a keenly commercial and financially calculating attitude towards their agricultural estates, something which was open to all regardless of whether they were lucky enough to own minerals or urban property as well. This development was greeted enthusiastically by the agriculturalists, who typically attributed much of the responsibility for efficient and productive farming to the energetic and well-informed management of resident landowners, and, in the words of the reporter to the Board of Agriculture on the North Riding of Yorkshire in 1794, where there were 'specimens of waste, neglect, barbarism, and poverty' these were on estates 'which are never visited by their owners, but abandoned to the care of a steward, perhaps a law agent, or other person still less acquainted with the management of land, and resident in London'.[14] Traditionalists regarded the development with dismay, and denounced landowners for abandoning their duty of treating their land and its agriculture as a form of trust for supporting the accustomed way of life of a whole community, and instead converting their property into a trading enterprise. Cobbett, with his highly individual brand of nostalgic conservative radicalism, continually harked back to a golden age of benignly benevolent gentry and plain honest farmers who ate at the same table with their labourers, and reserved most of his castigations for the new rich who purchased estates and treated them as mere sources of the greatest possible profit, and for the commercially minded farmers who indulged in frivolous luxury while grinding the faces of their underpaid labourers. But the old nobility and gentry were

[14] W. Marshall (ed.), *The Review and Abstract of the County Reports to the Board of Agriculture from the Several Agricultural Departments of England* (1808), i. 457.

not spared his contempt, and they were called 'these mean, these cruel, these cowardly, these carrion, these dastardly reptiles' for their share in commercializing and capitalizing the old way of life out of existence, and for becoming 'a prodigious band of spongers, living upon the labour of the industrious part of the community'.[15] Coleridge was a less vituperative witness to the same effect, complaining, in 1817, 'that our landowners have learnt their present theory of trading with that which was never meant to be the object of commerce' from a specious political economy which had led them to 'the most horrible perversion of humanity and moral justice', so that they managed their estates like tradesmen aiming simply at 'returns [that] shall be the largest, quickest, and securest possible; and secondly, with the least outgoings in the providing, overlooking, and collecting the same'.[16]

Coleridge's version of history, like Cobbett's, was that in some earlier epoch, presumably before the great waves of parliamentary enclosures, the landowners of old England had not been grasping, avaricious, calculating, and commercial in the handling of their property, but had been benevolently content deliberately to run their estates below the level of optimal output and maximum rents for themselves, in the interests of rural stability and maximum employment. That may not sound like the behaviour of some real historical Tudor landlords, but the point is that the general body of landowners was perceived, at the beginning of the nineteenth century, to have become sharply entrepreneurial in their handling of their agricultural estates in the very recent past, in contrast to their traditional 'feudal' or paternalist approach. This may or may not have been true, either in the sense that landowners had become markedly more market-driven in the four or five decades before 1815, or in the sense that by 1815 they were peculiarly grasping and self-centred, and uncaring for the welfare of their tenantry and dependants. There is plenty of evidence in the county reports to the Board of Agriculture in the early 1790s, as well as from individual estates which have been studied, which suggests widespread, though not universal, interest among the landowners in the productivity of their estates, and readiness to make the landlord's contribution to raising it, through enclosures, farm buildings, farm roads, and the creation of larger and more compact farm holdings. It does not suggest, however, that aristocracy and gentry had come to regard land simply as a commodity to be traded regardless of the effects on those who lived on their estates.[17] This combination of

[15] W. Cobbett, in *Political Register*, 1815 and 1834; *Rural Rides* (1833): quot. by Ian Dyck, *William Cobbett and Rural Popular Culture* (Cambridge, 1992), 72.

[16] S. T. Coleridge, *Second Lay Sermon*, 1817, quot. in R. J. White, (ed.), *The Conservative Tradition* (1950), 182–3.

[17] Marshall, *Review and Abstract*, 5 vols., for summaries of the county reports. The numerous estate histories are summarized by J. V. Beckett, 'Landownership and Estate Management,' in Mingay, (ed.), *Agrarian History*, vi., 545–640; and id., *The Aristocracy in England, 1660–1914* (Oxford, 1986), ch. 5.

contemporary perceptions and the record of contemporary estate activity is sufficient to make the agricultural case, which is the general case for the landed aristocracy and gentry, for the presence of some entrepreneurial spirit in the class during the reign of George III, without any need to invoke the special and selective case of the mineral and urban landowners. This was at the time when the conduct of some members of the order gave strong colour to the charge that the aristocracy had become rotten at its core, a time when the more dissolute and pleasure-seeking presumably had neither time nor energy for economically entrepreneurial activities.

Thus conflicting and contrary signals were coming from the example of aristocratic behaviour and the image of aristocratic manners in late Georgian Britain, and it would be unwise to conclude that there was any one single, or paramount, message that aristocratic culture conveyed to the rest of society. Much the same was true of early and mid-Victorian Britain, when the moral emphases are normally put into reverse: the aristocratic example could be taken as earnest, Godfearing, prudent, and businesslike, or as dissolute, adulterous, extravagant, and anti-commercial, according to taste. To be sure, the image which most impressed contemporaries was that of the 'bourgeois aristocrat', noted with dismay by Engels in 1858.[18] This was the aristocrat as devoted family man, leading an exemplary private life of comfortable domesticity, sincerely religious, scrupulous and painstaking in attending to business affairs, abhorring debt, drink, or gambling, and liberal in supporting good causes. Such an aristocrat, looking and behaving like any member of the wealthy upper middle class, was indeed a novelty, and it was little wonder that many observers, with the backing of many etiquette manuals, believed that a complete transformation had taken place thanks to the triumph of Evangelical precept and preaching, which had almost miraculously led the rakes to find salvation in respectability. All the same, unrespectables continued to survive in high places, and the chief effect of the new moral standards was to teach them to be more discreet and to keep their indiscretions out of the newspapers and law courts, an exercise in which they were not completely successful. To those outside the privileged circle of high society, however, provided they were not sympathetic to the nonconformist-radical view of the aristocracy as mere hereditary tax-eaters, the dominant mid-Victorian vision of the class was the respectable one, of propriety and industriousness. That was clearly a significant perception in determining the character and direction of any influence which aristocratic culture had on society at large.

A gallery of serious, sober-sided, Victorian grandees can be put on parade, most of them reacting against the follies and improvidence of their

---

[18] Marx-Engels, *Selected Correspondence, 1846–95* (1936), 115–16, quot. in Lawrence and Jeanne C. Fawtier Stone, *An Open Elite? England, 1540–1880* (Oxford, 1984), 411.

forebears, and most of them energetically applying themselves to business. Mid-Victorian favourites as exemplary noblemen, dedicated entrepreneurs in very different ways, were the 7th Duke of Devonshire and the 7th Earl of Shaftesbury. Devonshire inherited from his bachelor uncle, who had cohabited for years with a courtesan before going into a phase of remorse and seclusion, estates burdened with debts of over £1 million and flamboyant extravagances such as bananas growing in Paxton's great hothouses at Chatsworth. The 7th Duke, devout low churchman, star mathematician, austere in his private life, and already a widower when he inherited, devoted more than 40 years to unremitting labours in directing the development of Buxton and Eastbourne, and in pouring money into the Furness Railway, Barrow-in-Furness, and its steelworks and shipyards, almost single-handedly creating a new industrial complex. That these prodigious efforts far from clearing off the debts which he had inherited merely added to their total was not apparent to contemporaries, who saw only the brilliant success story of a virtuous, public-spirited, aristocratic industrialist operating on the grand scale.[19]

Shaftesbury, by contrast, was the outstanding, public-spirited, 'moral entrepreneur'.[20] Heir to Wilberforce as leader of the saints in politics, evangelical, anti-papist, invoking scripture at every turn, Shaftesbury was a thorn in the flesh of Whig and Tory governments with his uncompromising determination to obtain action on those social questions which he found worthy of moral crusading: chimney sweeps' climbing boys, the ten hours movement, ragged schools, dosshouses, and many more. One result of this was that the Shaftesbury estates in Dorset, already neglected, were left to mismanagement and peculation by a dishonest agent while the Earl was fully engaged in Parliament, in visiting mills and factories, and in improving tours on the Continent. Discovering the shocking state of labourers' cottages on his farms, he conscientiously did his best to improve them and escape the charge of being a hypocritical landowner who failed to put his own house in order, while attacking slum landlords with a will. It can scarcely be said that his brand of piety and social conscience was any help to business enterprise or efficiency, unless it had some vague relationship to the practices of welfare capitalism, and it would be more plausible to argue that Shaftesbury's was the acceptable face of anti-commercial, anti-industrial, aristocratic culture.[21]

[19] D. Cannadine, 'The Landowner as Millionaire: The Finances of the Dukes of Devonshire, c.1800–c.1926', Agricultural History Review, 25 (1977), 77–97.

[20] A concept explored in R. M. Hartwell, 'Entrepreneurship and Public Inquiry: The Growth of Government in Nineteenth-century Britain', in F. M. L. Thompson (ed.), Landowners, Capitalists, and Entrepreneurs: Essays for Sir John Habakkuk (Oxford, 1994).

[21] E. Hodder, The Life and Work of the 7th Earl of Shaftesbury (1887 edn.), 210–13, 449, 483, 583. See also G. B. A. M. Finlayson, The Seventh Earl of Shaftesbury, 1801–1885 (1981), 102–5, 126, 134–5.

There can be little doubt that of these two paragons of aristocratic virtue and rectitude Devonshire had more imitators from within his own class, and Shaftesbury had more admirers and supporters from outside it. On the virtuous front the alternative readings of the mid-Victorian aristocratic text were not in close harmony. High endeavour, great business enterprises, beneficent employment creation, and with luck great personal riches; or high endeavour, great philanthropic achievements, much righteousness and public esteem, at the price of poor management and mounting debt. Moreover the choice of images of aristocratic culture was not limited to these two, for there were also the disreputables to consider. True, the disreputables were not much in the public eye if they could help it, although they became extremely visible when their escapades spilled over into the pages of *The Times* and the *Morning Post*, which happened sufficiently often to furnish the strait-laced wing of the upper and middle classes with proof of the immorality and degeneracy of the aristocracy. A splendid instance of an encounter between two types of culture occurred when Shaftesbury, paragon of the virtuous, upright, Victorian philanthropist was the recipient of advice on prudent financial management from his mother-in-law's second husband, the cynical old reprobate Lord Palmerston, generally regarded as a hangover from the days of Regency frivolity and loose morals, about whom the story circulating in 1864 was that he was having an affair with Margaret O'Kane, the wife of an Irish journalist, the wag's version being that 'though the lady was certainly Kane, the question was, was Palmerston Abel?' he being 78 at the time.[22] This was never judicially tested, since the Prime Minister was not made to appear in the Divorce Court, it being rumoured that O'Kane had been bought off.

Appearance in the Divorce Court could certainly prove fatal to a woman's reputation, and ruined the careers of some men, notably Dilke and Parnell, but financial misbehaviour was more consistently reprehensible and disastrous. The 2nd Duke of Buckingham, for instance, was almost unimaginably foolish and reckless in his financial affairs, and was frequently unfaithful to his duchess, but for farmers and squires he had considerable virtues as the author of the Chandos clause in the 1832 Reform Act and as the Farmers' Friend who fought strenuously through the 1840s to stave off free trade. His complete ruin and virtual bankruptcy in 1848, however, forcing the sale of the entire contents of Stowe and most of his estates, stirred *The Times* not to sympathy but to denunciation of 'a most disgraceful event'. Its leader on the subject was typically pompous and self-righteous. 'Should we deal fairly if we spared the destroyer of his house, the man whose reckless course has thrown to the ground a pillar of the state,

---

[22] Hodder, *Shaftesbury*, Palmerston to Shaftesbury, 29 Nov. 1861, 582–3; *The Times*, 27 Jan. 3 and 5 Feb. 1864, quot. in Allen Horstman, *Victorian Divorce* (1985), 139.

and struck a heavy blow at the whole order to which he unfortunately belongs?' it asked. 'Public opinion respects the House of Lords, but not a degenerate aristocracy . . . In the midst of fertile lands and an industrious people . . . a man of property not unequal to his rank, has flung all away by extravagance and folly'.[23]

The aristocracy survived this heavy blow, and many others of a similar, if less spectacular, nature. Between 1830 and 1870 more than 60 members of the landed aristocracy were in and out of the bankruptcy courts, and although the great majority of these were the sons, or in one case a daughter, of noblemen who got into difficulties over rather small tradesmen's bills because they had rather small incomes, at least a dozen were peers in possession of their family estates and in serious financial trouble. Some went worthily if stupidly bankrupt, like the 5th Earl of Orkney, an Irish landowner with modest resources, who misguidedly backed his brother's attempt to develop a worthless patent for a new method of making steel, in an effort to show industrial spirit.[24] Others had simply got into the clutches of moneylenders before they had inherited, borrowing heavily on their reversionary expectations, a traditional eldest son's road to ruin. Among these, the 11th Earl of Winchilsea deserves notice by historians for having proposed the sale of the Hatton Collection to the British Museum as a contribution to paying off his debts. Hoping for £10,000, he was gravely disappointed when the Museum only offered £1,800, but in any case felt that the collection would not be missed by the family as 'their places . . . in the red room at Eastwell should be filled up by other works equally well bound'. 'The MS[s] have been buried for the last 200 years', he added, 'and have been of no use to anyone. By being sold to the B.M. everyone will be the better for the discovery, and I and my family will be relieved from the custody of such a collection, which ought always to be in the hands of proper officers to prevent that picking and stealing for which antiquaries have always been famous, and without which staff it would be almost impossible to permit the learned to have access to them'.[25]

Such a deft deflection of attention from the debts of a spendthrift to the sins of scholars might earn sympathy or even applause, but when horses and betting brought ruin *The Times* had no patience. The 6th Duke of Newcastle was bankrupted in 1870 with debts of over half a million, of which it seems that around £200,000 were the result of racehorse training and betting activities in partnership with the 12th Earl of Westmorland. In

[23] *The Times*, 14 Aug. 1848, 4. A full account of the Buckingham débâcle is given in J. V. Beckett, *The Rise and Fall of the Grenvilles: Dukes of Buckingham and Chandos, 1710 to 1921* (Manchester,1994); earlier accounts are in D. Spring and E. Spring, 'The Fall of the Grenvilles, 1844–8', *Huntington Library Quarterly*, 19 (1956), 165–90, and in F. M. L. Thompson, 'The End of a Great Estate', *Economic History Review*, 2nd ser. 8 (1955), 36–52.
[24] *The Times*, 8 July 1871, p. 11.   [25] Ibid., 26 May 1871, p. 11.

a repetition of the Stowe affair of 20 years before, the contents of Clumber and of the Duke's house in Carlton House Terrace were seized by bailiffs and auctioned off, while the Duke added to the scandal by scuttling off to Spa to evade jurisdiction. *The Times* scented another heavy blow at the aristocracy, claiming that Newcastle's bankruptcy 'has apparently shaken popular confidence in the character of our nobility'.[26] On the other hand confidence had not been shaken, by *The Times* measure, when Newcastle's father, then still the eldest son and known as Lord Lincoln, had suffered the shame of having his wife Susan run away with Lord Walpole, eldest son of the 3rd Earl of Orford, in a blaze of publicity because Lincoln was a prominent Peelite, former cabinet minister, and very upright Tractarian, and his Countess was from the top flight socially, the only daughter of the 10th Duke of Hamilton. Her flight took place in 1848, and divorce followed in 1850, after which she could not marry her lover as he already had a wife, and she eventually took a Belgian for her second husband and disappeared from the records. Meanwhile the affair had produced a splendid farce. Lincoln's close friend and political ally, Gladstone, went in pursuit of the Countess and, tracking her down to a villa near Lake Como, disguised himself as a guitarist and hid behind a pillar, thus obtaining the necessary evidence of adultery and pregnancy which he later presented to the House of Lords when the divorce Bill was heard. Since Gladstone was opposed to divorce on strongly held principle, and as he led the opposition to the 1857 Bill which became the first Divorce Act, his bizarre performance with the guitar did not improve his reputation for integrity.[27]

In the middle decades of the century London society did in fact clean up its image considerably, so much so that Hippolyte Taine was assured, in the 1860s, that he could spend 18 months visiting the best town houses in London without once meeting an adulteress.[28] That may have been because adulteresses did not care to come closer to London than Boulogne for fear of being ostracized, for there were quite a few divorces in the 1850s and 1860s which implicated aristocratic ladies, often seen in London houses, as well as the men. Male misbehaviour, unsurprisingly, was the more readily overlooked, as part of the prevailing double standard: although when, in 1859, the adulterous 2nd Marquess of Anglesey paid James Bell £10,000 damages for an uncontested divorce so that he, the Marquess, could marry Mrs Bell (Ellen Burnand) as his third wife, this looked uncomfortably like wife sale.[29] In 1889 Gladstone wrote an article in the *North American*

[26] *The Times*, 22 June 1869, p. 5, 23 June 1869, p. 9, 24 June 1869, p. 5, 25 June 1869, p. 6, 2 July 1869, p. 11, 4 Aug. 1869, p. 11, 29 Oct. 1869, p. 9, 17 Mar. 1870, p. 11, 25 Aug. 1870, p. 11, 27 Jan. 1871, p. 11, 13 Feb. 1871, p. 9.
[27] H. C. G. Matthew, *Gladstone, 1809–74* (Oxford, 1986), 80; Horstman, *Victorian Divorce*, 29–30, 61.   [28] Taine, *Notes on England*, 99.
[29] Horstman, *Victorian Divorce*, 144.

Review which claimed that the sexual morality of the upper class had dete-
riorated grievously in the 30 years since the Divorce Act, and as a direct consequence of it.[30] That was unprovable, and most likely not true. What can
be claimed with more confidence is that public awareness of the sexual
morals and normal behaviour of a section of the upper class had been
reawakened, or intensified, by the entry of the Prince of Wales into society
in the 1860s and his open identification with the fast set. In 1870 Bertie was
in the Divorce Court, if only to deny any adultery with Lady Harriet
Mordaunt, to whom he had written several indiscreet letters.[31] Five years
later he was involved, not well screened behind the scenes, in the great
Aylesford scandal, when he went off tiger-shooting in India with his
unsavoury friend 'Sporting Joe', the 7th Earl of Aylesford, while back home
his former friend, the Marquess of Blandford, ran off with the Countess,
who also had some compromising letters from the Prince. The Prince of
Wales's circle of mistresses later came to embrace Lady Brooke (later
Countess of Warwick) and Mrs George Keppel (sister-in-law of the 8th Earl
of Albemarle) among aristocratic ladies, and Lillie Langtry and Sarah
Bernhardt among the actresses; and the group of aristocrats he gathered
round him from the late 1870s in the Marlborough House set were notorious for infideltiy.[32] But it was possibly his part in the Tranby Croft baccarat
scandal of 1891 which made the deepest impression. Adultery, when
exposed in the divorce court, was disgraceful, but more frequently it was
kept concealed, and was tolerated; bankruptcy, when the subject of formal
proceedings, was both shameful and humiliating; but cheating at cards, or
defaulting on bets, was totally unacceptable.[33]

If the condition of the mid-Victorian aristocracy were to be read from
the law reports and the bankruptcy news rather than from the pages of
Taine's *Notes*, it would appear to have been almost as rotten at the core as
in the late eighteenth century; and the late-Victorian state, viewed through
Marlborough House glasses, distinctly more rotten. Had this been the
essence of what the aristocratic example had to offer to the middle classes,
then emulation would indeed have emasculated their industrial and professional vigour. Alternatively, since such an example clearly offended the nonconformist and respectable conscience, it might have strengthened a bourgeois
resolve to be as unlike the aristocracy as possible, which would have meant
a redoubling of industrial and professional vigour. In some circumstances
aristocratic decadence can act as a spur to the assertion of an independent
middle-class morality and identity, thus providing a cultural reinforcement
to the profit motive. That was what Cobden hoped would happen, and it is

[30] Ibid., *Victorian Divorce*, 164.   [31] Anita Leslie, *The Marlborough House Set* (1972), 53–4.
[32] Horstman, *Victorian Divorce*, 134, 137.
[33] Leslie, *Marlborough House Set*, 128–35, 151–2.

possible to detect a tendency of that kind in evangelicalism, although its message was complicated by upper-class and aristocratic participation.[34]

This was, however, never a very serious possibility, since disreputability and degeneracy were only one face of the aristocracy on view to the public. The other faces, of rectitude, propriety, industry, prudence, or philanthropy were equally on view, and if they exerted any general cultural influence it was of a rather different kind. Some contemporary observers made confident and one-sided pronouncements about the predominant flavour of aristo-cratic culture—haughty, arrogant, idle, time-serving, feudal, condescend-ing, patronizing, were favourite labels used by *The Economist, Reynolds News*, Carlyle, Dickens, Taine, and many more—and they have been followed by historians who confidently translate such characteristics into prejudices against trade and industry. The truth was more prosaic. The aristocracy as a class did not have just one, single, culture. In any case the aristocracy was neither sufficiently homogeneous nor sufficiently influen-tial, socially, intellectually, economically, or politically, for the course of cul-tural influences all to flow in one direction, from top to bottom: the different strands of aristocratic behaviour themselves responded to influences from outside their circle. Even the promiscuity and permissiveness of the fast set in the 1860s were not entirely self-induced by aristocratic self-indulgence, but owed something to the outside influence of the irresistible Skittles, the vivacious courtesan and hunting lady who counted the Prince of Wales, Lord Hartington, Lord Hubert de Burgh, Wilfred Scawen Blunt, and Napoleon III's finance minister Achille Fould among her close friends, and the masters of most of the fashionable Midland hunts among her champions.[35]

In the more serious world of business it is also not entirely a straightfor-ward matter to decide what signals the energetic part of the aristocracy were flying or which way influences were flowing, from aristocratic entre-preneurs to the wider economy, or from the market place to the aristocrats. The simple generalization is that in the comparatively undeveloped state of the economy in the eighteenth century those landowners who had resources on their estates which they wished to have exploited tended to become their own undertakers, investors, and managers, because independent capitalists and entrepreneurs willing and able to do the job for them were thin on the ground. Then, the argument runs, as the industrial economy became firmly established the supplies of capital and of businessmen increased, making it possible for landowners to lease out their resources and to withdraw into the role of rentiers, where they could combine financial security with a

[34] See above, pp. 13–14.
[35] H. Blyth, *Skittles: The Life and Times of Catherine Walters* (1970), 73–92, 112–21, 137–44, 170–6, 181, 191, 194, 226.

generous slice of participation in the profits of industrial and urban development. This is broadly correct. Landowners in general confined their
attentions to developing the assets of their own estates, and did not commit
their capital or skills to unconnected or remote enterprises, until, that is, the
development of limited companies and the stock market in the second half
of the nineteenth century made it possible to participate in such concerns
without much trouble, though not without risk.

There were always some exceptions to this pattern. A very few, the Earl of
Derby, Lord Dartmouth, or Sir James Graham, for example, tried their
hands at the new cotton or woollen mills in the 1790s and early 1800s,
without great success.[36] In the 1870s and 1880s there was a curious mix-
ture of aristocratic frivolity and serious business enterprise in the London
cab trade. Hugh Lowther, later 5th Earl of Lonsdale, Viscount Mandeville,
later 8th Duke of Manchester, Viscount Savernake, later 4th Marquess of
Ailesbury, and Sir John Dugdale Astley, all dabbled in cab ownership as a
sort of jolly prank 'by purchasing a well-appointed cab or two and setting
them to ply for hire when they were not using them'.[37] They all lost money
and reputation, Savernake at least becoming one of the more notorious of
the disreputables when he married the actress Dolly Tester and became
embroiled with cockfighting, ratting, and other unsavoury pastimes.[38] The
20th Earl of Shrewsbury, on the other hand, was a serious cab proprietor
and reasonably successful businessman who saw the potential of the new
development of fitting solid rubber tyres to the hansom and putting a superior quality cab on the street. He built up a thriving business, sold his fleet
of 134 cabs and 325 horses in 1888, and concentrated on his Noiseless
Tyre Company which provided solid tyres for the trade, later moving into
motor tyres and the motor industry, in which his family name, Talbot, long
survived him.[39]

A perhaps more impressive instance of late Victorian aristocratic enterprise was provided by Charles Parsons, 6th son of the 3rd Earl of Rosse,
who invented the steam turbine in 1884 at the age of 30, and not only initiated a revolution in marine transport and the technology of steam power
but went on to exploit his invention so successfully that when he died in
1931 he left a well-established Tyneside engineering firm and a personal
fortune of well over £1 million and a substantial Northumbrian landed
estate.[40] Such exceptions, the argument continues, however dramatic they

[36] Beckett, *Aristocracy in England*, 225–7.
[37] Trevor May, *Gondolas and Growlers. The History of the London Horse Cab* (Stroud, 1995),
68–70.   [38] Earl of Cardigan, *The Wardens of Savernake Forest* (1949), 310–12.
[39] May, *London Horse Cab*, 72–5.
[40] D. J. Jeremy and C. Shaw, (eds.), *The Dictionary of Business Biography*, 5 vols. (1984–6), s.v.
the Hon. Sir Charles Algernon Parsons (1854–1931). The Rosse family estates were in Ireland,
with an outlier in the West Riding.

may have been do not upset the contention that aristocratic enterprise was as a rule confined to minerals from under their estates, houses and buildings on top of them, and such transport undertakings—roads, canals, and railways—as promised to be of direct service to their estates. Enterprise in these areas had been quite common in the eighteenth century, although never in urban schemes, where landowners commonly acted as planners and providers of layouts, but not as speculative builders; by the mid-nineteenth century it had become fairly rare. The generalization is, however, rather too much of a simplification. First, the implication that landowners were reluctant industrialists, waiting for the chance to withdraw into a passive role, is mistaken. Second, many more than a mere handful of magnates and gentry remained in business into the late nineteenth century, even if by then they had, for example, become a minority of the whole group of mineral owners. Third, the rentier role was not so passive, detached, and unenterprising as Martin Wiener, for one, imagines when he claims that: 'The capitalism of the aristocracy . . . was basically rentier, not entrepreneurial or productive.'[41]

The impression that landowners were unenthusiastic about, even bored by, their business ventures owes a lot to the much-quoted remark of Lord Granville in 1859: 'I am here [Stoke on Trent] looking after my ironworks, a necessary but tiresome operation.'[42] In fact the 2nd Earl Granville, who owned and ran three collieries and an ironworks with eight blast furnaces and 1,500 workers, had been investing heavily in his business since the mid-1840s, and continued to run it up to the time of his death in 1891, long after most of his contemporary aristocratic industrialists had given up and leased out their works.[43] That looks more like an enduring enthusiasm for business and attachment to industrial profits than boredom, and indeed his comment in 1859 was no more than an affectation to please the Duchess of Manchester, who liked her correspondents to amuse her with gossip and flirtation. What could well pass for positive enthusiasm was discernible among some of the eighteenth-century entrepreneurs, such as the Duke of Bridgewater with his collieries and canal; the Grand Allies of the north-eastern coal trade, Lord Ravensworth, Lord Wharncliffe, and the Bowes family, with investments reputedly of half a million apiece in collieries and ruthless tactics of cornering the market and then undercutting one another which would have been a credit to any business management manual; or the 6th Earl of Crawford and Balcarres, who wrote of the family's position in Lancashire that 'the trade of Coalmaster was their vocation'.[44] Keenness

[41] Wiener, *English Culture*, 8.
[42] A. L. Kennedy, (ed.), '*My Dear Duchess': Social and Political Leters to the Duchess of Manchester, 1858–69* (1956), 69.
[43] J. T. Ward and R. G. Wilson, (eds.), *Land and Industry* (Newton Abbot, 1971), 30, 178, 183.
[44] Ward and Wilson, *Land and Industry*, 70.

was maintained well into the nineteenth century by those like the 2nd Marquess of Bute, with his personal drive to build docks at Cardiff and open up the coal measures of his great estates in the hinterland; the 3rd Marquess of Londonderry, driven by an ambition to rival the Earl of Durham as a great coalowner and greatly savouring annual accounts which showed 'so much greater a net profit than we in our most sanguine moments had ever calculated upon'; or King Jog himself, the 1st Earl of Durham—who had once gravely remarked at breakfast to Maria Copley that 'a man might jog on with' an income of £40,000 a year, to which little Cop had replied when discussing Lord Harewood's fortune that 'she believed it exceeded a couple of jogs'.[45] Durham and his son the 2nd Earl were so fond of money and their collieries that the returns from them were notched up to more than nine jogs at their peak in 1873, although along with other business tycoons the Lambtons had to accept several years of much lower profits, or even losses, so that they did not count themselves free from financial worries.[46]

The inconvenience of violent year-to-year fluctuations in profits, to which the coal trade was particularly liable, was one powerful motive for colliery owners to turn themselves into simple lessors of coal royalties. Such behaviour was neither unusual nor especially indolent or effete, since most businessmen, most of the time, try to minimize their risks and stabilize their income, or construct a floor below which their profits will not fall, using a variety of strategies of which achieving a rentier or pseudo-rentier position is a favourite. Nevertheless, against the grain, the Earls of Durham remained great coalowners until 1896, when their 14 collieries were sold to Sir James Joicey; the 7th Marquess of Londonderry and the 4th Earl of Ellesmere (descended from the Duke of Bridgewater) were still in business as colliery owners in 1919; and the 2nd Earl of Dudley survived into the 1920s as the most successful and longest-established aristocratic industrialist of them all, with a history of family involvement as leading colliery owners, iron and steel masters, brickmakers, and canal and railway proprietors in the Black Country stretching over more than 200 years and ten generations. Moreover, when the Dudley enterprises were finally sold in the mid-1920s the 2nd Earl's eldest son negotiated a deal with the successor company which left the family as major shareholders and himself as company chairman, another favourite device of businessmen when floating successful private firms as public companies.[47]

[45] J. Davies, *Cardiff and the Marquesses of Bute* (Cardiff, 1981), 113, 247, 250–1, 259, 298–9; R. W. Sturgess, *Aristocrat in Business: The Third Marquess of Londonderry as Coalowner and Portbuilder* (Durham, 1975), 22–5; J. Gore, (ed.), *Creevey* (1948), 219, Creevey to Miss Ord, 13 Sept. 1821.

[46] D. Spring, 'The Earls of Durham and the Great Northern Coalfield, 1830–80', *Canadian Historical Review*, 33 (1952), 237–53.

[47] Ward and Wilson, *Land and Industry*, 74–5; T. J. Raybould, *The Economic Emergence of the Black Country: A Study of the Dudley Estate* (Newton Abbot, 1973), 158–61, 216–18, 241–3.

The capital and managerial requirements of sinking pits to the deep and running collieries, and of setting up and running ironworks with the new technologies of the eighteenth century, had long meant that partnerships of non-landowners, or in some cases partnerships which included the mineral owner, were the prevalent form of business organization. Even at the full tide of landowner participation, in the half century or so before 1830, it is probably more accurate to think of the landowner-industrialists as simply joining in the race rather than as leading and dominating the field. By the second half of the nineteenth century the capital needed for collieries or ironworks, and for the transport infrastructure to support them, was dauntingly large even for the wealthiest landowners like the Dukes of Buccleuch and Hamilton, the Marquess of Bute, or Earl Fitzwilliam, and it is not surprising that they chose not to continue as sole proprietors of great industrial undertakings. Many like them, moving into the rentier position, were overtaken by the scale of business rather than by aristocratic laziness or indifference to industry. The snapshot taken for the 1871 Royal Commission on Coal Supply, before withdrawal from business had turned into a general retreat, shows in detail the scale of landowner involvement as it existed in the year 1869. Looked at in one way, it was inconsiderable: less than 4 per cent of the 2,786 separate collieries then operating in Britain were aristocratic concerns. Looked at in another way the continued participation was rather more impressive: there were more than 40 colliery owners with hereditary titles, with an average of three concerns each, and that was roughly 10 per cent of the peerage as a whole and possibly as much as a quarter of the fraction of the peerage whose estates contained coal measures that were being worked at the time.[48] If that estimate is even approximately correct, then given that 1869 is known to mark a point in the decline of landowner enterprises it becomes plausible to suppose that earlier in the century a clear majority of aristocratic owners of coal were their own capitalists and colliery operators.

In that light the image being transmitted by this fraction of the aristocracy was one of active involvement in business, with a pro-industrial culture. It would be stretching a point to call it active involvement in trade, for although these landowners certainly discussed with their agents such allegedly vulgar details as the price of coal, the level of wages, the state of the market, or the creditworthiness of customers, it was still a lordly kind of business conducted at arm's length through agents and managers, and it was not a business providing their sole source of support. Similarly, those mineral owners who took up the rentier position might be just as actively and positively involved in a lordly kind of business. The degree of involvement was a matter of scale and of location. Owners of tracts too small to

---

[48] R.C. on Coal Supply, BPP 1871, XVIII, App. 27.

support a colliery, or of large tracts divorced from ownership of the surface, as occurred in manors where the minerals belonged to the lord but the lord did not own the relevant bit of the surface, could well be no more than passive rent-receivers performing no noticeable functions in return for royalties based on the quantity and price of the coal extracted. Many of the more active rentiers, who employed specialist mineral agents and interested themselves in the state and prospects of the coal trade, and who were familiar with the general business conditions of their districts, were essentially engaged in the non-productive adverserial functions of getting and safeguarding the greatest possible rents from their coal for the longest possible time through vigilant policing of their lessees, whose interest on the contrary was to pay as little as possible while extracting the largest possible amount of coal at the lowest possible costs consistent with not actually allowing their workings to collapse before all the profitable coal had been extracted. On occasion, however, some external threat could draw lessor and lessee together in defence of a superior common interest in the health of their district's economy, which overrode the underlying tensions between them, and then the aristocratic rentier performed as a most active and assertive industrialist.

The identity of interest between lessor and lessee arose because both parties acquired over time a growing vested interest in the continuation of their relationship. The lessee had sunk capital into an enterprise and feared that new competitors might destroy it, and the lessor, who might also have some dedicated infrastructure capital at stake, feared that new competitors might destroy his rental income. It is true that determined entrepreneurial defence by an aristocratic–business alliance was not necessarily successful. Thus the Taff Vale Railway, conceived in opposition to the 2nd Marquess of Bute by the ironmasters of Merthyr, and, as lessee of one side of the Bute Dock, in an almost continual state of hostility and friction with the Bute estate, nevertheless closed ranks with the 3rd Marquess in the 1880s: their united opposition to the proposal to build rival coal-shipping docks at Barry was strenuous, resourceful, and costly, but unavailing. The promoters of the Barry Dock and Railway, themselves supported by their local aristocrat, Lord Windsor, obtained their Act, the new dock was opened in 1889, and the coal trade and revenues of both Bute and Taff Vale were hit as predicted by the new competition.[49] Other alliances of lessors and lessees were equally vigorous in opposing outside competition, and rather more successful: a good example of this comes from Tyneside. Here the dukes of Northumberland were major landowners and royalty owners in the manor of Tynemouth, and controlled the best shipping place on the north bank of

[49] Davies, *Cardiff*, 288–91, 299; M. J. Daunton, *Coal Metropolis: Cardiff, 1870–1914* (Leicester, 1977), 20–1, 33–4.

the Tyne used by many private colliery lines, all paying wayleave rents based on the amount of coal carried. The 4th Duke's influence with the Admiralty and in Parliament was invaluable in steering the 1851 Bill for the construction on that site of the Northumberland Docks through the intricate shoals of the pretensions of the venerable and incompetent Tyne Conservancy Commissioners and the touchy civic pride of the City of Newcastle, while contriving to find no more than a tithe of the finance from his own pocket. This was achieved, as the Duke's agent told him, 'without Your Grace taking a prominent part in a measure which cannot be otherwise than galling to the inhabitants of the most important Town in the North of England'.[50]

It is even more significant that over the following two or three years the Duke formed a united front with his chief lessees, the Blyth and Tyne Railway and the colliery proprietors who owned it, to fend off a dangerous intruder in the shape of a rival railway line and dock company, which had the support of the Earl of Carlisle, a major mineral owner in the northerly hinterland of the region. The Blyth and Tyne had grown in a rather casual and unplanned way out of a simple colliery line, and was about as unpopular with parliamentary counsel, who found the concept of a passenger-carrying railway which paid wayleave rents objectionable and extortionate, as it was with its passengers, who were squeezed into carriages the size of coal tubs which they christened 'bumler boxes'. The Duke, however, had an important slice of income at stake, and the railway partners had considerable capital tied up in the line, and this formed a strong bond whatever their earlier differences may have been over the scale of wayleave rents and the obligation to ship exclusively through the Duke's spouts. In this situation the Duke and his chief agent devised a sophisticated business strategy. First they pushed through, at the Duke's expense, the parliamentary incorporation of the Blyth and Tyne Railway, in the face of much muttering that the wayleave principle was contrary to public policy. Then they reduced the level of wayleave rents, based on the tonnage of coal carried, to about half their former rate, in return for the new company signing a 1,000-year agreement to pay them, so that the company could now argue that its charges per ton-mile were comparable to those of any ordinary public railway. Thus prepared, they defeated the proposed rival line in private bill committee, and steered through an alternative bill giving the Blyth and Tyne powers to build more wayleave lines, making it into a small-scale regional monopolist.[51]

[50] Alnwick MS, Alnwick Castle, Northumberland, Business Minutes [of 4th Duke], ix, 24 Oct. 1851, pp. 64–8; and see F. M. L. Thompson, 'English Landed Society in the Nineteenth Century', in Pat Thane, G. Crossick, and R. C. Floud, (eds.), *The Power of the Past* (Cambridge, 1984), 205.
[51] HLRO, Blyth and Tyne Railway Bill, HL 1852, IV, fos. 3–5; Blyth and Tyne Railway, HC 1853, XXI, fos. 22, 36, 235–60; Blyth and Tyne Railway, HC 1853, XXII, fos. 1–71, 150–260; Tynemouth and Morpeth Direct Railway, HC 1853, XXII and XXIV, *passim*.

In the regional setting this was a business triumph of the first order for a landlord–lessee alliance; if it did not by itself determine the pattern of the district's economic development, it did determine how the profits of that development were to be shared out over the next FIFTY years or more. The capital of the Blyth and Tyne partners was secured and their future prosperity as a company was assured; so much so that within a decade they were playing railway politics with the North Eastern and the North British, scheming to become a link in the Edinburgh–Newcastle route. The Duke's income dipped temporarily because of the rent reduction, but rapidly recovered and went on increasing as coals from further and further to the north were carried over the system for shipment on the Tyne. Above all, the principle of wayleave rents was secured for a thousand years to come, and the misfortune that the agreement was not proof against the 1921 railway reorganization could scarcely have been foreseen. In situations of this kind the lines of division ran between competing landowners and competing businessmen, not between landowners as a group and entrepreneurs as a group; and an aristocratic landowner could well be of immense value to the whole business community of a region as a champion of their interests as well as his own, almost a latter-day baronial head of an industrial affinity. Moreover, although an aristocratic rentier like the Duke of Northumberland was financially cautious and ran much lesser risks than aristocratic entrepreneurs like the Earls of Durham or Dudley, there was little to choose between them in terms of business acumen and efficiency. It would be extremely hard to conclude from the example of this sub-group of the aristocracy that they were hostile to industry, indifferent to its problems, or ignorant of its nature.

Yet it is not difficult to understand how a historian of the very wealthy, W. D. Rubinstein, can conclude 'that from the beginnings of the Industrial Revolution down to the 1880s, the British landed aristocracy was increasingly becoming a caste-like and socially-isolated group, distancing itself from, and distanced from, the newer business magnates,' and how a cultural historian, Martin Wiener, can speak confidently of the domination of twentieth-century British society by 'preindustrial aristocratic and religious values . . . that inhibited [the] quest for expansion, productivity, and profit'.[52] The evidence shows that there was no one, single, unchanging set of aristocratic values. There were frivolous, extravagant, improvident, self-indulgent, and immoral aristocrats, more conspicuous and publicly visible at some periods than at others, who lent colour to the stock anti-aristocratic lines of popular radicalism, which were not wide of the mark in depicting their values as those of arrogance, parasitic privilege, and contempt for the industrious part of the population. There were businesslike and entrepreneurial

---

[52] W. D. Rubinstein, *Men of Property* (1981), 219; Wiener, *English Culture*, 127.

aristocrats, whose interest in money and wealth may have remained constant, but whose methods of pursuing them tended to change as the scale of business and the forms of business organization changed; their values were not those of undiluted Smilesian hard work and thrift, but were no further adrift from those values than were the majority of successful and moderately indulgent businessmen. Finally one should add a third group of aristocrats who were neither industrial entrepreneurs, because their estates were purely agricultural, nor particularly extravagant or fast-living, because a high-spending life in London society did not suit their disposition or their pocket.

In many ways this last group was the solid central core of the aristocracy. Its values were essentially of the rural, paternalist, hunting-shooting kind; its contacts with trade were at the retail level, which it regarded with condescension or distaste; and its general outlook could well be termed anti-industrial. This group was possibly the dominant ingredient in the aristocratic image in the middle of the eighteenth century; yet by the third quarter of the nineteenth century it was arguably the least influential of the three, because its wealth had not kept pace with the others and because its sphere of influence was increasingly restricted to rural local communities. The first group, the dissolutes, may well have become more influential, not because their escapades necessarily became more ruinous or more sensational so much as because they happened mainly in the metropolis and attracted press attention, both from the court newpapers and from the new populars like *Reynolds News*. The influence over the public mind of the second group, the aristocratic entrepreneurs, may have increased most of all. Not only did this group thrust ahead in the hundred years after 1780 and establish itself as the wealthiest subset of the aristocracy, the elite within the elite, but also by definition its wealth and its entrepreneurial qualities were on view essentially in the coalfield districts, the districts where industrialization was happening. Thus whatever this group had to say about the industrial spirit and entrepreneurial vigour was said in the heartlands of the new industrialists, while at the same time through its great wealth and possessions the group held a powerful position in London society and was much noticed in metropolitan circles.

At the end of the day, however, it remains arbitrary and unhistorical to claim that one group represented the true essence of aristocratic culture, to the exclusion of the others. The message is of horses for courses: the aristocracy sent out a range of different signals, and which ones were picked up depended on the character and disposition of those who received them.

3

Entrepreneurs as Aristocrats

Gentrification is a concept which has slid steadily downhill in the last thirty or forty years, like the gentry themselves. In the hands of estate agents, journalists, and urban geographers it has been transferred from people to things, and is used to describe the social uplifting and prettifying of previously run-down residential areas. For social historians gentrification is something which happens to individuals and families, the social uplifting and prettifying of the upwardly mobile as they seek to move from some previous more lowly social position and pass themselves off as gentry. There is, also, a third sense in which the term is used, when cultural historians speak of gentrification as a process which transmits a particular set of values, or even imposes them, through schools, universities, and the pervasively infiltrating power of elite opinions and manners. In this sense the concept is imprecise and nebulous, distanced from direct contact with the lives of real landed gentry or aristocracy, so that it tends to resist serious analysis. Observe, however, that Lawrence Stone grasps at this meaning in order to square the circle and argue that the upper middle class was gentrified by cultural mimicry of the landed elite although they were unable, or unwilling, to gentrify themselves by founding true landed families.[1] It is also a meaning affording great potential for indulgence in mental gymnastics, since it can be taken to imply a cunning upper-class subversion of late Marxist hegemony theory, in which the landed classes exercised an aristocratic-gentry hegemony to bewitch and bemuse the bourgeoisie at the very time when they were supposed to be exercising a bourgeois hegemony to morally discipline and socially control the toiling masses.

The first two meanings are less exciting than this, and more amenable to dispassionate appraisal. Oddly, however, the greatest passion in the recent historiography of the subject has been aroused by gentrification as a conceptually simple and straightforward process in which businessmen, new men of wealth, acquire landed property and some of the true characteristics of the older landed elite.[2] Estate agents' debasement of language can,

[1] Lawrence Stone and Jeanne C. Fawtier Stone, *An Open Elite? England, 1540–1880* (Oxford, 1984) 409–11.

[2] Ibid. David Spring and Eileen Spring, 'The English Landed Elite, 1540–1879', *Albion*, 17 (1985), 150–66; Lawrence Stone, 'Spring Back', ibid., 167–80. David Spring and Eileen Spring, 'Social Mobility in the English Landed Elite', *Canadian Journal of History*, 2 (1987), 333–51. W. D. Rubinstein, 'New Men of Wealth' *Past & Present*, 92 (1981), 125–47; id., *Men of Property*

however, be helpful here as a reminder that a property can itself be gentrified, by the character and reputation of its occupier more than by its fixtures
and fittings; and that the properties amenable to this process do not necessarily have to be ostentatiously large and grand, although admittedly they
need to be more landed, for a country gentry status, than a terraced house
in Islington which may pass muster for the urban pseudo-gentry.

The issue of the size of landed estate which reflected, or conferred, gentry status has generated its share of heat and misunderstanding among historians, and although it may not be possible to settle the matter once and
for all, it is possible to stake out a reasonably clear and tenable position. A
variety of thresholds has been proposed for gentry-ranking estates: with
nineteenth-century English conditions in mind, where an average acre produced a rental income of roughly £1 a year, figures of 1,000, 2,000, 3,000,
and on occasion as much as 5,000 acres have been advanced as the minimum required to support a gentry family.[3] How should we choose between
them? As a start it should be remarked that if some stipulated income from
land was a necessary part of the qualification, then rents per acre of agricultural land varied according to quality and location from less than half, or
even a quarter, of the average to as much as four or five times, so that the
size of estate required to furnish an income of, say, £1,000 a year might
range from 200 acres up to 4,000 acres depending on the part of the country it was in. The rental extremes, particularly the very high rents per acre,
were to be found in special situations, such as dairying or market garden
land on the edge of large towns, and perhaps should not be applied to the
gentry, whose estates were most unlikely to consist entirely of such land—
although the very low rents per acre, characteristic of poor upland grazing,
were often found on gentry shooting estates. A more appropriate rental
spread for gentry measurement is provided by James Caird's estimates of
normal rents in 1850–1 for the counties which he visited, which run from
15s. to 45s. per acre, implying that a £1,000 income could be supplied,
depending on its location, by an estate in the range 444–1,333 acres.[4]

Income, and the acreage needed to provide it, was clearly very important,
but recognition as a landed gentleman depended on other attributes and

(1981). F. M. L. Thompson, 'Life after Death: How Successful Nineteenth-century Businessmen
Disposed of their Fortunes', *Economic History Review*, 2nd ser., 43 (1990), 40–61; W. D. Rubinstein,
'Cutting up Rich', *Economic History Review*. 2nd ser., 45 (1992), 350–61; F. M. L. Thompson,
'Stitching it Together Again', ibid., 362–75; id., 'Business and Landed Elites in the Nineteenth
Century', in id. (ed.), *Landowners, Capitalists, and Entrepreneurs* (Oxford, 1994), 139–70; W. D.
Rubinstein, 'Businessmen into Landowners: The Question Revisited', in Negley Harte and Roland
Quinault (eds.), *Land and Society in Britain, 1700–1914* (Manchester, 1996), 90–118.

³ Rubinstein, 'New Men of Wealth', 135–6, rather suddenly introduces a 5,000-acre threshold
into a discussion previously grounded on a 2,000-acre measuring rod.

⁴ Caird's observations are usefully mapped in M. E. Turner, J. V. Beckett, and B. Afton, *Agricultural Rent in England, 1690–1914* (Cambridge, 1997), fig. 2.2, p. 47.

qualities besides possession of an estate, notably on blood, lineage, family connections, and long occupation of the same country seat by the family; and on the style of living, the household establishment, the scale of entertaining, and the participation in the local or county community by the resident owner. One might expect that the older the family the smaller the minimum acreage qualification, and that social arbiters might exact a much higher territorial stake from newcomers who brought nothing but their wealth, and perhaps a fabricated pedigree, on to the social scene. Supreme among the arbiters was Burke's *Landed Gentry*, launched in 1833, a more rigorously and exclusively landed social register than contemporary alternatives, such as Walford's *County Families*, started in 1860 and essentially a directory of the 'upper ten thousand' with wide coverage of the administrative and military classes as well as the landed. Until 1914 'a strict requirement of landed property was enforced, and if a family sold its estates the pedigree was ejected from the book [the *Landed Gentry*]', and although this 'strict requirement' was never more closely defined than possession of 'a considerable country estate', that was generally assumed to have been one of at least £500 a year. The original arbiter, J. B. Burke himself, in 1861 addressed the question of the minimum amount of landed estate which he considered essential to support hereditary titles, and pronounced the criteria to be £500 a year, from land, for a baronetcy, and £2,000 a year for a peerage. This permits the inference that an untitled landed gentleman might get by on a bit less than £500 a year.[5]

With that yardstick in hand an interesting comparison can be made between entries in the 1871 edition of *Burke* and entries in the New Domesday Book of 1873, which recorded, with some errors, all the landowners in Britain and the exact sizes and annual values of their properties.[6] These two registers are so close together in date that, in a 5 per cent sample of the *Burke* gentry, 98 per cent can be positively identified in the New Domesday Book. The larger landowners are well represented, with a quarter of the *Burke* gentry owning estates of 3,000 acres or more, among them a sprinkling of the untitled aristocracy with estates of over 10,000 acres. A further 10 per cent of the *Burke* gentry had estates in the 2,000 to 3,000 acre range; but the tail was very long, with another quarter having estates of 1,000 to 2,000 acres, and well over one-third owning less than 1,000 acres

---

[5] *Burke's Landed Gentry*, preface to the 18th edn., vol. iii (1972); preface to 16th edn. (1952), p. xviii; J. B. Burke, *The Vicissitudes of Families*, 2nd ser. (1861), 6.

[6] For the landowners with 2,000 acres and more the revisions of the New Domesday figures by J. Bateman, in various editions of *The Great Landowners of Great Britain and Ireland* (1876, 1878, 1879, and 1883), have been preferred to those in the *Return of Owners of Land, 1873, England and Wales* (C.1097, 2 vols., 1875) [The New Domesday Book] as being more accurate. For owners of fewer than 2,000 acres, who were not noticed by Bateman, the New Domesday entries have been used; as these are arranged county by county some of the smaller estates which lay in two, or more, counties may have been missed.

each. One way of looking at these figures is to say that a clear majority of those socially accepted as being landed gentry, roughly two-thirds of them, passed the 1,000-acre threshold. The other way of looking at them is to say that a clear majority of the landed gentry, roughly two-thirds of them, failed the 2,000-acre test. Those with the smallest estates, of less than 1,000 acres, held properties ranging from 11 to 954 acres. The 11 acres belonged to William St-Julian Arabin of Beech Hill Park, Essex, apparently purchased by his grandfather, a successful lawyer and judge, in the 1830s; it was closely matched by the 12 acres of the Right Reverend Francis Kerrill Amherst of Field Gate House, Kenilworth, no doubt accepted by *Burke* on the strength of his dignity as Roman Catholic Bishop of Northampton, though presumably he did not entertain the ambition of founding a landed family. The 954 acre estate, although small, supported two country houses: it belonged to the long-established Staffordshire family of the Adderleys of Coton Hall, Uttoxeter, who acquired a second seat, Barlaston Hall, Stone, through marrying an heiress in 1816.[7]

The tiddlers in this group of sub-thousand acre gentry estates were indifferently the product of recent purchase, complicated inheritance patterns, or fresh starts by younger sons, and showed no bias towards any particular type of origin. Atherley of Northbrook House, Hampshire, was a Southampton businessman who purchased his 'estate' of 37 acres from a double-barrelled colonel in the 1850s; Armstrong of Hemsworth, near Pontefract, the son of an East India Company servant, inherited his 54-acre estate from his grandmother through his aunt; and Attye of Ington Grange, Warwickshire, was the youngest son of a minor Yorkshire gentry family, and made his own way into his 84-acre 'estate'. Such minute estates, smaller than most farms, were obviously incapable of making more than a token contribution to financing the style of a landed gentleman, and their owners were no more than pseudo-gentry, living on some other, non-landed, source of income. All the same, most of them were JPs and Deputy Lieutenants in their counties in the 1870s, indicating a degree of formal acceptance into county society, and some had contrived rather convoluted marriage connections with the established aristocracy through marriage to the granddaughter of the younger son of a baronet, or to the daughter of a younger son of a bishop who was the brother of a baronet, connections painstakingly and lovingly recorded in *Burke*. In any case the tiddlers, located somewhere on the fringes of the seriously landed gentry, did not seriously affect the normal estate-size of the sub-thousand acre gentry as a whole: the average size of estates in this group was 417 acres, and the median size 455 acres.

---

[7] The sample consists of all entries under the letter 'A' in *Burke's Landed Gentry* (1871 edn.) with English or Welsh seats, a total of 90 families, linked to their landowning as recorded in Bateman or the New Domesday Book.

No one would dispute that there were many respects in which the owners of estates of the order of four or five hundred acres, whether they were
members of long-established families or newcomers from the business or
professional world, could not look the greater gentry or the magnates in the
eye. They were, after all, the merest of the mere parish gentry, whose total
obscurity and intensely parochial interests and culture place them completely outside the pale of the Stones' great study of the landed classes.[8]
Their inferiority in acres and income clearly made them inferior in influence
and social standing. Yet their inferiority was perhaps a matter of shades of
distinction more apparent to insiders within the landed classes than to outsiders. In the sample of sub-thousand acre gentry estates 80 per cent of the
owners were JPs, and two-thirds were related to aristocratic or greater
gentry families by descent or by marriage. To the rest of the world these five-
hundred-acre men must have looked like authentic members of the local
ruling class, an elite group into which the quarter of the set who were newcomers who had purchased their estates since 1800 appear to have been
fully assimilated.[9]

These families may not have offered any great catches in the marriage
market, but their proven eligibility for providing partners for the younger
daughters or sons of the more substantial gentry and aristocracy suggests
that they were accepted as more or less social equals and were not consigned
to the parochial isolation which the Stones seem to imply. This was achieved
almost as frequently by the new men as by long-settled members of the
lesser gentry, by the Allens of Clifford Priory in Herefordshire, recently
arrived on their 390 acre estate, whose first owner married the daughter of
a cousin of the Earl of Derby in 1845, or by Awdry of Seend, Wiltshire, settled on their estate of 573 acres since the seventeenth century, whose father
had married in 1794 a daughter of the third son of the Duke of Somerset.
Admittedly, for either type in this set, whether old or new families, the great
majority of marriage partners were found among their own kind and from
clerical or military families. Still, the evidence is plain enough that a modest estate of four or five hundred acres could support a gentry family which
moved in the same circles, at least for purposes of some social intercourse
and intermarriage, as their grander and wealthier neighbours, and that this
was possible for newcomers as well as for old families. It is hardly surprising that the owner of such an estate might have a prominent local position,
since it could comprise up to half a dozen tenanted farms and a number
of cottage properties, quite sufficient to confer control over many a village
or parish. The surprise is that the Stones should have been so dismissive
of the mere parish gentry, and so gullible as to take at face value the stock

---

[8] Stone and Stone, *Open Elite?*, 6–7, 184–7, 402.
[9] There were 2 MPs in the group, both of them among the recent purchasers.

stereotype of the mere parish gentry as bucolic, ill-educated, and boorish, 'the butt of the London wits, poets, and playwrights from Shakespeare to Sheridan and beyond', as they emphasize.[10]

A family such as the Harpurs of Burton Latimer Hall, Northamptonshire, with an estate of no more than 578 acres, which they inherited at the end of the eighteenth century, were not ill-educated by the standards of the time, and if their outlook was parochial it did not prevent them from finding all their marriage partners from outside the county. Between 1780 and 1914 one Harpur went to Worcester College, one to Corpus Christi, Cambridge, and one to Trinity Hall, Cambridge, while two went to Bradfield School and two to Hurstpierpoint College; two of them were rectors of Calthorpe, Leicestershire, and another two were Northamptonshire JPs. Deeply obscure and undistinguished they may have been in any national sense, but they rated entries in *Burke's Landed Gentry* and in *Kelly's Handbook to the Titled, Landed, and Official Classes*, and were plainly of some consequence locally. The Brooks of Flitwick, Bedfordshire, were no less parochial, with their estate of 660 acres acquired by the marriage of a London banker to an heiress in 1789, but the boorishness of John Thomas Brooks, an enthusiastic and experimental horticulturalist of more than local renown in the 1840s and 1850s, is open to question.[11] It is not suggested that two swallows make a summer, merely that modest landed estates—in both these cases the income from land was around £1,000 a year in the mid-nineteenth century—were consistent with definite, if modest, landed gentry status.

Not surprisingly the equation of landed gentry with small estate does not necessarily work the other way round. All the landed gentry who were socially recognized as such obviously owned landed property—until, that is, the 1930s, when the social register began to record families who had parted with their land, in the interests of continuing the record of gentry pedigrees, thus moving the goalposts and converting the 'landed gentry' into a hereditary caste which might be completely landless.[12] All the owners of small estates, however were not necessarily recognized as being gentry. Taking the two counties of Bedfordshire and Northamptonshire as passably representative of

---

[10] Stone and Stone, *Open Elite?* 6, repeated on p. 398. Interestingly, they view with extreme scepticism the 'stock theme of social commentators as well as playwrights' about 'the decline and disappearance of the established families of the county and their replacement by self-made newcomers from the City' (p. 17.) Playwrights may clearly be believed or not believed at will.

[11] *Burke's Landed Gentry* (centenary edn., 1937); F. M. L. Thompson, *English Landed Society in the Nineteenth Century* (1963), 132–3.

[12] *Burke's Landed Gentry* (centenary edn., 1937), preface, p. xv, explained that the inclusion of landless gentry, for the first time, was necessary to sustain the value of the 'book as being a record of the history and inter-relationship of what was, and still is, an important class', and their omission 'would have left a serious gap in the matrimonial cross-references from the accounts of those families which still retain their land ... some families which had been omitted from previous editions because of the loss of their properties now reappear as "formerly of" estates which in some cases serve as the qualification of other families newly admitted to these pages.'

TABLE 1. *Gentry status and estate size: Bedfordshire and Northamptonshire*

	Total number untitled	Outliers	Net number small estates	*Landed Gentry families*	percentage of net number in *Landed Gentry*
400–2,000 acres	200	26	174	68	39.0
400–999 acres	141	11	130	41	31.5
1,000–2,000 acres	59	15	44	27	61.0

Sources: Return of Owners of Land, 1873; Burke's Landed Gentry (1871 edn.).

All owners with hereditary titles have been excluded. Owners who were younger sons, or descended from younger sons, of peers or baronets have been counted as 'gentry'.

Midland agricultural and rural England where landownership was likely to have been more stable over a long period than in either the Home Counties or strongly industrializing and urbanizing counties, and hence likely to have the highest levels of gentry recognition, a test of the relationship between gentry status and estate size has been conducted. As expected, practically all of the owners of estates of 2,000 acres and above were either members of the landed nobility or appeared in *Burke's Landed Gentry*. In 1873 there were 200 lesser estates, in the range of 400–1,999 acres, of which 26 were outlying parts of larger family holdings in other counties which in aggregate were above the 2,000-acre threshold. There were thus 174 lesser estates, all in the possession of untitled owners, and of these some 40 per cent were recorded in the pages of the *Landed Gentry*. Subdivision of this group produces a gratifying size correlation: just over 60 per cent of the estates of 1,000–1,999 acres were in the hands of authentic gentry, while barely 30 per cent of the smallest estates of 400–999 acres were so, as indicated in Table 1. The social status of the non-gentry owners, a minority of the first sub-group and a majority of the second, is anyone's guess: they could have been, variously, genuine old-fashioned yeomen, owner-occupying farmers, absentee landowners, or upwardly mobile owners whose aspirations to gentry standing had not yet been accepted.[13] The absentee landowners, in turn, would include some who had inherited a family holding and were away in town pursuing a professional or business career, and others who had invested in land as a low-risk security in the same way as some men of property put their savings into house property.

The object of this excursion into the territorial definition of a landed gentleman was to arrive at some tenable acreage guidelines. Those guidelines

---

[13] Upward mobility was shown by 8 of the owners in the 1,000–2,000 acre group and 9 of those in the 400–999 acre set, who were not recorded in *Burke's Landed Gentry* in the 1871 edition but whose direct descendants were listed in the 1937 edition.

are suggestive and permissive, not prescriptive. There was a high probabil-ity, virtually a certainty, that anyone owning more than 2,000 acres would be accepted as landed gentry; a reasonable prospect that an estate of more than 1,000 acres would qualify; and about a one-in-three chance that own-ership of fewer than 1,000 acres might be acceptable. From the point of view of a new purchaser one could say that going for an estate of 2,000 acres would almost guarantee assimilation into the ranks of the gentry, sooner or later, while it would not by any means have been foolish to har-bour aspirations for gentry status in return for an investment in little more than 400 acres of well-placed land.

These conclusions are highly pertinent when confronted by the colli-sion between Wiener's high degree of gentrification of businessmen, and the low level of gentrification favoured by the Stones and Rubinstein. Martin Wiener would probably regard his thesis as immune to vulgar measure-ment, except possibly in the counting of apposite quotations from Matthew Arnold, Charles Dickens, William Morris, John Ruskin, and a few more of the Victorian intelligentsia; there are indeed remarkably few numbers or measurements of any kind in his book, but if his argument were to be sus-ceptible of verification it would presumably adopt the lowest possible size of gentry estate for its scale, to maximize the gentrification effect. The Stones and Rubinstein, on the other hand, explicitly or implicitly use the highest possible minimum estate size for the bottom rung on their scale of gentrifi-cation, in the cause of minimizing the effect. The Stones counted country houses, not acres, those which they found by a complicated system of meas-urement to have been large enough and grand enough to house a member of the county elite or a landed grandee and his family and establishment. They claimed a rough correspondence between the owners of their country houses and the owners, in the 1870s, of estates of 3,000 acres—rather more country-house owners than estate-owners in two of their sample counties, Hertfordshire and Northamptonshire, and considerably fewer in the third county, Northumberland. By their definitions, therefore, the gen-trification of businessmen through land and country house purchase was bound to be much less, perhaps two-thirds less, than gentrification meas-ured by the criteria of *Burke's Landed Gentry*. A curiosity is that in Northamptonshire some half dozen of the houses owned by 'mere parish gentry' with estates of fewer than 2,000 acres appear in the Stones' list of elite houses: these were Marston St Lawrence, on an estate of 1,894 acres; Wadenhoe (1,819 acres); Glendon Hall (1,417 acres); Welton Place (1,066 acres); Thorpe Manor (958 acres); Boughton Hall (404 acres); and Brixworth Hall (1,094 acres).[14] Rubinstein, claiming that there was very

<hr />

[14] Martin Wiener, *English Culture and the Decline of the Industrial Spirit, 1850–1980* (Cambridge. 1981), 12–13, merely remarks in general terms on the tendency of British industrialists to buy

little gentrification of businessmen in the nineteenth century, has an implicit disagreement with the Stones, since he contrasts a low level of estate-purchasing after 1780 with allegedly higher levels in previous centuries, while the Stones argue for consistently low levels for the entire period 1540–1880, and provide statistics which in fact show a higher level of business purchasers in the nineteenth century than in the two hundred years before 1760.[15]

Rubinstein is, indeed, concerned with acres, not country houses, when measuring the land-purchasing activities of businessmen, and goes out of his way to dismiss the mere possession or occupation of a country house, in the absence of evidence that a sizeable quantity of land was attached to it, as evidence of gentrification. His choice of the 13 members of the Crawshay ironmasters' dynasty listed in the 1895 edition of *Walford's County Families* to illustrate this point is a little unfortunate, although the point itself, that owning a 'house in the country' was not the same as owning a country estate with a house on it, is valid. *Walford* listed 15 country houses as belonging to Crawshays, dismissed by Rubinstein as merely impressive country addresses with no land behind them. In fact in 1873 the 15 living members of the Crawshay dynasty owned between them at least 8 country houses (a further 6 were probably rented), each with land attached, and a total of 4,069 acres worth £9,728 a year. The houses dismissively named by Rubinstein—Cyfarthfa Castle, Haughton Castle, Scole Lodge, Bradbourne Hall—were all owned by Crawshays and all had land attached; he misses Hingham Hall, Oaklands Park, and Dany Park, and above all Caversham which had become the chief Crawshay house and estate.[16] Just how many acres Rubinstein had in mind when declaring that one of the most distinctive and significant features of nineteenth-century social and political developments was the absence of land purchasing on any scale by the new men of wealth is not altogether clear. The firm ground is that no blocks of land of fewer than 2,000 acres entered into his calculus. But there is more than a suspicion that his most cherished aim was to prove the somewhat obvious point that very few, if any, new men of wealth, regardless of whether that wealth came from finance, commerce, or industry, were

country estates; there are no entries in the index for 'country houses', 'land', 'landed estates', or 'landed gentry'. Stone and Stone, *Open Elite?*, 11, 62, App. II; the Northamptonshire houses in their sample are listed on pp. 432–3.

[15] W. D. Rubinstein, *Elites and the Wealthy in Modern British History* (Brighton, 1987), 157–9; id., *Men of Property*, 218–19; Stone and Stone, *Open Elite?*, table 6.2; the figures show that in the period 1540–1759, 26 per cent of the purchasers of country houses were from business origins and 42 per cent in the period 1760–1879, in absolute numbers 68, business-purchasers in the first 219 years and 84 in the next 119 years.

[16] Rubinstein, *Men of Property*, 218; *Return of Owners of Land, 1873*; John Habakkuk, *Marriage, Debt and the Estates System. English Landownership, 1650–1950* (Oxford, 1994), 553–4, 555, 590.

capable of acquiring land on a truly ducal scale (most dukes having acquired by royal or parliamentary grant anyway, rather than by purchase). This leads him to speak of the 10,241-acre estate purchased by Giles Loder, a Russia merchant, and his son, in the 1860s and 1870s, as being only 'moderate' and of little consequence. Hence, also, the major conclusion he draws from his study of the relationship between new wealth and landownership is that the collective weight of business fortunes made little impact on the structure of landed society, because it failed to transform, and did not attempt to transform, the character of either the super-elite of the magnates, or that of the gentry.[17]

There is some confusion of thought here. It is quite true that very few businessmen at any time in the two hundred years since 1780 bought their way into the company of the landed magnates. In the list of the 29 individuals with the largest incomes from land in 1883, £75,000 a year or more, only one was a businessman: the banker, Samuel Jones Loyd, Lord Overstone, whose land purchases and those of his father totalled over 54,000 acres.[18] Rubinstein found ten new men of wealth who owned estates of more than 25,000 acres in 1883, many of them household names from the classic period of the Industrial Revolution: among ironmasters, the Guests of Dowlais (later Lord Wimborne), the Baileys of Glanusk (later Lord Glanusk), the Bairds of Lanark (later Lord Stonehaven), and the Cunninghames of Craigends, near Paisley; from cotton, the Peels, from brewing the Guinnesses, and from commerce, the Mathesons of Jardine Matheson; banking furnished three grandees: the Barings, the Rothschilds, and the Scotts. Some were more obscure, like James Morrison, textile warehouseman and wholesaler, the richest commoner of the nineteenth century.[19] One, Lord Eldon, came from the pre-1832 days when truly immense fortunes could be made from the law and 'old corruption'. To these a few should be added who were overlooked by Rubinstein: the banker William Joseph Denison, whose own land purchases plus his large fortune in personalty were incorporated into a 52,000-acre estate by his heir, his sister's fourth but second surviving son Lord Albert Conyngham, who adopted the Denison name and was created Lord Londesborough; another banker, Thomas Leyland of Liverpool, whose three successors owned 40,000 acres between them in 1883; and two more ironmasters, William Orme Foster of Staffordshire, who combined his uncle's fortune with his own to set up a 21,000-acre estate in Shropshire, and William Thompson, ironmaster of

[17] Rubinstein, *Men of Property*, 218; id., *Elites and the Wealthy*, 158–9.
[18] Id., *Men of Property*, table 7.1; R. C. Michie, 'Income, Expenditure, and Investment of a Victorian Millionaire: Lord Overstone, 1823–83', *Bulletin of the Institute of Historical Research*, 58 (1985), 59–77. In 1883 Overstone himself owned nearly 31,000 acres, having given a further 20,000 acres to his only daughter and eventual sole heiress on her marriage in 1858 to James Loyd-Lindsay (created Lord Wantage in 1885).   [19] Rubinstein, *Men of Property*, 215–17.

Pennydarren and Tredegar and banker in the City, whose lands and fortune went to his only daughter and heiress, married to the Earl of Bective. Thompson tried to make sure that the estates purchased with his money should remain separate from the hereditary estate of the Marquess of Headfort by stipulating that they should descend to his daughter's second son, or failing that to her eldest son (whose courtesy title was the Earl of Bective) only until he should inherit the marquessate, but unfortunately his daughter's early death in 1864 leaving only one son and that son's predeceasing his father somewhat upset these plans.[20]

Even with these additions there is no cause to dissent from the conclusion that no more than 10 per cent of these very large estates were owned by new men in 1883, although it should be noted that among those new men the industrialists were a clear majority, while fortunes derived from banking and commerce came only in second place. In the hundred years since 1883 there have not surprisingly been considerably fewer purchasers at this magnate level. In the 1890s Samuel Cunliffe-Lister used part of the fortune he had made from wool-combing to put together an estate of 34,000 acres in Yorkshire, taking the title of Lord Masham from one of his villages; Weetman Pearson salted away some of the profits of Mexican oil and his construction businesses, on either side of the Great War, in a comparably sized estate in Sussex and Scotland, being called Lord Cowdray after his polo ground; William Lever, 1st Lord Leverhulme, reputedly bought as much as 100,000 acres from the proceeds of Sunlight soap; more recently, with the continued popularity of sporting estates, the financier Christopher Moran bought the Glenfiddich property of 45,000 acres in the heart of whisky and Balmoral country, in the 1980s, and there may be other examples of vast tracts of relatively low value Scottish grouse moors and deer forest acquired by new men, such as Lord Dulverton who had turned some of the Wills' tobacco money into 263,000 acres in Scotland, as well as into a lowland estate in Somerset.[21] The last hundred years has indeed produced scarcely more than a handful of new landed magnates with more than 25,000 acres each; but in the same period the total number of such estates has dwindled as the old-established aristocracy have sold off large parts of their inheritance. In the 1980s there were probably no more than 30 such estates in Britain, two-thirds of them in Scotland; of that 30 a quarter were owned by

[20] Barbara English, *The Great Landowners of East Yorkshire, 1530–1910* (Hemel Hempstead, 1990), 30; F. M. L. Thompson, 'Life after Death: How Successful Nineteenth-century Businessmen Disposed of their Fortunes', *Economic History Review*, 2nd ser., 43 (1990), App. 2; id., 'Desirable Properties: The Town and Country Connection in British Society since the late Eighteenth Century', *Historical Research*, 64 (1991), 156–71.

[21] F. M. L. Thompson, 'English Landed Society in the Twentieth Century: II, New Poor and New Rich', *Transactions of the Royal Historical Society*, 6th ser., 1 (1991), 1–20.

new men, so that the relative penetration of the super-elite by new money had actually increased.[22]

That statistic has curiosity value rather than any great social significance. At no time has it been possible for a new man of wealth to contemplate entering into serious territorial competition with the greatest ducal grandees like Bedford, Buccleuch, Devonshire, Northumberland, or Sutherland. These owed their great empires to the fortunes of war and rebellion, plunder, royal favouritism, and above all to generations of accumulation and fortunate marriages. In more settled and law-abiding times like the eighteenth and nineteenth centuries, where outright theft or confiscation were impossible, it was inconceivable that anyone could make a large enough fortune in a single lifetime to be able to buy such an estate on the open market, and it would be foolish to assume that any businessman, however proud and ambitious, ever tried to do so. Even the shortcut to aggrandisement, heiress marriage, could not be made to catapult wealthy businessmen up the territorial ladder. Heiresses with money, which businessmen might produce, could be attractive to needy landowners and could be a great help in keeping old families afloat; but heiresses with large acres were carefully reserved for large-acred husbands, and were never, until recently, allowed to squander their attractions on men of no social position, however wealthy. The one identified case of a large landed heiress marrying into a non-landed family appears to be that of Elizabeth Millicent, only daughter of the second son of the 4th Duke of Sutherland, who was heiress-presumptive to the earldom of Sutherland and those estates which were attached to that title (which included Dunrobin Castle, the family seat) at the time of her marriage in 1946 to Captain Charles Noel Janson, whose father had a house in Belgravia, but no other known position. On the death of her uncle the 5th Duke of Sutherland in 1963 she became Countess of Sutherland in her own right.[23] Sensible businessmen do not set themselves unattainable targets, and it is not meaningful to say that if they had set out to rival the largest ducal estates the record shows that they signally failed to do so. It is arguable, however, that some families originating in business wealth suc-

---

[22] The new landed magnates extant in the 1980s were:

Viscount Cowdray (Pearson)	17,000 acres Sussex 60,000 acres Aberdeen
Viscount Leverhulme (Lever)	90,000 acres Cheshire 23,000 acres Scotland
Lord Vestey	4,500 acres Gloucestershire 93,000 acres Scotland
Christopher Moran	45,000 acres Scotland
Lord Dulverton (Wills)	263,000 acres Scotland over 3,000 acres in Somerset
Lord Thorneycroft	44,000 acres Scotland
Viscount Wimborne (Guest)	32,000 acres Dorset

Sources: Sunday Times, 'Britain's Rich, the Top 200', (2 Apr., 1989); J. McEwen, Who Owns Scotland? (Edinburgh, 1981); R. Norton-Taylor, Whose Land is it Anyway? (1982).

[23] *Burke's Peerage and Baronetage* (1949 edn.); *Who's Who* (1977 edn.).

ceeded, over the generations, in exuding as much power and influence, and in attracting as much public notice, as any of the dukes, irrespective of the size of the estates that they acquired: Barings, Carringtons, and Rothschilds (from banking), Gladstones and Peels (from cotton and the cotton trade), Guinnesses (from brewing), Courtaulds (from silk and mourning crepe), and Ridleys (from coal and glass), are cases in point, while coal was also the foundation of the Bowes-Lyon family.

In any case it was not in the interests of new men of wealth to attempt to revolutionize the character of the landowning set, whether the grandees or the mere parish gentry, if their intention was to join the established elite and be accepted by it, and not to overthrow it or replace it by a new-fashioned elite modelled in their own image. In this sense the acquisition of a 10 per cent share of the group of really large estates could have been evidence of highly successful penetration of the old landed order and compatible with assimilation into it, while some hypothetically higher rate of invasion might have meant failure through overkill, as it might have undermined the old order and destroyed its social attraction.

Approaching the question of the gentrification of businessmen through examination of the proportion of landowners who were new men is not, however, unproblematic. It is, of course, the approach adopted by the Stones in their assessment of the *Open Elite?* Their precise answers to the question have been disputed, but leaving aside those arguments the method itself is designed to show how many members of the landed elite were new men, not what proportion of the new men of wealth succeeded in joining the landed elite. The answers given by the Stones are that some 4 per cent of all owners of country houses in the first half of the eighteenth century were purchasers from the world of business, about 11 per cent of the owners in the period 1760–1819, and 9 per cent in the period 1820–79.[24] If one assumes that most of the families who had been purchasers between 1760 and 1819 remained in possession in 1879, then an alternative way of expressing these findings would be to say that about one-fifth of the owners of large country houses in 1879 represented families who had arrived from business origins at some point since 1760. The triumphant declaration that these figures prove that 'the traditional concept of an open elite . . . is dead' appears a trifle premature.[25] Their figures do prove that the landed elite remained rather stable in composition, with considerable continuity of

[24] Stone and Stone, *Open Elite?*, table 6.2. Purchasers from office-holding and the law accounted for 5 per cent of the 1760–1819 and 3 per cent of the 1820–79 owners.

[25] Stone and Stone, *Open Elite?*, 403. The statement on the same page that the bulk of purchasers were 'men enriched by public office or the law', as in the rest of Europe, is also at variance with their own figures, which show 157 businessmen-purchasers in the entire period 1579–1879 as against 142 from office and the law; and for the 1760–1879 period 89 from business and 36 from office and the law: table 6.2.

membership, over a long period of time, and that at any given point of time older-established families easily outnumbered recent arrivals. They also prove that the elite was not closed, and was always open to some new men. Possibly they prove that there never were great throngs of merchants and manufacturers knocking at the door and seeking admission. But they are silent on the question of the propensity of the very wealthiest businessmen to seek to join the elite. If there was only a small number of wealthy merchants and manufacturers, many or most of whom succeeded in entering the elite, then the elite was as open as it could possibly be. If, on the other hand, the business-purchasers of country houses or very large estates were no more than a small fraction of the total number of very wealthy businessmen, then the elite, although not closed, was certainly an exclusive club that excluded, or had little attraction for, the mainstream fortunes created by the commercial and industrial revolutions.

The attempt to get round this difficulty by approaching the question from the other side, trying to establish what proportion of all businessmen did in fact acquire landed estates, was pioneered by Bill Rubinstein. Since it is impossible to define or identify a population comprising 'all businessmen' or even one consisting of 'all successful businessmen' or 'all wealthy businessmen', he took as his criterion wealth left at death in the form of personalty assessed to probate duty, and studied the land-purchasing activities of all millionaires and half-millionaires. This procedure produces a clearly defined group of wealthy businessmen (and others with non-business sources of their fortunes), but it has well-understood limitations as a proxy for 'all wealthy businessmen'. Probate duty was levied only on assets left at death so that any disposals during the lifetime of the deceased were not recorded. While gifts *inter vivos* may have been randomly distributed over different levels and types of fortunes, it is equally possible that they were more common among certain types of family businesses where control was often passed to sons during the father's lifetime than in others, where family connection with a business was ended by death. An attempt was made in 1881 to bring gifts *inter vivos* into the probate duty net, but it was an entirely voluntary tax impossible for the Inland Revenue to monitor and was only ever paid by a few scrupulously honest individuals, among whom the biggest payer was the Duke of Bedford.[26] The 1910 (1909) Finance Act introduced the concept that gifts were liable to death duties unless made more than three years before death (a period subsequently changed to five years before death, then seven years, and later back to five years), and from then on it became more likely that estate valuation figures included recent gifts *inter vivos*.

---

[26] Finance Act 1881, 44 Vict. cap. 12, sec. 38, known as 'Account Duty'; and see *25th Report of the Commissioners of Inland Revenue*, PP 1882, XXI, 39.

Of rather more importance, probate valuations were of personalty only and excluded all real property (from 1898 'unsettled' real property was included, and from 1926 'settled' land also came within the net). The effect of this is that the probate figure does not necessarily reflect the total wealth of an individual, and can in individual cases lead to misleading classifications of businessmen as millionaires or half-millionaires. For example, John Bailey, ironmaster, who died in 1858 leaving £600,000 in personalty, was in fact a millionaire since he had purchased the Glanusk estate in Brecon of over 28,000 acres, worth £19,921 a year, with a capital value of at least another £600,000.[27] Several industrialists who left less than £500,000 in personalty were half-millionaires when their estate purchases are taken into account: among them were Robert Heath, Staffordshire ironmaster, who left £320,045 when he died in 1893, and had laid out more than £300,000 in purchasing the Biddulph Grange, Knypersley Hall, and Clough Hall estates, probably of more than 8,000 acres in all; Samuel Morley, the hosiery manufacturer, left £484,291 at his death in 1886, and had also purchased the 1,400 acre Hall Place, Tonbridge, estate, which would have cost him at least £50,000; or there was Sir Joseph Whitworth, the famous engineer and machine tool manufacturer, who died in 1887 worth £462,928 in personalty, who had acquired the Stancliffe estate, near Matlock, where he kept a noted Shorthorn herd in the park; the extreme instance is perhaps the financier Whitaker Wright, who died in 1904 with personalty of £148,200, having bought Lea Park, Godalming, for £250,000 and spent £400,000 on landscaping, building a theatre under one lake and a billiard room under another—all the dodgy companies he had floated went bankrupt in 1900, and in the end he committed suicide while awaiting prosecution for swindling.[28]

How many businessmen there were whose land purchases when added to their probate valuations would propel them into the half-millionaire category it is not possible to say, although one can be reasonably confident that anyone who becomes a millionaire when land acquisitions are taken into account was already a half-millionaire in personalty. The groups of half-millionaires and millionaires defined by probate valuations of their personalty are, therefore, something less than definitive identifications of 'all wealthy businessmen' even if, as is questionable, a fortune of half a million pounds is accepted as the threshold for 'wealthy'; they are, all the same, rough proxies for the 'super-wealthy' which are convenient for historical analysis. The results of Rubinstein's analysis showed that 38 per cent of all millionaires dying between 1840 and 1899 (not counting those who were established landowners) had purchased estates of 2,000 acres or more, and

[27] Probate and Legacy Duty Register, PRO, IR26/2159, fos. 89–98 (Bailey, 1858).
[28] D. J. Jeremy and C. Shaw, (eds.), *The Dictionary of Business Biography* 5 vols. (1984–6).

that 23 per cent of all half-millionaires from the same period had done like-wise. The inverse of these percentages, indicating that a decided preponder-ance in both groups did not buy land, has been interpreted as showing that business and landed society became sharply dissociated in the course of the nineteenth century, that new men of wealth withdrew from the world of the landed aristocrat, and that the landed aristocracy itself became a closed group, hostile to new entries and jealous of any infringements of its status and its sphere.[29]

Interpreting statistics is largely a matter of taste. It could equally well be argued that the positive percentages indicated a well-sustained inclination on the part of the very wealthy to acquire landed status, although the urge was less than universally experienced. As it happens, these particular statis-tics have occasioned vigorous, not to say fierce, debate, and they turn out to be seriously flawed. The revised figures show that 60 per cent of the nineteenth-century millionaires and half-millionaires acquired landed estates during their lifetimes, and a further 20 per cent generated landed successors in the next generation which frequently acted under directions to apply their inheritance in the purchase of lands. Moreover, the residue of 20 per cent who spurned the landed milieu was very largely composed of wealthy men who were childless and therefore had at most exceedingly slender encour-agement to play the game of founding landed families.[30] It thus becomes dif-ficult to imagine that the new super-wealthy could have acquired more landed estates than they actually did, although the theoretical possibility of acquiring larger ones than they actually did certainly existed. It also becomes necessary, presumably, to stand the commentary on its head and claim that business and landed society grew closer together in the course of the nineteenth century, and that new men of wealth poured into the coun-tryside, where the landed aristocracy welcomed them with open arms.

Neither the first interpretation, alleging a widening gulf between the new wealthy and the old aristocracy, nor the second, picturing a happy fusion of the two groups, can properly be deduced from either set of figures since these deal only with the ownership of estates and say nothing about life-styles or social relations; although the second set of figures does effectively re-establish the openness of the landed elite to the super-wealthy. Where there has been general agreement is on the decline from the 1890s in the propensity of the very rich to buy land, despite the fact that this was the time when land suddenly became very cheap and when there were plenty of prime estates in the market. The purchase price of land, which had not uncommonly been pushed up to 40 years' purchase in the booming land

---

[29] Rubinstein, *Elites and the Wealthy*, table 6.1, and commentary on pp. 157–64.
[30] Thompson, 'Life after Death', 39–61; Rubinstein, 'Cutting up Rich', 350–61; Thompson, 'Stitching it Together Again', 362–75; id., 'Business and Landed Elites in the Nineteenth Century', 139–70. See App. 1 for listing of the 1809–93 millionaires.

market of the 1860s and early 1870s, was down to 18 or 20 years' purchase in the 1890s, and the rents on which these prices were calculated had themselves fallen by around one-fifth on average. Hence estates could be purchased in the 1890s, or indeed in the 1900s, for a good deal less than half the price they had been fetching a decade or so earlier.[31] A rational business calculation, however, was that even at low prices land might not be cheap, since there was little confidence that rents, and therefore land values, would not go on falling. A rational social calculation was that it was becoming markedly less necessary to acquire land in such large amounts as before in order to gain social acceptance, and quite unnecessary to convert a major part of a personal fortune into real estate.

This perception is, however, not entirely accurate. These considerations damped down the eagerness of the rich to acquire country estates, but they by no means killed off their ardour altogether. Among the millionaires who died between 1894 and the end of 1914, of whom there were 96 'new men' (plus 17 from the established landed class), 21 acquired estates of 2,000 acres or more, including the giant estate of 30,000 acres of Lord Furness of Grantley Hall, Ripon, otherwise known as Christopher Furness, the Hartlepool shipowner, another 29 had smaller estates in the 400–1,999 acre range, and 26 had houses in the country with little land attached; 10 had London town houses, while 6 lived at undistinguished addresses of no social pretensions. The remaining 4 millionaires were not recorded in *Who Was Who*, the *Dictionary of Business Biography,* the *Dictionary of National Biography, Burke's Landed Gentry,* or *Burke's Peerage and Baronetage,* the sources used to identify residences and landownership, and most likely owned no land and had no links with the countryside, although it is possible that some of them did. The majority of these estates had been acquired since 1883, and therefore did not appear in Bateman's *Great Landowners.* The evidence for their existence comes mainly from the self-descriptions which the millionaires gave in their entries in *Who's Who,* claims which have been checked against entries in *Kelly's County Directories* (and *Streeter's Directories for Scotland*) which describe them as 'principal landowners' in the relevant parishes. In itself the fact that so many of them wished to claim landownership, and to state how many acres they owned, says something about their desire to impress the world, or the elite part of the social world, with their landed possessions: none of them, of course, stated that they were worth a million pounds, for it was vulgar to mention sums of money, but not areas of land.[32]

[31] F. M. L. Thompson, 'The Land Market in the Nineteenth Century', *Oxford Economic Papers,* NS, 9 (1957), 285–308; id., *English Landed Society in the Nineteenth Century* (1963), 317–19; Avner Offer, 'Farm Tenure and Land Values in England, c.1750–1950', *Economic History Review,* 2nd ser., 44 (1991), 1–20.

[32] All the millionaires who died between 1894 and 1914, who were not old-established landowners, taken from Rubinstein, 'British Millionaires, 1809–1949', checked against entries in

These figures for the 1894–1914 cohort of millionaires are comparable, without being closely comparable, with those for the nineteenth-century millionaires who died before 1894, and they tend to understate their land purchases. Reliance on statements in *Who Was Who* is one clue, for aside from the possibility that some millionaires may have elected not to reveal, or assert, their landholdings, more than one-third were not included in *Who's Who* at all. Apart from a handful of giants of industry and finance who were household names, *Who's Who* noticed people for their public roles, as MPs or perhaps as mayors of large towns, not for their wealth or success in business.[33] Many millionaires chanced to have been MPs, and more had been mayors, High Sheriffs, or Deputy Lieutenants, thus earning notice; but many others had not held any office. The other clue is the concentration solely on the estates acquired in the lifetimes of the 1894–1914 millionaires, because of the great difficulty of tracing heirs who might have bought land in the years after the nineteenth-century records of the legacy and succession duties effectively give out in 1894. For these reasons the 52 per cent of the 1894–1914 cohort who acquired estates during their lifetimes, of gentry size and above, can be compared, cautiously and conservatively, with the 60 per cent of purchasers in their own lifetimes in the pre-1894 group: a definite decline, but not a precipitate one. In terms of the actual numbers of millionaire-purchasers to be seen on the ground there had, indeed, been a steady increase: an average of one purchaser every two years between 1809 and 1879 grew to 1.5 each year in 1880–93, and to two per year between 1894 and 1914. Not a rate of penetration likely to have alarmed the old order, but not one suggesting declining interest in country properties, either.

Throughout the Victorian and Edwardian periods some of the very rich who bought land were uncomplicated social climbers intent on passing off themselves and their descendants as real aristocrats, while others who bought land did so chiefly because they liked to have country houses and estates for pleasure, hunting, shooting, and playing at being landlords, and at the same time liked to remain powerful businessmen at the head of family firms. What seems to have happened after 1918 is that the first stream of purchasers declined to little more than a trickle, while the second stream

Who Was Who, 1897–1916 (1920), *DBB, DNB,* and *Burke's Landed Gentry* and *Burke's Peerage and Baronetage.* See App. 2 for a listing of the 1894–1914 millionaires.

[33] Interestingly, the *DNB* picked up 3 millionaires who were not in *Who's Who*: George Salting (1836–1909), a major art collector who left his pictures to the National Gallery, the British Museum, and the Victoria and Albert Museum; Vyell E. Walker (1838–1906), cricketer and one of the founders of the MCC, a powerful hitter and a deceptive slow lob bowler, who happened to join the family brewery, succeed to the family estate at Southgate in 1889, and leave a fortune of £1·598 million; and William Whiteley (1832–1907), the 'universal provider', who left a million pounds for endowing the Whiteley Homes at Burr Hill, Surrey.

continued to flow quite strongly. Thus the overall decline in the business-wealth-into-land process was composed of clearly differentiated rates of decline in these two main elements, a matter of considerable significance when it comes to trying to interpret the relationship of land purchase to entrepreneurial vigour. The decline was in any case modest, and between 1915 and 1940 a rather steady 47 per cent of the 185 'new' millionaires who died in that period purchased country properties of around 400 acres and upwards, and most of them found their way into the *Landed Gentry* or the *Peerage and Baronetage*. A few of these were very large estates, but most were on the small side, and any decline was evident in the size rather than in the number of estates being acquired. The acquisitions of Lords Cowdray, Dulverton, Leverhulme, and Masham have already been noticed: they fell to be recorded in the inter-war group because the millionaires in the family died then. The Wills family in particular produced millionaires like rabbits, three just before 1914 and four more in the inter-war years (and a further couple in the 1940s): the tobacco money was poured into Bristol University, but it was also employed in sprinkling Somerset and Gloucestershire with their country houses and estates. Sewing thread did just as well for J & P Coats, supplying five pre-1914 and five inter-war millionaires, out of which amongst other things came the 29,000-acre Glen Tanar estate in Aberdeenshire, from which George Coats took his title in 1916. Sewing thread did not do badly for the Clarks of Paisley, whose fortune supplied the Saltwood Castle estate in Kent as a backdrop for Sir Kenneth and his Civilization, and enabled his son Alan to perform what could be mistaken, in the absence of strong competition, for an authentic aristocratic act.

Other newly acquired estates of this period were more modest, such as the Hampshire manor of Landford purchased by Alfred Mond, the chief architect of ICI, just as he was becoming Lord Melchett, and the Kentish estate bought by Marcus Samuel, creator of the British part of Royal Dutch Shell and 1st Viscount Bearsted, a property which Wiener describes as 'a great country estate' although it was less than 3,000 acres. The mystery men of the inter-war years were the Vestey family, meat-packers, founders of the Union Cold Storage and the Blue Star Line, owners of the Dewhurst chain of butchers and of the supply sources in Argentina, notoriously among the wealthiest businessmen of the time. They were already practising the tax-dodging techniques for which they became famous, and avoided being caught in the net which recorded millionaires for probate and death duty purposes: the property press, nevertheless, did record the purchase of the 4,000-acre Stowell Park estate in Gloucestershire, by William, 1st Lord Vestey, and of the 8,000-acre estate of Warter Priory, Yorkshire, by his second son, George. Interestingly the vendor of Warter Priory was the dowager Lady Nunburnholme, widow of the Hull shipping magnate

C. H. Wilson who had bought the house and estate in 1878: a neat example of passing the aristocratic parcel from one new man of wealth to another.[34]

This inter-war tranche of millionaire-purchasers was far from negligible, but it has not been much noticed because the entire subject of land and the landed aristocracy has tended to be written out of the agenda of national history since the Great War. The more technical reason for overlooking this tranche is that the millionaire-purchasers played a very small role, almost an invisible role, in absorbing the immense quantities of land which came on to the market in the inter-war years. If it was true, as the press claimed at the time, that a quarter of England changed hands in the hectic years of land sales between 1918 and 1921, it implied the transfer of 8 million acres; with more than a trickle of sales continuing after the collapse of the land market boom in 1921, a total of the order of 9 to 10 million acres was sold in the inter-war period as a whole, in England alone, and a great deal more in Britain when the massive acreages of Scottish sales are taken into account. The millionaire-purchasers are unlikely to have taken up as much as 5 per cent of all this land, probably less. The concentration of land market historians on the rise of a new breed of owner-occupiers through purchases by sitting tenants, and on the activities of speculative land syndicates, which between them were the principal purchasers, and their neglect of the inter-war nouveaux riches, is in this perspective both understandable and justifiable. The obverse of this coin is that there were superabundant supplies of land on the market, at bargain prices, especially after 1921, so that every wealthy businessman with an appetite for land could easily satisfy it. There were no supply constraints on gentrification—although in view of persistently gloomy expectations about the future course of land values there were indeed strong investment reservations—and one can assume that the demand from the very rich for great landed estates was fully satisfied, and that it had become a decidedly minority taste, with most purchasers looking for small to middling sized properties. The contrast with the nineteenth century before the 1880s, when land prices were high and rising and there were supply constraints since existing large landowners were generally loath to sell, is instructive: in seemingly discouraging land market

---

[34] Rubinstein, 'British Millionaires', 214–20 records 182 'non-landed' millionaires dying between 1915 and 1940. The land-purchasing activities of many of them can be identified in the *Estates Gazette*, and some from self-description in *Who's Who*, but the status of those who simply gave country house addresses remains uncertain. Some 86 out of the 182 appear to have acquired estates of 400 acres or more. Specific references: George Coats, Lord Glentanar: R. F. Callander, *A Pattern of Landownership in Scotland* (Finzean, 1987), 97; Alfred Mond, Lord Melchett: *Estates Gazette*, 8 June 1929, p. 840; Marcus Samuel, Lord Bearsted: Wiener, *English Culture*, 146–7; William and George Vestey: *Estates Gazette*, 22 Sept. 1928, p. 401; DBB, V., 848. See App. 3 for listing of the 1915–40 millionaires.

conditions large estate-acquisition had then been the majority taste of millionaires.[35]

It was only after 1945, however, that the appetite of millionaires for acquiring some land of their own became a definitely minority taste, and it continues to flourish; having languished in the aftermath of the Second World War it received a stimulus from the tax advantages of 'hobby farming' and the generous treatment of agricultural land for death duties, and was strengthened in the 1970s and 1980s by a move into land as a hedge against inflation backed by a revival of confidence in the future of agricultural land values—which petered out after 1990—and the reinstatement after 1979 of political approval for the amassing and display of great wealth. Out of the 200 people judged to be the wealthiest in Britain in 1989, with assets valued at £30 million or more (which is approximately equivalent to the nineteenth-century millionaire), one-half represented the new money of self-made multimillionaires. One-quarter of these hundred new men and women of wealth had already bought landed estates, as sidelines or indulgences rather than as major receptacles for the investment of their fortunes, and not as avenues for retreat from their business enterprises. In size their properties ranged all the way from the 500 acres or so of Michael Heseltine to the 45,000 acres of Christopher Moran. The new landowners included some transients like Alan Bond, who laid out £10 million on the 2,000-acre Glympton estate in Oxfordshire only to be compelled to sell it again the following year when his business empire collapsed. Most of them, however, looked to be set to be landowners for their lifetimes, and some perhaps to found landed families.[36]

Perhaps the star of this 1989 list was Lord Sainsbury of Preston Candover, who over several years had pieced together a prime Hampshire estate of over 3,000 acres round a prime, but not gargantuan, country house, buying from earlier millionaire-purchasers: Preston House from Peter Cadbury, chocolate money, and the Lockerley estate from the Dalgety family, a grain and cattle food fortune. Others, however, had equally imposing acquisitions. Vivien Duffield, daughter and heiress of Charles Clore the property tycoon, was settled on the 18,000-acre Brechin estate which she had bought from the Earl of Dalhousie in 1987 for £2.5 million; Anthony Bamford, the maker of JCB bulldozers, acquired the Daylesford estate in Gloucestershire of 2,000 acres for £12 million in 1988; Andrew Lloyd Webber turned some of the takings from *Cats* into the splendid Sydmonton estate of 1,200 acres in Hampshire, while Paul McCartney, with even more millions from Beatles' records, bought the Mull of Kintyre as a retreat; the Vesteys had added to

[35] *Estates Gazette*, 31 Dec 1921; *The Times*, 19 May 1920; Thompson, *Landed Society*, 330–3. For the role of syndicates as purchasers see Pam Barnes, *Norfolk Landowners since 1880* (Norwich, 1993), 70–8. Land prices in the 1920s and 1930s were roughly half their pre-1870 level: ibid., 70, citing Ph.D. thesis by J.T. Ward.   [36] *Sunday Times, Britain's Rich: the Top 200*, 2 Apr. 1989.

their previous holdings a sporting estate of 100,000 acres in Sutherland; and Lord Vinson, founder of Plastic Coatings and Margaret Thatcher's earliest industrial adviser, as Director of the Centre for Policy Studies from 1974 to 1980, had bought 4,000 acres in Northumberland. A few years before 1989 lifetime landowners had included J. Arthur Rank, whose 10,000 acre estate in Hampshire was sold to an insurance company soon after his death in 1972, and Sir Thomas Sopwith, aviation pioneer, whose 2,000 acres at Kings Somborne, also in Hampshire, went on the market after his death in January 1989.[37]

The living millionaires of 1989 are not strictly comparable with the dead millionaires whose land-purchasing proclivities in earlier periods have been examined: but the fact that around one-quarter of them have acquired estates while still in their entrepreneurial prime indicates that the minority taste for landed possessions is very much alive, and may even have increased in comparison with the inter-war period. Using millionaires as the control group for measuring gentrification, however, has one apparent advantage and several drawbacks. The advantage is that a population of businessmen has been defined by an apparently consistent criterion that can be applied over a long stretch of time: that is, all those who did not inherit landed wealth whose assets at death were worth £1 million or more (the criterion for the 1989 set being the different one, roughly adjusted for inflation, of all those who did not inherit landed wealth whose assets, while they were still alive, were worth £30 million or more). The apparent consistency of the definition is the first drawback. Until 1926 the valuation of assets at death was substantially only a valuation of the personalty owned by the deceased, that is the stocks and shares, the plate and jewellery, and other moveable property, excluding any land or house property; before 1898 the valuation was exclusively of personalty.[38] The exclusion of land from the probate values means that the 'millionaire' of pre-1926 vintage is not the stable and constant entity he seems to be. A probated millionaire who also owned land was worth more than a landless millionaire, and a sub-millionaire who owned land could well have been worth more than a million: this is a second pitfall in using the millionaire yardstick. An extreme case was furnished by George Philips, who in partnership with the highly entrepreneurial and innovative George Lee rose to be one of Manchester's largest cotton spinners in the early decades of the nineteenth century. Philips spent about £700,000 between 1817 and 1830 in building up the Weston estate in Warwickshire to over 3,000 acres and in rebuilding Weston Hall, gave most

---

[37] J. Scott, 'Landed interest renews itself', *Country Life*, 23 Feb. 1989, pp. 116–17; F. M. L. Thompson, 'English Landed Society in the Twentieth Century, ii., New Poor and New Rich', *Transactions of the Royal Historical Society*, 6th ser. 1 (1991), 1–20. The *Observer*, 20 May 1990, stated that Lord Sainsbury had built up an estate of 17,000 acres, but other sources put it at about 3,000 acres.   [38] Rubinstein, 'British Millionaires', 204.

of the rest of his money during his lifetime to his son and his granddaughters, and died almost insolvent in 1847. Here was a successful businessman who died penniless according to the probate records, but who had succeeded in founding a landed family; by 1873 his son had built up the estate to well over 6,000 acres.[39] This is also a good example of a more technical disadvantage of treating the millionaires as a consistently defined group. A businessman, or indeed any wealthy person, might choose to give away large sums during his life, and although this has become more common in the twentieth century as a way of avoiding death duties it was not unusual in the nineteenth century. Such gifts might be to charities or for philanthropic and educational purposes; or they might be made for business reasons to enable an heir to carry on a family business.

Other instances were less extreme, but they were quite numerous. The Botfields, for example, were great coalmasters in North Staffordshire and they laid out over £650,000 in buying land between 1798 and 1858, so that Beriah Botfield was reckoned 'by far the richest commoner in Shropshire' in the 1850s; yet he left not more than £50,000 in personalty when he died. Another coalmaster, W. B. Harrison, the leading man on the Cannock Chase field, did rather better in leaving £270,000 when he died in 1912; on top of that he had bought the Wychnor Park estate in Staffordshire, and had already handed that and most of his business interests over to his son, and that son appeared as the first recorded millionaire in the family, in 1937.[40] Rubinstein searched diligently for the 'hidden' millionaires among the nineteenth-century landowners, that is those of the landed aristocracy and gentry whose probated wealth was small but whose total assets topped the million mark when the capital value of their landed estates was added, and he rightly pointed out that until the 1880s the majority of the really wealthy men in Britain were landowners.[41] He remains, however, extremely sceptical about the existence of a corresponding group of 'hidden' new landowners, that is of wealthy businessmen who escaped listing among the millionaires or half-millionaires because they had invested a significant part of their fortunes in landed estates.[42]

The scepticism may well be justified, for any rigorous and conclusive testing of the hypothesis would be difficult to the point of impossible, since there is no objective definition of 'wealthy businessmen' and hence no source which identifies them all. A proxy is to be found, not altogether a

[39] D. G. Brown, 'From Cotton Lord to Landed Aristocrat: The Rise of Sir George Philips, bart, 1766–1847', *Historical Research*, 69 (1996), 62–82.

[40] Ibid.; Rubinstein, 'British Millionaires', 220 (William E. Harrison, died 1937, probate £1,392 million).   [41] Rubinstein, *Men of Property*, 59–61.

[42] Id., 'New Men of Wealth', 135–7; id., 'Cutting up Rich', 356–9; id., 'Businessmen into Landowners: The Question Revisited', in Negley Harte and Roland Quinault (eds.), *Land and Society in Britain, 1700–1914* (Manchester, 1996), esp. p. 105.

satisfactory one, in the entries in the five volumes of the *Dictionary of Business Biography*. They contain entries for 324 businessmen who died before 1914, among whom are ten 'hidden' new landowners who might have been counted as millionaires if the estates which they had purchased had been valued with their other assets, and a further sixteen who for the same reason would have qualified as half-millionaires: a very small proportion of the total number of businessmen in the group, but a not insignificant addition to the number of very wealthy estate-purchasers in the period. The possible 'true' millionaires in the group included well-known entrepreneurs such as the iron and steel magnates Sir Isaac Lowthian Bell and Henry W. F. Bolckow, both of whom bought country estates and large houses in the hinterland of Middlesbrough and both of whom had probate values of around £800,000, and Samuel Cunliffe Lister, wool-comber and textile manufacturer, who purchased the Swinton and Jervaulx estates in Yorkshire in the 1880s for £710,000, and died in 1906 with a probate value of £633,637; and such lesser-known businessmen as the glove maker, J. Derby Allcroft, who bought an estate of 8,500 acres in Shropshire, restored Stokesay Castle, and then built himself another 100-room country mansion, leaving £492,063 in personalty when he died in 1893. The potential half-millionaires included the Sheffield steel maker Charles Cammell, who left a personal fortune of £250,000, but also three separate estates which he had purchased, totalling more than 6,500 acres; the department store owner Owen Owen, who left £477,800 in 1910 plus estates at Penmaenmawr and Machynlleth; the marine cable and telegraph pioneer Sir John Pender, who left £337,180 in 1896, and estates in Kent, Argyll, and Linlithgow, plus some land in Lancashire and Denbigh; and John Walter, the owner of *The Times*, who had a personal fortune of £310,229 and a country house, Bearwood, which had cost him £120,000 to build, sitting on its Berkshire estate of 5,678 acres.

Instance may be piled upon instance to produce an effect, but hardly a conclusion. The one definite conclusion is that it is unwise to rely on the class of probated millionaires as a consistently and uniformly defined group which constituted a club that continuously enrolled all the wealthiest businessmen in Britain. Indeed, one can find an entrepreneur who left no more than £84,000 when he died, yet had an estate of 5,052 acres in Sussex, the proceeds of the pianos made by Henry Fowler Broadwood; while one of the great Black Country ironmasters, John Nock Bagnall, left only a little over £5,000 although he had acquired a country seat, served as High Sheriff of Staffordshire, and had a place in *Burke's Landed Gentry*.[43] This points the

[43] *DBB*, vol. i. Richard Trainor, 'The Gentrification of Victorian and Edwardian Industrialists', in A. L. Beier, David Cannadine, and James M. Rosenheim (eds.) *The First Modern Society* (Cambridge, 1989), 182; John Nock Bagnall's estate was very small, but sufficient along with his local standing to gain him recognition as a country gentleman; the Bagnall ironworks were a family business, and other members of the family also purchased estates.

way to the chief disadvantage of using millionaires as the yardstick for measuring gentrification, beside which the others are scarcely more than technical hitches. Businessmen who left a million when they died were clearly successful in the business of making money; and since one of the objects of an entrepreneur is to make money, wealth must be one measure of success in business. It is not self-evident, however, that accumulated wealth left in a lump sum at death is a better indicator of success than wealth spent during a lifetime, for example on houses, horses, women, politics, steam yachts, or on more worthy objects like churches, schools, universities, libraries, museums, or galleries. Still less is any particular level of wealth, or expenditure, a universal indicator of success. The trouble with millionaires, then, is that so many of them were simply extremely wealthy but not especially notable as entrepreneurs.

It would be very difficult in principle, and impossible in practice, to define and identify the total population of successful entrepreneurs at a single date, let alone over the entire period since 1780. Nevertheless, the collective decisions of the editors and contributors to the *Dictionary of Business Biography* do provide an alternative set of definitions and listings to the millionaires, even if this alternative is skewed towards those individuals who business historians happen to find interesting.[44] The populations are disturbingly different. One hundred business millionaires died between 1894 and 1914, but only 14 per cent of them are noticed in the *Dictionary*; and of the 324 businessmen who died before 1914 drawn from the *Dictionary*, only 9 per cent were millionaires. The mismatch is not quite so extreme as appears on the surface, since the *Dictionary* includes a number of salaried people such as Post Office administrators, building society managers, and railway managers, who were in no position to make vast personal fortunes; and the editorial policy was to include some instances of patently unsuccessful entrepreneurs who through bad luck, incompetence, or downright dishonesty left very little, or nothing at all, at the end of careers containing exciting and original episodes. For example, Sir Samuel Morton Peto is in the *Dictionary*, leaving nothing when he died in 1889 because he was bankrupt; he had an important career as a railway contractor, he was an MP for nearly 20 years, received a baronetcy in 1855, and in his prime had owned the 3,224-acre Somerleyton estate in Suffolk and had rebuilt the vast house at huge expense—which he had had to sell, to Sir Frank Crossley, the Halifax carpet maker, in 1863.[45] All the same, the discrepancy is so large

[44] Recent attempts to rubbish the *DBB* as being haphazardly if not eccentrically selected, and hence being useless as a database of businessmen, by W. D. Rubinstein, 'Wealth Making in the Late Nineteenth Century', *Business History*, 42 (2000), esp. pp. 142–4, have been robustly countered by Tom Nicholas, 'Wealth Making in the Late Nineteenth Century', ibid., 41 (1999) and id., 'The Rubinstein Hypothesis Revisited', ibid., 42 (2000), 155–68.

[45] Mark Girouard, *The Victorian Country House* (New Haven, Conn. and London, 1979), 211–12, 420.

that it is obvious that business historians have different criteria than simple wealth for judging the significance, success, and historical interest of businessmen. Whatever the criteria used for deciding the interest and importance of a businessman within his own industry or occupation, the aim was in any case to provide a very large, and illustrative, cross-section of the field, not a comprehensive and exhaustive listing of all businessmen. At present it has to be accepted that no database of all businessmen active between 1780 and 1980 exists, and probably never will. The quest for complete certainty on the propensity of entrepreneurs to acquire landed estates may thus be futile.

Nevertheless, the estate-purchasing activities of the 324 businessmen from the *Dictionary* who died before 1914 support a less pessimistic conclusion. More than one-third of them acquired country properties during their own lifetimes, ranging from a few hundred acres up to the 34,000 acre estate of Samuel Cunliffe Lister, 1st Lord Masham. When these purchasers are analysed according to the size of their probated estates, as in Table 2, they reassuringly conform to rational expectations. Four-fifths of the millionaires and nearly 70 per cent of the half-millionaires purchased estates, but only just over one-third of those leaving between £100,000 and £500,000. Curiously, in the light of Rubinstein's difficulty in finding any evidence that 'wealthholders with as little [as] £100,000 purchased significant amounts of land',[46] 22 per cent of those whose fortunes lay between £50,000 and £100,000 were purchasers, and no less than 11 per cent of those whose fortunes were less than £50,000. Most of these two last groups bought only small quantities of land, which could be called insignificant on some definitions, although they were significant enough on the gentry scale to qualify the purchasers as members of county society fit to be JPs, DLs, and High Sheriffs; a very few, like Broadwood of the pianos with his 5,052 acres, or Sir Charles Mark Palmer, coal and iron master and Jarrow shipbuilder, who bought Grinkle Park in the North Riding and 4,000 acres but left only £15,226 at his death in 1907, acquired sizeable estates which represented the major slice of their total assets, as at a humble level did the land of the Worcestershire needle maker John English (1789–1878) which yielded him £700 a year, more than his income from needles and worth much much more than his £2,000 personalty. Whatever the correlation between business success and wealth, there was certainly a correlation between amount of wealth and estate acquisition. Those who had placed a large proportion of very small fortunes in land were perhaps oddities. What is striking is that the actual number of purchasers from the group with middling fortunes of £100,000 to £500,000 was larger than the number of millionaire and half-millionaire

---

[46] Rubinstein, 'Cutting up Rich', 357.

TABLE 2. *Land purchases by businessmen who died before 1914*

	Probate values of personalty (000s)				
	< £50	£50–£100	£100–£500	£500–£1,000	> £1,000
Total number 324	85	45	131	33	30
Landed 114 (35%)	10 (12%)	10 (22%)	48 (37%)	22 (67%)	24 (80%)

Source: Dictionary of Business Biography (complete count of all entries for those dying before 1914). See Appendix 4 (i) (a) for detailed listing.

purchasers, although they tended to buy smaller properties, for example William Adam (1828–98), Kidderminster carpet manufacturer, with his 2,000-acre estate in Gloucestershire and his £211,291 personalty; John Charlesworth Dodgson Charlesworth (1815–80), West Riding colliery owner, with estates in Yorkshire, Worcestershires, and Shropshire of 3,469 acres and personalty of £200,000; Edward Greene (1815–91), Suffolk brewer who formed Greene King in 1887, Master of the Suffolk Hunt, a national authority on horses, MP, purchaser of Nether Hall, Pakenham of nearly 1,000 acres, leaving £393,929 in personalty; or Alfred Waterhouse (1830–1905), architect, who left personalty of £163,575 and the 700-acre Yattendon Court estate, near Newbury, which he had bought and on which he built a country house for himself.

Not surprisingly the appetite for investing in landed properties declined further in the following generation of businessmen, but was far from vanishing. A second set has been extracted from the *Dictionary of Business Biography*, consisting of all those who were born before 1870 and died after 1914, chosen so as not to overlap with the first group, but restricted to those who had reached maturity, literally and in terms of their business careers, before 1914 and thus had largely formed their family and social aspirations from pre-1914 models. There were 379 businessmen in this group. Most of them died during the inter-war years, although many survived into the 1950s. Their land purchases, also, were concentrated in the inter-war years, and over all a quarter of the group acquired some land, usually in small amounts. As the breakdown in Table 3 shows, the largest number of purchasers was once again provided by the set with middling-sized fortunes, which included one of the largest purchasers, Sir Amos Nelson (1860–1947), textile manufacturer, who in 1922 bought the 6,000-acre Gledstone estate near Skipton and commissioned Lutyens to design him one of the most magnificent houses in Yorkshire; he left a fortune of £444,246.[47] He was

---

[47] Clive Aslet, *The Last Country Houses* (New Haven, Conn. and London, 1982), 318.

TABLE 3. *Land purchases by businessmen born before 1870 who died after 1914*

		Personalty (000s)				
		< 50	50–100	100–500	500–1,000	> 1,000
Total number	379	89	65	136	42	47
Landed	97 (25%)	7 (8%)	9 (14%)	39 (29%)	12 (28%)	30 (64%)

Source: Dictionary of Business Biography (complete count of all entries for those born before 1870 who died after 1914). See Appendix 4 (ii) for detailed listing.

substantially outclassed by the managing director of Harrods, Sir Richard Burbridge (1847–1917), who contrived to acquire the 11,000-acre Littleton Park estate, another 1,500 acres in Shepperton, Middlesex, 52,000 acres in western Australia, and more in Canada, while leaving no more than £186,262 in personalty. The 4,000-acre Hall Barn estate in Buckinghamshire acquired by Edward Levy Lawson (1833–1916), 1st Lord Burnham of Hall Barn, owner of the *Daily Telegraph* and one of the Prince of Wales's set, who left £267,871, was less exceptional; while the 1,000 acres of Pottersbury Lodge, Northamptonshire, bought by the food retailer and vice-chairman of the Home and Colonial stores George Beale (1864–1953) who proceeded to become Master of the Grafton Foxhounds, one of the hunting world's premier positions, was more typical of someone whose fortune was a rather modest £276,599. It was, indeed, closely matched by the estate of the founder of the Home and Colonial stores, Julius Charles Drewe (1856–1931), who left £207,700, and after first buying Culverton Castle near Tunbridge Wells in 1890 and then Wadhurst Hall in Sussex in 1900, finally settled on the 1,500-acre Drewsteignton estate in Devon and commissioned Lutyens to build Castle Drogo there.

It is difficult to establish the size of estates which were acquired after the 1880s, unless the owners volunteered the information in *Who's Who* or the contributors to the *Dictionary of Business Biography* discovered it. In those cases where these two sources are silent there is no knowing how large, or small, was the property which went with the country houses acquired by those who have been counted among the 'landed' in Tables 2 and 3, although where the individuals were JPs and DLs, and served as High Sheriffs, in rural counties unconnected with their places of business it is a reasonable presumption that they had been accepted as members of county society. If all those whose acreages cannot be identified are assumed to have acquired 'houses in the country' with no more than garden ground attached, the proportions of the groups who became 'landed' would be reduced to one-quarter in Table 2 and one-fifth in Table 3, showing that the inclination to acquire estates was still a substantial minority taste, one that was certainly weakening from the 1880s onwards but was far from vanishing. Some of those who acquired land in large enough quantities for it to be accorded the status of a 'named estate' in the sources possessed no more than a couple of hundred acres or so, and would have failed to clear the old nineteenth-century gentry hurdle, while very few even of those who dealt in thousands of acres would have met the newfangled gentrification test of placing around half of a total fortune in real estate. As Rubinstein found when examining instances of the personalty:realty ratio, the super-wealthy who purchased landed estates were unlikely to commit more than a small proportion of their total wealth to land, which consigns the large-scale purchasers among the millionaires to the position of 'businessmen with some land on the side, rather . . . like an English tourist who claims to be Spanish on the basis of acquiring a suntan on the Costa Brava'.[48] So much for any idea that the Barings, Rothschilds, Peels, Guests, Tennants, Pearsons, and their kind might have succeeded in joining the landed elite while still remaining prominent businessmen. Those with modest fortunes, who purchased estates, were likely to have attained low ratios of personalty to realty, and it may well be that the likes of Henry Fowler Broadwood (1811–93) who invested about £94,000 in land and left £84,000 in personalty, John English (1789–1878) with £21,000 in land and £2,000 in personalty, Sir Charles Mark Palmer (1822–1907) with nearly £100,000 in land and only £15,226 in personalty, and Whitaker Wright (1845–1904) who put £650,000 into his estate and bizarre country house and left just £148,200 in personalty, were the most convincing examples of businessmen who converted themselves into landowners. If so, they were hardly the most striking examples of successful founders of landed families.[49]

It was quite possible for someone to invest only a small part of his fortune in a small quantity of land, and become accepted into county society provided the little estate had the right sort of house on it and its new owner adopted the lifestyle approved by the 'county'. Such a person can properly be termed 'gentrified' although remaining in business (though probably not 'in trade' unless of a superior wholesale variety), and remaining reliant on non-landed sources for his income. On other definitions he was not 'gentrified' because he had not transformed himself into a landowner capable of sustaining his lifestyle from the income from land. Even if the gentrification of businessmen is gauged solely by the measure of the acquisition of land in gentry or aristocratic-sized portions it can be concluded that there was considerably more of it than implied in the works of the Stones and Rubinstein; and if it is measured by acceptance into landed society there was almost certainly a great deal less of it than implied by Wiener. The

[48] Rubinstein, 'Businessmen into Landowners', 97. See also Tom Nicholas, 'Businessmen and Landownership in the Late Nineteenth Century', *Economic History Review,*. 2nd ser., 52 (1999), 27–44.   [49] Details from *DBB*.

crude measures, however, have nothing to say about the effects of landownership on businessmen. The questions whether businessmen who acquired
estates actually became country gentlemen, and if they did, whether that
turned them into indifferent, indolent, and unenterprising entrepreneurs,
remain to be addressed.

4

Entrepreneurial Culture and the Culture of Entrepreneurs

The enterprise culture is a very recent ideological and managerial construct, but like many concepts fabricated in right-wing ideas factories, and indeed in business schools, it claims to be a late twentieth-century restatement of a Victorian condition. 'The great car society' may be an exception to this rule of dressing up policy objectives in Victorian clothes: even then, that could be translated as saying 'we are all carriage folk now', except that carriage folk were generally thought of as being the idle rich and not notably entrepreneurial. The enterprise culture is generally supposed to have existed during the workshop-of-the-world days of Britain's industrial hegemony that came to an end roughly in the 1880s, and to have consisted of a dominant set of values and institutions which was particularly encouraging and stimulating to commercial and industrial enterprise and to the pursuit of profit. A paramount aim of government between 1979 and 1997—and apparently since then as well—has been, it is said, to restore this culture after the battering and rejection it has undergone in the last hundred years, assailed from all directions by gentrification, by welfarism, by corporatism, by socialism, and by red tape. Strangled and stifled, the once dominant enterprise culture has been replaced, it is alleged, by the nanny state and an insidious dependency culture. The deliberate use of state power to create private enterprises and to foist pseudo-market mechanisms on public services may, or may not, be appropriate to our contemporary economic and social condition, but it bears little relation to the Victorian enterprise culture, which itself was largely mythical.

Victorians themselves never used such an expression as 'the enterprise culture', nor the variant of 'the entrepreneurial ideal' which was formulated many years ago by Harold Perkin to describe the powerful myth of the self-made man and the ideal type of competitive capitalist.[1] What they talked about was self-help and self-reliance, thrift, abstinence, hard work, diligence, and perseverance, and for them 'culture' meant art, literature, a liberal education, gentility, and good manners. It can perhaps be claimed that the mid-Victorians had a dominant laissez-faire ideology, although it was almost ceaselessly challenged and compromised in particulars in practice,

[1] Harold Perkin, *The Origins of Modern English Society, 1780–1880* (1969), 221–30.

and was disowned by dissident intellectuals. That ideology entrusted the working of the economy to free market capitalism, an economy, apart from utilities such as railways, gas, and water, of individuals and family firms, not of great companies; and within the ideology there was indeed a specification for the ideal type of individual entrepreneur. For the rest, there was never much mileage in the pretence that free market capitalism, acting through individual capitalists, could, or did, provide for the moral, spiritual, educational, or cultural needs of society, and much doubt whether it made a very good job of satisfying material needs, for instance in nutrition or housing. Officialdom and central government were viewed with considerable suspicion, and there was a cult of self-reliance, localism, and voluntaryism to which most capitalists subscribed; but this cult was fed by other, independent, streams and not simply by the great capitalist river. What the Victorians did not have was an enterprise culture which was dominant or hegemonic, in the ungainly jargon of the Gramsci-ite school. Indeed, it is a matter of keen debate whether the standard-bearers of the free market ethos, the middle classes, ever had the self-confidence, the self-knowledge, or the power to put their own stamp on Victorian society by breaking free from the culture and values of the aristocracy and gentry who controlled the world in which they had risen to prominence.[2] What the Victorians did have was, in short, an entrepreneurial culture which in general infused the conduct and definition of business affairs, but whose influence in wider spheres of government, social policy, let alone in elite society, was at best patchy and most of the time was not in serious contention with older and more powerful traditions. Moreover, this entrepreneurial culture was an abstraction, partly the creature of contemporary theorists, mainly the invention of hostile critics from the arts and literature. In real life it was endlessly qualified and compromised by the actual culture of real flesh and blood individual entrepreneurs, and by the particular customs and rituals of individual firms which had their idiosyncratic habits—as did counting houses, government departments, schools, universities, or cathedral closes—that modern analysts would term 'cultures'.

The Victorians' favourite political economist was undoubtedly John Stuart Mill. He had plenty to say about capital, and labour, as factors of production. He held that 'the business of society can best be performed by private and voluntary agency', with certain carefully defined exceptions. But, in the Olympian manner of economists, he had little to say about flesh and blood capitalists beyond the assumption that they behaved in an economically rational way in their pursuit of profits. His one stray observation that bears

---

[2] The debate on the mid-nineteenth-century 'failure' of the industrial bourgeoisie in Britain was initiated by Raymond Williams, *The Long Revolution* (1961) and Perry Anderson, 'Origins of the Present Crisis', *New Left Review*, 23 (1964), 26–54, and has rumbled on since: see, for example, R. J. Morris, *Class, Sect and Party. The Making of the British Middle Class: Leeds, 1820–50* (Manchester, 1990), esp. pp. 1–19.

on the matter of entrepreneurial culture is deadpan, but revealing: 'to carry on a great business successfully,' he remarked, 'requires that the directing mind should be incessantly occupied with the subject; should be continually laying schemes by which greater profit may be obtained, or expense saved.'[3] This reads like an endorsement of the businessman as dessicated and tireless calculator; but it was placed in the context of a discussion of the advantages and disadvantages of the joint stock company form for large-scale manufacturing concerns, and was designed to affirm the superiority in commitment and zeal of the owner-manager capitalist over the hired manager. A long tradition that owners were the best qualified to look after their own interests, and that salaried managers or agents could be indolent, neglectful, or dishonest—a tradition founded in agricultural estate experience as much as in anything industrial—lay behind such a view. It did not necessarily mean that Mill thought the best businessmen were philistine Gradgrinds, and his own personal intellectual, literary, and romantic tastes suggest otherwise.

Vulgar popularizers and apologists for the capitalist spirit and laissez-faire economics certainly did give the impression that the archetypical entrepreneur was a ruthless captain of industry in single-minded pursuit of profits. Harriet Martineau, for one, did this in her exposition of the laws of political economy as storytelling, and John Stuart Mill thought that her reductionism made laissez-faire look ridiculous.[4] The recently rediscovered Samuel Laing, a minor Scottish businessman turned didactic travel writer in the 1830s and 1840s, was another apologist who regarded industrial capitalists as the standard bearers of civilization and portrayed the efficient ones as wholly materialist, utilitarian profit-seekers who never turned aside from the pursuit of money to indulge in any frivolity or luxury, and who held that any deviation from this path into unproductive expenditure or leisure was evidence of falling into the decadence of the aristocratic embrace.[5] In the main, however, the standard impression of the industrial capitalist as a kind of ogre of crass materialism and unfeeling avarice, and as a social pariah, derives from the hostile critics like Dickens, Engels, or Matthew Arnold. The pro-industrial didacts, after all, were illustrating what they held to be the iron laws of economics, particularly the wages fund theory, and in describing how the economy worked did not claim to be giving a full account of how society functioned or, by derivation, a full picture of the character of capitalists and their culture.[6]

---

[3] J. S. Mill, *Principles of Political Economy* (1848: 1915 edn.), 978, 139.

[4] R. K. Webb, *Harriet Martineau: A Radical Victorian* (New York, 1960), 109.

[5] B. Porter, '"Monstrous Vandalism": Capitalism and Philistinism in the Works of Samuel Laing, 1780–1868', *Albion*, 23 (1991), 253–68.

[6] J. S. Mill made this point most explicitly: W. Ashley, 'Introduction' to 1915 edn. of *Principles*, pp. xiv–xxiii.

The critics, on the other hand, felt free to attribute fully rounded charac-
terizations to their capitalists, warts and all, with considerable relish for the
warts. The features of Engels's ogre are well known: 'I have never seen a
class so deeply demoralised, so incurably debased by selfishness, so cor-
roded within, so incapable of progress, as the English bourgeoisie,' he wrote
in 1844. 'For it nothing exists in this world, except for the sake of money. . . .
It knows no bliss save that of rapid gain, no pain save that of losing gold. In
the presence of this avarice and lust of gain, it is not possible for a single
human sentiment or opinion to remain untainted.' And in support he cited
Carlyle's 'splendid description' in *Past and Present* 'of the English bourgeoisie and its disgusting money greed'.[7] It is less often noticed that in the
Preface to the English edition of his book, in 1892, Engels retracted his 1844
views to the extent of admitting that 'the largest manufacturers, formerly
the leaders of the war against the working class, were now the foremost to
preach peace and harmony' and that they had abandoned shortsighted selfishness and money greed, and no longer remorselessly ground the faces of
their workers, although they no doubt maximized profits even more effi-
ciently by using such kid-glove methods.[8]

Matthew Arnold was withering in his contempt for the ill-educated, ignorant, narrow-minded, money-grubbing industrialists, and the 'philistines' he
pilloried in *Culture and Anarchy* (1868) were memorably captured and
pressed like rank weeds in its pages. '[Consider] their way of life,' he wrote,
'their habits, their manners, the very tones of their voices; look at them
attentively; observe the literature they read, the things which give them
pleasure, the words which come forth out of their mouths, the thoughts
which make the furniture of their minds; would any amount of wealth be
worth having with the condition that one was to become just like these
people by having it?'[9] The answer was probably yes, some amount of
wealth, provided it was large enough, was worth having on almost any conditions, and that was the answer given subsequently by the professional
classes Arnold so much admired as well as by the aristocracy which he
found a shade too barbaric and uncultured for his taste.

In the mean time the 'philistine' label stuck, and entered the stereotype of
the Victorian industrialist carried in the mental baggage of generations of
students. But above all that baggage was packed by Charles Dickens. It is true
that he presented genial, warm-hearted, generous, caring, if paternalist, capitalists in the Cheeryble brothers of *Nicholas Nickleby* (1838–9), who were
closely modelled on the real life Grant brothers, benevolent calico printers

    [7] F. Engels, *The Condition of the Working Class in England in 1844* (first published in English
in the USA in 1885 and in London in 1892: 1950 edn.), 276.
    [8] Ibid., 'Preface' (1892 edn.), pp. vii–viii.
    [9] M. Arnold, *Culture and Anarchy* (1868), quoted by Wiener, *English Culture*, 37.

from Manchester, although the Cheerybles were regarded as totally implausible romantic inventions by most contemporary reviewers. And in *Bleak
House* (1853) the great ironmaster, Rouncewell, replete with his country
house as well as his multifarious business affairs, is a great deal more polite,
well-mannered, and quietly self-assured than the crusty old aristocrat Sir
Leicester Dedlock with whom he has dealings over his son's projected marriage. Although Dickens has these, and other, images of industrialists on
offer, it is *Hard Times* (1854) and its Coketown, Gradgrind, and Josiah
Bounderby the manufacturer, that have created the most enduring impression (possibly sharing top billing with Scrooge, the pitiless tight-fisted mon-
eylender, who, however, is softened by bad dreams and the Christmas spirit
into donning the more benevolent and acceptable face of capitalism). Bounderby could have stepped straight from the pages of Engels into those of
Matthew Arnold. He is greedy, self-centred, heartless, ignorant, pompous,
hypocritical, thoroughly nasty, and he makes a lot of money.[10] Dickens, of
course, besides writing for money, was writing what would later be called
'social problem' novels. He was deeply shocked and disgusted by what he
saw when he visited Manchester in 1838, and proceeded to use the Cheerybles to suggest one solution to the condition of the working classes and
industrial towns, that of humanitarian employers and what would later be
termed welfare capitalism, and Bounderby to suggest another, that of rous-
ing public opinion against the indifference and iniquities of employers.
There was no pretence that he was recording in the one type or the other the
typical or representative capitalist, and it was his readers and reviewers who
were ready to believe that Bounderby was real and to be found in factories and mills throughout the land, while the Cheerybles were fanciful and
implausible.

   Bounderby is the supreme anti-industrial image of the industrialist, a car-
icature of mean, harsh, narrow materialism of production for production's
sake and wealth for wealth's sake seized on by those who denounced industrialism and all its works. Yet by a curious inversion the Bounderby type
seems, in the hands of Martin Wiener, to represent what was commendable,
progressive, and productive in the industrial spirit before it was crushed by
the dead weight of English culture. It is true that Wiener does not attempt
a profile of the praiseworthy entrepreneur, but rather allows one to be
inferred from his one extended account of an entrepreneur who let the side
down, lost the industrial spirit, and joined the enemy camp. This was Marcus
Samuel, creator of one of the world's great oil companies, Shell Transport
and Trading, who instead of keeping up a ceaseless and single-minded quest
for more profits like his rival Henry Deterding who controlled Royal Dutch,

[10] Analysis of Dickens in I. Melada, *The Captain of Industry in English Fiction, 1821–71*
(Albuquerque, N. Mex., 1970), 103–15, 157–60.

eased up after buying a country estate in Kent in 1895, devoted his energies to non-business goals, and allowed Shell's dynamism to falter to the point where he had to accept a minority position in a merger with Royal Dutch. Samuel's non-business goals were: 'Eton and Oxford for his sons; affluence for his more remote descendants, a country house for his family; horses, gardens, angling, watching cricket in comfort, the devotion of subordinates and servants, the respect of acquaintances, the chance to be charitable on a large scale and to give generous hospitality.'[11] If one substitutes Groton and Harvard for Eton and Oxford, and deletes the reference to cricket, this sounds remarkably like the profile of many American super-entrepreneurs of the same period: the Whitneys, Vanderbilts, and Goulds, John D. Rockefeller, Henry Clay Frick, and Randolph Hearst, for instance, all seem to fit this model, adding for some of them an ambition to watch their daughters marry British aristocrats instead of watching cricket, and it is not generally thought that there was any waning of their acquisitive instincts.[12]

Marcus Samuel's mistake seems to have been that he left a fortune of only £4 million, and not one of £40 million, and that he abandoned the unremitting pursuit of wealth for unworthy and frivolous reasons that a Bounderby would never have countenanced, like personal pleasure, family betterment, public service (he was Lord Mayor of London in 1902), and philanthropy. In truth, Samuel does not seem to have done too badly for the ninth son of an East End trader in Oriental shells, and in any case he was more of a lucky speculator than an outstanding entrepreneur even in his business prime. It is true that he built up valuable experience and contacts in trading with the Far East in the 1880s, but the vision for starting the oil tanker business came from Fred Lane, the London representative of the French Rothschilds; finding oil in Borneo was a lucky strike; and Samuel's ignorance of the technicalities of the oil business and his lack of organizational or managerial skills, coupled with his arrogant and offensive manner in dealing with government, probably meant that his progressive loss of interest in running the business was good for Shell rather than harmful.[13] Gentrification, which Samuel certainly embraced with enthusiasm, might rescue industry from capitalists whose economic energies were flagging, rather than cause the energy to flag; and ennoblement, frequently a means of kicking outworn politicians upstairs and out of the way, might perhaps perform the same service for extinct entrepreneurs. In any case, while Samuel achieved his

[11] Martin Wiener, *English Culture and the Decline of the Industrial Spirit, 1850–1980*, (Cambridge, 1981) 146–7, and quoting R. Henriques, *Marcus Samuel* (1960), 87. Wiener's outburst is a trifle strange, since Deterding himself built an expensive country house, Kelling Hall, Norfolk, in 1912: C. Aslet, *The Last Country Houses* (1982), 74–6.

[12] F. C. Jaher, 'The Gilded Elite: American Multi-Millionaires, 1865 to the Present', in W. D. Rubinstein (ed.), *Wealth and the Wealthy in the Modern World* (1980), ch. 5, esp. pp. 197–205.

[13] *DBB*, v, 1st Viscount Bearsted (1853–1927).

goals of Eton and Oxford for his sons, a country estate, and a peerage, that lifestyle did not prevent his eldest son, and two grandsons, from having successful, if unspectacular, business careers in Shell, Lloyds Bank, and Hill Samuel; the Kent estate was lost, but they continued to live grandly in other desirable parts of the country. A three-generation business dynasty, still open-ended, was quite an achievement, not all that common in any industrialized country. It was more than the Vanderbilts or Rockefellers could manage; and it was some evidence that the industrial spirit could continue to flow in the blood of public school and Oxbridge-educated progeny of gentrified businessmen.

Martin Wiener, to be sure, is concerned with the quality and strength of the industrial spirit, which he considers to have declined well below 40 per cent proof since 1850, the proof of that view being the supposed poor performance, whether relative or absolute, of the British economy, itself a matter of opinion rather than fact which has attracted a prodigious literature.[14] At the individual level it is hard to say whether the business performance of the 3rd and 4th Viscounts Bearsted has been better or worse than that of their grandfather; it has certainly been different, for they have done more or less routine and bureaucratized directorial jobs, while he was a buccaneer in uncharted waters making up his own rules as he went along. It is equally difficult to say with complete certainty whether the performance of the British economy has been consistently poor and below the reasonably attainable for the entire period since 1850, though that seems highly unlikely, and even if it has been it would remain almost impossible to say how much of the underachievement can be attributed to something termed 'entrepreneurial failure'. That also raises the question whether the qualities appropriate to entrepreneurial success in an economy of family firms where a one-man band could make a lot of noise and money are also appropriate in an economy of large companies, let alone one of multinational corporations. Such questions attracted much attention from the Harvard Research Center in Entrepreneurial History in the decade after 1948, but it closed down in 1958 without having found an answer.[15] In the mean time the point of immediate concern is that the type of entrepreneur and of entrepreneurial culture awarded the seal of approval by those of the Wiener persuasion seems to be, in Dickensian terms, some kind of cross between Bounderby,

---

[14] The course of the debate on decline can be followed in Michael Dintenfass, *The Decline of Industrial Britain, 1870–1980* (1992); Bruce Collins and Keith Robbins (eds.), *British Culture and Economic Decline* (1990); W. D. Rubinstein, *Capitalism, Culture and Decline in Britain, 1750–1990* (1993); and most recently and most convincingly in Peter Clarke and Clive Trebilcock (eds.), *Understanding Decline. Perceptions and Realities of British Economic Performance* (Cambridge, 1997).

[15] T. A. B. Corley, 'The Entrepreneur: The Central Issue in Business History?', in Jonathan Brown and Mary B. Rose (eds.), *Entrepreneurship, networks and modern business* (Manchester, 1993), 13–15.

Scrooge, and Rouncewell, while the Cheerybles emphatically could have tried harder and done better. On this scale, in non-fictional terms, James Morrison, 'probably the richest commoner of the 19th century, leaving between £4 million and £6 million at his death', who devoted himself wholeheartedly to drapery and textile wholesaling and apparently never gave away a penny in his life, must rank as a much better entrepreneur than, say, Sir Henry Tate, who collected pictures and founded a Gallery as well as making Golden Syrup, and left no more than £1.2 million at his death.[16]

The ideal entrepreneur, the hero of the Victorian success story as told by Samuel Smiles, was the self-made man who by his own unaided efforts and through self-improvement, self-help, abstinence, thrift, hard work, acquisitive drive, innovative flair, and grasp of market opportunities rose to the top, and on the way created jobs, added to human happiness by flooding the world with his cheap products, even into the darkest corners of Africa, and thus brought about continuous and unprecedented economic growth. The self-made bit, in particular, was a myth, since the great majority of the early industrialists, let alone those of the mid-nineteenth century, had a head start, if not in formal education, then in family capital and business connections.[17] There have always been a few examples, however, of great men and business tycoons rising from very humble origins. The lawyer Eldon was often paraded as an anti-industrial Tory example, but in fact his father was a Tyneside coal-fitter, not a collier, and coal-fitters were fairly wealthy merchants, not workingmen. But George Stephenson, son of a colliery fireman, was an authentic instance and a Victorian cult figure; and so, much later, was Lord Nuffield and his bicycle shed, and the decades since 1945 can offer John Hall, a miner and the son of a miner, who has played the Tyneside property market to the tune of £50 million, the Metro Centre, and the Wynyard estate which he has bought from the Marquess of Londonderry. There are indeed perhaps as many, or as few, self-made top business people around in the 1990s as there were in Samuel Smiles's day. There are, for example, Lord Weinstock, the orphaned son of a Polish-Jewish immigrant tailor brought up by a hairdresser elder brother (although he then got a kick start by marrying the heiress of Sir Michael Sobell, founder of Radio and Allied Industries, which formed the base on which Weinstock built GEC); Alan Sugar, the East End barrow boy who created Amstrad; or Sir John Moores, post office messenger boy, founder of Littlewoods and chief benefactor of a new university. Robert Maxwell, son of a Czech labourer, used to be reckoned one of this band before his downfall.[18] A myth with some slender basis in fact, it was a potent force in shaping Victorian opinion, and

[16] Rubinstein, 'British Millionaires', 207, 211.   [17] Crouzet, *First Industrialists, passim.*
[18] *Sunday Times* 'The Sunday Times Rich List' (6 Apr. 1997), and earlier editions, from ibid., 'Britain's Rich, the Top 200', (2 Apr. 1989), onwards.

its decline as a talisman, rather than as a slender basis in fact, may well have misled and confused those who offer either entrepreneurial or cultural explanations for Britain's alleged economic decline.

Much less mythical was an enterprise culture, or 'entrepreneurial ideal' as it has been called, which was constructed by the early nineteenth-century opinion-formers in the treatises and tracts of political economy, Benthamite utilitariansim, and philosophical radicalism, and popularized as the creed of the Manchester School. Elements of this culture, the emphasis on the virtues of competition, free trade, curtailment of patronage and inherited privilege, and minimalist government, became generally accepted by educated opinion by the 1850s and 1860s—a little late in the day for those who date the decline of the industrial spirit from 1850—and were strongly reflected in the nation's institutions and policies. It was tempting to suppose that the victory of free trade, the rhythmic throbbing of the workshop of the world, the market-testing of elementary education under the Revised Code, and indeed the apparent triumph of evangelical morality as the foundation of mid-Victorian respectability and prudery, represented nothing less than the political, legislative, and cultural enactment of the triumph of the entrepreneurial ideal.[19] All was not what it seemed. Manchester ideas were fine for commercial policy, and with some tampering, for fiscal policy as well, but in other spheres they failed to impress or dominate; neither Manchester men, nor businessmen more generally, were on top, in control of government, policy, or opinion. What had happened was much more like a series of mental adjustments, compromises, and concessions by the old aristocratic order as it manœuvred to stay in the saddle. Somewhat paradoxically, when the old ruling elite did begin to slip out of the saddle from the 1880s onwards, and the professional and business men moved in in serious numbers, the institutional forms of the entrepreneurial ideal were challenged and eroded at an accelerating pace. Between 1880 and 1914 businessmen had far greater political and social power than ever before, but they were not united or vigorous in defending the basic tenets of the enterprise culture. Free trade, competition, inherited privilege, minimalist government, all these became issues in internecine disputes amongst businessmen, not battle standards in a class war.[20]

---

[19] Perkin, *Origins of Modern English Society*, 221–30, 271–319, gives a full account of the entrepreneurial ideal and its triumph which is strong on concepts but weaker on politics and the economy.

[20] Harold Perkin has a version of 'the decline of the entrepreneurial ideal' in *Origins*, 437–54, which is basically a recitation of the accumulation of departures from laissez-faire over social questions between the 1830s and the 1880s, and this does not mesh closely with his later version of the onward march of 'the professional ideal' in his *Rise of Professional Society: England since 1880* (1989), nor with the latest version, in which entrepreneurs themselves become professionals, in his *Third Revolution. Professional Elites in the Modern World* (1996).

Faced with this situation one is inclined to echo the Countess de Montijo's response to the rumour that Lord Clarendon had fathered her daughter, the Empress Eugenie, while he was British Minister in Madrid in the 1830s: '*les dates ne correspondent pas.*'[21] The spirited efforts of British entrepreneurs had propelled Britain to the leading position in the world in the 50 or 60 years before 1850, at a time when the enterprise culture or entrepreneurial ideal was apparently little more than a gleam in the eye, an aspiration but not an accomplished fact. In the 50 or 60 years after 1850, when the entrepreneurial ideal was entrenched as orthodoxy, even if being challenged by the professional ideal towards the end of the period, the steely resolve of the entrepreneurs seems to have softened and Britain began to go downhill. There seems to be a serious mismatch here. There also seems to be a serious confusion between opinion and theory, on the one hand, and the business scene which the theories were trying to interpret, on the other. The selections made by historians from the writings and sayings of a collection of political economists, essayists, novelists, and others are good evidence of what these people thought about the capitalists, their functions and their behaviour; they are not necessarily reliable evidence of how businessmen actually behaved. There are several ways in which the veracity of the role models, or the extent to which actual entrepreneurs diverged from them, could be tested historically. Here, two are chosen: the effects of literal gentrification, that is the acquisition of landed property, on entrepreneurial performance; and secondly, the extent to which successful entrepreneurs abided by the prescribed rules of abstaining from unproductive and wasteful expenditure on luxuries, frivolities, and amusements. These are two touchstones for the thesis that entrepreneurs who departed from the straight and narrow path of abstemious acquisitiveness were betraying the cause of economic growth as well as compromising their own chances of business success.

In the past it has been too readily taken for granted that when a successful businessman purchased a country estate he ceased to be a businessman and set out on the path of becoming its antithesis, a landed gentleman of leisure. The process has frequently been termed 'a haemorrhage of capital and of talent', a switch from the productive employment of capital in trade, finance, or industry into its unproductive use in status display in country mansions and as low-risk rentier capital.[22] Many estate purchases did have

---

[21] Kennedy (ed.), *My Dear Duchess*, 6: Clarendon went to Madrid as British Minister in 1833, and while it is true that he became the Countess's lover, her daughter Eugenie had been born in 1826.

[22] See, for example, M. W. Flinn, *Origins of the Industrial Revolution* (1966), 46–8 and, for a case study of this 'draining of capital', E. L. Jones, 'Industrial Capital and Landed Investment: The Arkwrights in Herefordshire, 1809–43', in id. and G. E. Mingay (eds.), *Land, Labour and Population in the Industrial Revolution* (1967), 48–71. Wiener, *English Culture*, 145–6 takes haemorrhaging for granted, but the concept is critically examined in F. M. L. Thompson, 'Landownership and Economic Growth in England in the Eighteenth Century', in E. L. Jones and S. J. Woolf (eds.), *Agrarian Change and Economic Development* (1969), esp. pp. 54–7.

this effect, and particularly when a landed family has been founded which has successfully endured over several generations the 'loss' to the trading economy has apparently been permanent. In general terms there were three possible cases of the relationship of new men to the land. The first case was the foundation of a landed family and complete severance of connections with commercial or industrial origins. The second was the transient or life-cycle purchase, the rich man's version of acquiring a retirement home which would be resold after his death. The third case was the more complicated and ambivalent evolution of a hybrid type of landed businessman, some-times termed an aristocratic bourgeois, who sought to combine the pleasures and status of a landed position with continued activity in the world of business from which he had sprung; a subdivision of this category would distinguish the active businessmen who purchased land simply as an invest-ment and kind of adjunct to the business, perhaps to try to insure the future of the family firm, perhaps in order to find a safe outlet for surplus capital not required in the firm.[23]

Only the first type had a direct and seemingly obvious effect on the supply of entrepreneurial talent and capital. It is arguable, however, that a clean break with business origins, and successful adoption into the landed sphere was not necessarily a serious blow for the productive part of the economy. Landowners were not inherently unenterprising, although it is fair to say that the enterprise of new landowners was more likely to be focused on the latest agricultural gimickry than on the kind of industrial undertakings with which many of the longer-established landowners were concerned. The remains of a fine example of this may be seen at Leighton Hall on the Shropshire–Montgomeryshire border, where John Naylor, great-nephew and heir to one-third of the fortune of a Liverpool banker, Thomas Leyland, spent a large slice of his inheritance on a state-of-the-art mid-Victorian model farm complete with a patent roundhouse for the efficient manage-ment of dairy cattle and pigs, a kind of agricultural version of railway architecture, an internal rail system for transporting fodder and manure, and a steam and hydraulic-powered network of pipes and pumps for the dis-tribution of liquid manure direct on to the fields. Of course, he built a large and ornate country house as well, a kind of Italianate-Gothic mongrel, tur-reted and gilded, but the ostensibly productive part of his investment was clearly also little more than another form of display and conspicuous con-sumption, since however clean and efficient his farming operations were they can never have been commercially competitive or profitable.[24]

[23] For examples of this subdivision see M. J. Daunton, 'Firm and Family in the City of London in the Nineteenth Century: The Case of F. G. Dalgety', *Historical Research*, 62 (1989), 154–77.

[24] Legacy and Succession Duty Registers, PRO, IR 26/1136, fo. 968 (T. Leyland, died 1827, personalty £800,000); IR 26/1683, fo. 897 (Richard Leyland, died 1844, personalty £360,000); IR 26/1843, fo. 681 (Christopher Leyland, died 1849, personalty £670,000). The landowning great-

In more general terms it can be maintained that when a businessman, and more particularly his sons or other heirs, showed the inclination to transform themselves into landed gentlemen of leisure they were probably little loss to the cause of economic growth, as with such dispositions they would most likely have made poor businessmen. Moreover, to hold that their departure from trade and industry represented a deplorable or irreplaceable 'haemorrhage of talent' implies adherence to a simplistic theory of entrepreneurship equivalent to the 'wages fund theory', which would hold that there was a very small and fixed number of potential entrepreneurs in any society, and that when one of them neglected to fulfil his destined mission no substitutes or replacements could be expected to step forward. It would be more convincing to argue that the landed route acted as a safety valve for the economy, allowing impure or half-hearted capitalists to escape from the industrial system and make room for bright young things better endowed with the industrial spirit.

Even if one sweeps all these qualifications aside and persists in regarding the foundation of landed families by new men as a dead loss to the productive economy, there still remain the two cases in which the acquisition of a landed estate was not in itself an important denial of business values and aspirations. The transient, who retired to the country after a successful business career—or, indeed, after a successful political, professional, military, or ecclesiastical career—was a very traditional figure: examples can be drawn from the fifteenth century, and the type was well-known to Defoe. After death the estate would normally be sold again, leaving no permanent mark on landed society and causing no long-term damage to entrepreneurial opportunities. If a deceased transient's estate was resold to another transient from the next generation of elderly businessmen, as sometimes happened, a country house and its land could become a long-serving retirement home for the wealthy.[25] The arrangement may have been of positive benefit to the economy: it provided a form of pension for ageing and flagging entrepreneurs without encouraging any flagging of the entrepreneurial spirit, and it was an agreeable way of storing capital for later release to nourish the ventures of the next generation.

If that type of behaviour was neutral, or mildly stimulating, in its effects on enterprise, the case of the hybrid who ran with the business fox and

nephews of Thomas Leyland in 1883 were: John Naylor of Leighton Hall, Montgomery, 11,000 acres, £12,729 annual value; Thomas Leyland of Haggerston Castle, Northumberland, 21,070 acres, £52,979 annual value; and Richard Christopher Naylor of Hooton Hall, Cheshire, 11,610 acres, £19,896 annual value. On Leighton Hall see the *Sunday Telegraph*, 17 Jan. 1993, p. xvi.

[25] There are examples of this in Lawrence Stone and Jeanne C. Fawtier Stone, *An Open Elite? England, 1540–1880* (Oxford, 1984), 164–9, and in H. J. Habakkuk, *Marriage, Debt, and the Estates System: English Landownership, 1650–1950* (Oxford, 1994), 599–606.

hunted with the aristocratic hounds is more problematic. The type had been foreshadowed by the lifestyle of some of the wealthiest sixteenth- and seventeenth-century London merchants, who anticipated the 'retirement' model by moving out into the country while still continuing to attend to business in the City, no doubt with something less than the unremitting vigour of their youth. From around the middle of the eighteenth century this developed into a distinctive way of life available to rich and successful businessmen, able to operate from country seats farther afield than in the inner ring of the Home Counties; by the end of the nineteenth century this was a well-established social form among the very wealthy, who might have country seats far removed from their places of business without ceasing to be active in them. There is no compelling reason why an entrepreneur should not enjoy hunting and shooting and the means of indulging such tastes, and still remain an entrepreneur. The question must arise, however, whether an entrepreneur who tarred himself with the brush of gentlemanly pursuits was as good an entrepreneur as the one who did not. That is a question which business historians might be able to answer, although the answer given by the most able business historian who has addressed this issue, Donald Coleman, is strangely hesitant and ambivalent. For while he concludes that the gentlemen in business, who may have preferred 'to pursue foxes rather than profits', probably 'produced a tendency somewhat to depreciate the aim of maximising profits and somewhat to appreciate the aim of securing stability and order' and may have contributed to 'some lag in industrial advance' in the period 1870–1950, he also reveals that in the firm he made his own, Courtaulds, it was the non-gentry at board and managerial levels in the 1930s—the 'practical men', the 'players'—'who were both the most stubborn opponents of new ideas and scientific research and the least willing to recognize trades unions or the need for change in the face of labour unrest', and the gentlemen on the board 'who showed initiative in bringing in scientists or in making organizational changes which the practical men opposed.'[26] The means of measuring the quality of entrepreneurship remain elusive, and have failed to advance beyond the yardstick of profits and the accumulation of wealth, despite the recognition that profit maximization has not been the sole or even the prime aim of most entrepreneurs. Hence one is entitled to assume that an aristocratic-bourgeois businessman who continued to make money was an effective entrepreneur whose chosen lifestyle did not sap the strength of his industrial spirit.

It follows from this that the bare fact of the acquisition of landed estates by new men of wealth is not a measure of outright gentrification, if by gentrification one understands absorption into an old-style landed elite

[26] D. C. Coleman, 'Gentlemen and Players', *Economic History Review*, 2nd ser., 26 (1973), 92–116, esp. 113–15.

antithetical to business pursuits. To gauge the impact and extent of gentrification it then becomes important to know not just who bought estates, but
also their motives and the influence that had on their subsequent careers and
those of their families. That is easier said than done, since the motives for
land purchases may never have been recorded at all or at best lie hidden in
as yet undiscovered or unresearched private papers. It may be simpler to
identify the baddies in this story, those who founded landed families and
withdrew from productive economic activity, than the goodies whose links
with land had neutral or positive implications. In all cases it is a matter of
proceeding by examples and instances, groping towards some valid generalizations. It is not without significance that out of the couple of dozen individuals who were Samuel Smiles's paragons of industrial achievement in the
heroic age of the Industrial Revolution just over half used their new found
wealth to buy landed estates, and half of those in turn spawned industrial
dynasties as well in the sense of producing descendants who carried on in
business—although Smiles himself did not find it necessary to comment on
these outcomes, preferring instead to indulge in a homily on the comparative unimportance of making money: 'Worldly success, measured by the
accumulation of money, is no doubt a very dazzling thing,' he said,

and all men are naturally more or less the admirers of worldly success. But though
men of persevering, sharp, dexterous, and unscrupulous habits, ever on the watch to
push opportunities, may and do 'get on' in the world, yet it is quite possible that
they may not possess the slightest elevation of character, nor a particle of real good-
ness. He who recognizes no higher logic than that of the shilling, may become a very
rich man, and yet remain all the while an exceedingly poor creature. For riches are
no proof whatever of moral worth.[27]

Few modern commentators would place moral uplift among an entrepreneur's objectives, and fewer still would volunteer to say whether, and how
much of it, had been achieved. There is firmer warrant for saying that many
famous names from this heroic age founded landed families and then vanished from the pages of economic history. Several were prolific begetters of
gentry families. Arkwright's water-frame spun off no fewer than four of
them; the cotton businesses of the Peels early in the nineteenth century
(though in the case of the Tamworth estate it was initially a business investment in a proposed new centre for cotton mills away from Manchester), and
the Fieldens in mid-century, generated three landed families apiece, as did
Ricardo's stockbroking and financial dealing, while Marshall's linen managed four. This tradition was fully maintained in the late nineteenth century
by the three landed Brasseys who stemmed from Thomas Brassey, the great
railway contractor; and in the twentieth century by the extensive landed

[27] Samuel Smiles, *Self-Help* (1866: 1996 edn., with a foreword by Lord Harris of High Cross),
ch. 2, 'Leaders of Industry', 17–40 and 189.

progeny of W. D. & H. O. Wills's cigarettes.[28] To be sure, the Fieldens did not altogether lose interest in cotton and the welfare of Todmorden until the third and fourth generations. While a couple of the sons of H. O. Wills, and the first tobacco baron, Lord Dulverton, served the Imperial Tobacco Company as directors or presidents: but judging from the list of the recreations of one—which included shooting, fishing, deer stalking, motoring, bicycling, riding, rowing, lawn tennis, foreign travel, and music—and the political career of another, they did not have a great deal of time to spend on the tobacco business. All the rest of these families disappeared from the business scene after their founder's death, although they were far from sinking without trace, being well enough known in other spheres as MPs, racehorse owners, lords lieutenant, masters of foxhounds, and the like. It might be noted, however, that a Peel turned up in industry once more, in the 1930s, after an absence of a hundred years and five generations: this was the 2nd Earl Peel, and he was chairman and managing director of James Williamson & Son, a director of the Lancashire Steel Corporation, and deputy chairman of the LMSR until the nationalization of the railways. He owed this Peelite reincarnation as an industrialist to his mother, the Williamson linoleum heiress. No doubt he ran this family business competently, in harness with the large estates in Lancashire and Yorkshire that had been acquired with part of the linoleum money, but not competently enough to save Lancaster's linoleum industry from the onslaughts of plastic floor coverings; his son, the 3rd Earl, retreated to the position of a Yorkshire landowner, defending his grouse moors against the threat of a 'right of access'; he lacked any other visible means of support.[29]

Others were more restrained in creating landed families, and contented themselves with one. The well known did this, and not uncommonly sooner or later acquired a peerage. From banking came Abel Smith and the later Lords Carrington; from cotton Jedediah Strutt and the Lords Belper; from wool Samuel Cunliffe-Lister and the Lords Masham and Earls of Swinton; from iron Josiah Guest and the Viscounts Wimborne; and from shipping Christopher Furness and the Viscounts Furness. The somewhat less well

[28] Arkwright of Sutton Scarsdale, Derby.; Arkwright of Willersley, Derby.; Arkwright of Mark Hall, Essex; and Arkwright of Hampton Court, Hereford. Peel of Tamworth, Staffs.; Peel of Knowlsmere, Yorks.; and Peel of Wallington Hall, Norfolk. Fielden of Todmorden Castle, Lancs.; Fielden of Grimston Park, Yorks.; and Fielden of Nutfield Priory and Beachamwell, Norfolk. Ricardo of Bromesberrow, Hereford; Ricardo of Gatcombe Park, Glos.; and Ricardo of Kiddington Hall, Oxford. Marshall of Patterdale Hall, Westmorland; Marshall of Cookridge Hall, Yorks.; Marshall of Monk Coniston Park, Westmorland; and Marshall of Weetwood Hall, Yorks. Brassey of Normanhurst, Sussex; Brassey of Preston Hall, Kent; and Brassey of Heythrop House, Oxford— the next generation added a fourth Brassey, of Apethorpe, Northants. Wills of Batford Park, Glos.; Wills of Blagdon, Somerset, and Wills of Miserden, Glos., are a few of the Wills tribe.

[29] B. R. Law, *Fieldens of Todmorden* (Littleborough, 1995), esp. p. 202; *Who Was Who*, vii; *Who's Who* (1993 edn.).

known did it also, and generally did not acquire peerages: the insurance broker Julius Angerstein, virtual creator of the National Gallery, set up a Norfolk
landed family; Matthew Boulton of the Soho Works fathered the gentry
family of Tew Park, Oxfordshire; Samuel Eyres, a Leeds woollen manufacturer, succeeded in planting a gentry family in Gloucestershire through his
daughter's children; and a Russia merchant, Giles Loder, equiped his son with
estates in Northamptonshire and Sussex; while the builder, Thomas Cubitt,
founded both a substantial landed establishment in Surrey and Devon and the
Ashcombe peerage. These examples of the creation of landed families were
spread over the whole period from the 1780s to the 1920s, and each family or
cluster of families had rather different life histories, integrating at different
speeds and different social levels into the old elite, through intermarriage
with the aristocracy or gentry, or with church or army families, through
school and university, and through different kinds of public service and sporting interests. A perceptible shortening of the time taken to win full social
acceptance, from two or three generations down to one, was the most obvious change over time. But in broad terms these all conformed to a constant
type: new men who themselves, or through their immediate descendants,
entered the old elite by becoming country landowners, whereupon the descendants turned their backs on the original source of the family fortunes, maybe
retaining a symbolic memory of whence they had come through some device
in their new-granted coat of arms, and deployed their talents in politics,
administration, the army, the hunting field, the racecourse, or conceivably in
the professions, but never in business. Until, that is, reduced circumstances
forced some of them back on to the labour market after 1945, when they
mostly found comfortable positions in the City without great difficulty.[30]

Here was a group whose family histories run true to the stereotype of
gentrification as fatal to the entrepreneurial spirit. Other families, however,
tell a different story. The transients among the estate-purchasers were, by
definition, ephemeral, which makes it difficult to form an impression of how
important they were as a social phenomenon. The length of their stay in
the countryside varied considerably. William Armstrong, armaments and
hydraulics baron of Tyneside, spent the last thirty years of his life building
Cragside and its surrounding estate, which, with the separate property of
Bamburgh Castle, came to cover 16,000 acres, engaging in a moderately
friendly rivalry with Lord Salisbury as to whose house should be the first to
be lit by electricity, but in no more than semi-retirement from his engineer-

---

[30] Estates in 1883 were: Carrington, 25,809 acres, £42,254 annual value; Belper, 4,945 acres,
£9,509 annual value; Guest (Wimborne), 52,860 acres, £46,856 annual value (subsequently
extended); Angerstein, 19,731 acres, £17,512 annual value; Boulton, 7,947 acres, £13,537 annual
value; Eyres (Eyres-Kettlewell), 4,183 acres, £6,274 annual value; Loder, 10,241 acres, £11,527
annual values; Cubitt, 6,789 acres, £8,509 annual value. Estates acquired after 1883 were: Cunliffe-
Lister (Masham), 34,000 acres (*Who Was Who*, i); Furness, 30,000 acres (*Who Was Who*, i).

ing works and his passion for mechanical gadgetry; and he used the astonishing Norman Shaw house at Cragside both to accommodate gadgetry and
to entertain visiting naval customers from Japan. He left no children when
he died in 1900, but his great-nephew William Henry Fitzpatrick Watson,
who had in anticipation assumed the additional name of Armstrong in
1889, inherited the property and in 1903 contrived to secure the re-creation
of the Armstrong peerage. The twentieth-century Armstrongs were no
businessmen, the second baron of the new creation occupying himself as
Siamese Consul-General in Canada from 1924 to 1942, although his
son, the third baron, who succeeded in 1972, became a Lloyds underwriter, one of the by then traditional ways for the upper classes to make a
normally effortless living in the City. He retreated to Bamburgh Castle and
Knightsbridge, and the Cragside estate was sold and the house and grounds
were acquired by the National Trust, as subsequently was Bamburgh Castle.
J. Arthur Rank, flour-miller, cinema-proprietor, and entrepreneurial father of
photocopying, enjoyed his 10,000-acre estate of Micheldever in Hampshire
for less than twenty years, and after his death in 1974 it was sold to the
Eagle Star Insurance Co., which has been biding its time for a propitious
moment to implement its scheme for developing the site as a private enterprise new town. At the other end of the scale, no one can have been in and
out more rapidly than Alan Bond, Australian speculator, brewer, press
baron, and yachtsman, who bought the 2,000-acre Glympton estate in
Oxfordshire in 1988 for £10 million and was obliged to sell it again in less
than twelve months when his financial empire collapsed. Whether they
owned a country estate for a few months or for many years wealthy businessmen such as these showed their taste for running a large agricultural
estate and a large country house in conjunction with an active business life,
and although Alan Bond would presumably be counted as an entrepreneurial success in 1988 and an entrepreneurial failure in 1989, there is no sign
that this combination of business with country living on the grand scale was
in itself damaging to the industrial spirit or a significant cause of bankruptcy.[31] It is entirely possible that most of those multimillionaire businessmen who own large country estates in the 1990s, like Lord Sainsbury or
Anthony Bamford, will turn out to be transients, single-generation landowners. Such, at least, was the opinion of the editor of the 1952 edition of
Burke's Landed Gentry, who remarked that 'whereas in J. B. Burke's day the
successful businessman acquired an estate so that he might settle there, and
his children and children's children after him, now an estate is bought purely

[31] Armstrong: DBB, i; Who Was Who, i and vi; Who's Who (1975); and see F. M. L. Thompson,
'Private Property and Public Policy', in Lord Blake and H. Cecil (eds.), Salisbury: The Man and his
Policies (1987), 259. Rank: Who Was Who, vii. Bond: The Times, 2 Sept. 1988; Country Life,
23 Feb. 1989. Interestingly, Glympton had three post-1945 owners before Bond, including Garfield
Weston, biscuit magnate: The Economist, 23 July 1988, p. 27.

for the benefit of the actual present owner. People do not look to posterity, present taxation will not let them.'[32]

Twenty years later, in a preface to the 18th edition of *Burke's Landed Gentry* Hugh Montgomery-Massingberd gave the impression that the transients had long been a major element among the landed gentry at large. 'Up to 1914,' he stated, 'a strict requirement of landed property was enforced, and if a family sold its estates the pedigree was ejected from the book. For example, of the families included in 1863 at least 50 per cent had disappeared by the 1914 edition.'[33] It is difficult to interpret this statement, since it included the disappearance of old-established but recently impoverished gentry and the extinction of families through demographic failure, who were not transients, and it probably also included vanishing Irish gentry who had been part of the 1863 register but had their own separate volume from 1899 onwards. But since Massingberd was talking about a turnover of something like 2,000 families it is likely that casualties on such a scale included considerable numbers of genuine ins and outs. In any case, for present purposes the important point is that many of these transients were not tired old businessmen putting themselves out to grass, but very wealthy men in the prime of their business careers who were joining the club of the aristocratic bourgeoisie, the amphibians, equally at home in the counting house and the country house, with the one difference that they did not seek, or were unable, to found dynasties.

The amphibians' club indeed had many eminent members, and the wealthy businessmen who treated their landed estates in this fashion possibly outnumbered those who took the traditional path of merging themselves into landed society. It is fair to regard the banking Hoares, specifically Henry Hoare 'the magnificent', as the founders of this club in its modern form. He purchased the Stourhead estate in Wiltshire, built the house, landscaped the grounds, and pieced together a great estate, in the second half of the eighteenth century, accompanying this with the cultivation of a network of aristocratic marriages and friendships, and a leading position in county society, whilst never surrendering his place as one of London's leading private bankers.[34] The dynastic principle has fared well with the land, but even better with the banking. The family transferred Stourhead to the National Trust in the 1960s, but has maintained an unbroken connection with the bank for more than 300 years, so that 1990 saw four Hoares, including the bank chairman, in the partners' parlour in Fleet Street. This may, conceivably, be an example of the kind of exasperatingly durable, highly traditional

---

[32] *Burke's Landed Gentry* (1952 edn.), p. xvii.   [33] Ibid. (1972 edn.), iii, p. ix.
[34] C. G. A. Clay, 'Henry Hoare, Banker, his Family, and the Stourhead Estate', in F. M. L. Thompson (ed.), *Landowners, Capitalists, and Entrepreneurs. Essays for Sir John Habakkuk* (Oxford, 1994), 113–38.

and conservative, family business much disliked by business schools and progressive economists as obstacles to innovation, economic efficiency, and the growth of large-scale firms, and hence it may not be regarded as a good advertisement for the entrepreneurial virtues of gentlemanly capitalism or the aristocratic bourgeoisie.

The same could hardly be said of the Rothschilds, who were responsible for elevating the working life of the high Victorian banking landowner into an art form. The English branch of the Rothschilds was founded when Nathan Mayer arrived in Manchester in 1799 to muscle in on the cotton trade; within ten years he was in London and high finance, and by the 1830s was also installed in a comfortable country house with 600-acre estate at Gunnersbury, within easy commuting distance of the City. One hundred and sixty years later the Rothschilds are still in the forefront of innovative and internationally competitive merchant banking, and the family continues to excel in zoology, social science, and public life as well as in banking, so that their credentials as high achievers are impeccable. Meanwhile, three of Nathan Mayer's four sons set themselves up as great landowners—the fourth went to mind the Paris branch, taking his picture collection with him. The eldest son, Lionel, lived at Gunnersbury for most of his banking and political career, but eventually bought the Tring Park estate, which initially he had rented. His brothers settled at Mentmore (which eventually went to Lord Rosebery by marriage), and at Aston Clinton. This settlement of the Vale of Aylesbury was consolidated in the 1870s when Lionel bought the Halton and Ascott estates for his own two younger sons, and by the arrival of cousin Ferdinand in the 1880s to build his astonishing chateau at Waddesdon. Thus at the peak there were half a dozen Rothschild mansions and great estates all within a short ride of one another. The reason, it was said, was so that they could call on each other in case none of the local gentry condescended to know them. The real reason was their passion for hunting, and their passion for business. They were keen foxhunters, and they also introduced staghunting to the district, keeping a pack of staghounds at Tring and providing a supply of stags, which were carted to the meet and then turned out to be chased. Tring, it may be noted, is on the London and Birmingham Railway, opened in 1838; the original stables and kennels for the Rothschild Staghounds were rented, at Tring, in 1839. Rapid access from London was the key to their lifestyle. Lionel not infrequently took a day off from banking to go hunting, and it was not unknown for him to catch an early train from Euston, take a gallop round his brother's place at Mentmore, and be back in town for an afternoon's business or attendance at Westminster.[35]

[35] R. Davis, *The English Rothschilds* (Chapel Hill, NC, 1983), 25–30, 48, 92–4, 174; José Harris and Pat Thane, 'British and European Bankers, 1880–1914: An Aristocratic Bourgeoisie?', in Pat Thane, G. Crossick, and R. Floud (eds.), *The Power of the Past* (Cambridge, 1984), 215–34.

The Rothschilds were indisputably *grand seigneurs*: they had broad acres, large and luxurious country houses, aristocratic friends—although because of the double bind of their Jewishness and the clannishness of all bankers, only one aristocratic marriage, that of Hannah to Rosebery—aristocratic tastes, and, unique mark of social acceptance, a begging letter from Queen Victoria asking to be invited to Waddesdon. It would be misleading to draw the conclusion from all this that they had simply climbed into the ranks of the old landed aristocracy, repudiated the ladder by which they had ascended, and adopted the supposedly anti-entrepreneurial 'aristocratic values' of the old school. Neither had they become high-level sycophants, toadying to the aristocracy and high society in pursuit of patronage and custom, although one would not deny a streak of instrumentality in their style. They were, much more simply, successful and dedicated bankers and financiers who happened to enjoy hunting and spending their money on country houses, and who with the aid of the railway were able to develop a pattern of living which comfortably combined both business and social worlds without diminishing their appetite for profits or their ability to make them. In the long run they can be seen as the trend setters, foreshadowing the business takeover of the upper class and setting the guidelines for the fusion of aristocracy and plutocracy: for it is by adopting some variant of the Rothschild recipe of business mixed with country houses that the surviving members of the old landed aristocracy have been able to continue and to survive into the 1990s. Symbolically it was Rothschilds who rescued and restored in all its gilded opulence and splendour Spencer House, almost the last survivor of the great aristocratic town houses in London, restoring it as part bank, part town house.[36]

Some have maintained that bankers, specifically private bankers, international financiers, and merchant bankers, were peculiarly suited to the Hoare–Rothschild gambit. Martin Wiener goes so far as to claim that the world of finance was little 'different from the traditional world of the aristocracy', and that, unlike industrialists, bankers led an easy existence far removed from the grime of actually making things, and became 'indistinguishable from the old aristocracy', placing the cult of amateurism above the pursuit of economic enterprise.[37] If the Rothschilds were amateurs one can only conclude that the economy was well rid of professionals. Youssef Cassis, the authority on *fin de siècle* aristocratic bankers, concludes that industrialists were on the whole excluded from the new upper class elite.[38] Certainly the aristocratic bankers frequented the same social world as the

[36] F. M. L. Thompson, 'Moving Frontiers and the Fortunes of the Aristocratic Town House, 1830–1930', *London Journal*, 20 (1995), 76.   [37] Wiener, *English Culture*, 145.
[38] Y. Cassis, 'Bankers in English Society in the Nineteenth Century', *Economic History Review* 2nd ser., 38 (1985), 212.

landed elite and London society as a matter of course and of business, which the less rarified or less elevated managers and directors of joint stock banks—the later High Street banks—did not. Certainly Barings, Glyns, Grenfells, Mills, and Meinhertzhagens were to be found treading the same path, with the Gurneys, Peckovers, Goslings, Barclays, and Gilletts following on behind in slightly less grandeur. But there was no bankers' monopoly or patent on the aristocratic-bourgeois game, and many others from many different trades and industries learnt to play it. Brewers were probably the first to follow the Hoares, when Samuel Whitbread I built up the Southill estate in Bedfordshire to over 10,000 acres between 1760 and 1795; a couple of hundred years later, in 1990, Samuel Whitbread VI was still at Southill, he still owned over 10,000 acres there, and he was still chairman of the brewery, assisted by at least four other members of the Whitbread family.[39] The Guinnesses delayed their entry on to the English landed stage until the 1890s, when Lord Iveagh bought the Suffolk estate of Elveden to add to the family's considerable Irish holdings, having been frustrated in his earlier attempt to buy the Savernake estate from the dissolute 4th Marquess of Ailesbury. The family continued to control and manage the brewery with almost disastrous vigour, for we are informed that it was the 3rd Earl of Iveagh's overweening ambition to see his firm rival Rothschilds as a global economic power which propelled Guinness into the great financial scandal of the Distillers' takeover of the late 1980s, which led to the imprisonment of Ernest Saunders, the managing director of Guinness; it also led to the unceremonious exit of all Guinnesses, who had formed half the board of directors in 1985, from all connection with the business, except as shareholders.[40]

Brewing and banking are often coupled together as inherently gentlemanly occupations, in which the emergence of the aristocratic-bourgeois style was neither difficult nor surprising. What, then, should we make of the Crawshays, who produced five generations of ironmasters, until Cyfarthfa was taken over by Guest, Keen, and Nettlefold in 1902, and combined this, after a hesitant beginning, with a landed position, admittedly not a grandiose one, in Berkshire, Gloucestershire, and Glamorgan? Or of Sir Lowthian Bell, whose son and grandson in turn performed as leading ironmasters, colliery owners, and directors of Dorman Long, as well as being the owners of Rounton Grange and its 3,000 acres? Bookstalls produced W. H. Smith, estates of more than 15,000 acres, the Hambleden viscountcy, and three more generations of chairmen of the company, which thus

[39] D. Rapp, 'Social Mobility in the Eighteenth Century: The Whitbreads of Bedfordshire, 1720–1815', ibid., 2nd ser., 27 (1974), 380–94; Burke's Landed Gentry (1972 edn.), iii; Debrett's Distinguished People of Today (1990 edn.).

[40] Earl of Cardigan, The Wardens of Savernake Forest (1949), 318, 325, 327; Obituary of 3rd Earl of Iveagh, The Times, 20 June 1992.

remained under family management fron the 1840s to the 1970s. Civil engineering and Mexican oil floated the Pearsons into large landowning, polo, and high society, and after an interlude when the 2nd Viscount Cowdray did little more than perform as the Master of the Cowdray Hounds, the third generation returned to an active business life, chairman of the family firm for more than thirty years and President of Pearson PLC into his eighties. Bovril brought its inventor, George Lawson Johnston, a bizarre and costly town house in Edwardian London, a 3,000-acre estate at Odell Castle in the 1920s, and a peerage as Lord Luke; his son, the 2nd Lord Luke, is a leading figure in the county and has been Master of the prestigious Oakley Hunt, but he has also had a long business career with Electrolux, with Ashanti Goldfields, and with the Bovril family firm. Likewise, the Vesteys have been large landowners for two generations while remaining in charge of their meat-packing and butcher's shops; neither have the Palmers abandoned biscuits, nor have the Sainsburys given up supermarkets.[41]

Naturally, instance can be piled upon instance without proving anything much more than that it has been perfectly possible, for more than 200 years, for particular individuals and families to combine the operation of businesses—in manufacturing and retailing as well as in finance and brewing, though finance does seem to predominate—with the possession of country houses, large landed estates, and indulgence in country pursuits. That has nothing to say about the relative importance, within the total land-purchasing activities of new men as a whole, of the aristocratic-bourgeois group as against the landed families group; and it has nothing to say about the significance of the aristocratic-bourgeois group in relation to the business community as a whole. Two observations can be hazarded in conclusion. First, it seems likely on general grounds that country-house and land-purchasing designed to support an aristocratic-bourgeois style of businessman became more common from the 1830s onwards, as the construction of the railway network made it a more widely available and sustainable way of living and doing business. From the 1880s and 1890s it was likely to have become increasingly the dominant type of land-purchasing, because the traditional objective of founding a landed family in the hope of being assimilated into the old landed elite was ceasing to make sense: land values were falling, it was imprudent to contemplate being able to live on agricultural rents, and above all, joining the old elite when it was in decline and clear transformation into a branch of the plutocracy was a diminishing attraction for ambitious men. Second, it is quite difficult to find any business dynasties, owning, managing, or controlling what amounted to family firms over

[41] For the Crawshays see Habakkuk, *Marriage, Debt, and the Estate System*, 469–70; for other families in this paragraph, information from *DNB, DBB, Who Was Who*, i–viii, and *Who's Who* (1993 edn.).

several generations, which were not associated with the possession of country houses and estates, with the exception of the chocolate Quakers, Cadburys, Frys, and Rowntrees, who did not abandon their principles enjoining simplicity and abjuration of outward display and aristocratic airs with quite such readiness as banking or brewing Quakers like the Gurneys, Gilletts, or Barclays. For most of the long-running family concerns it seems that a landed position may have been a vital ingredient in perpetuating the dynastic impulse and maintaining family cohesion. No doubt there have always been many small businesses which were family concerns, lasting for generations, just as there have been many father-and-son professional practices, which had no truck with landed possessions. And no doubt the great mass of the business community at any one time has generally consisted of single-generation, one-off entrepreneurs, and latterly it has consisted of corporations run on meritocratic rather than hereditary principles by salaried managers.

The argument, however, is not that these landed business dynasties have dominated the British economy, nor even that they have nurtured the most dynamic enterprises. It is the more modest and less assertive argument that a significant fraction of successful businessmen acquired the trappings of estates and country houses, and that a growing proportion of those showed that that had no harmful effects on their immediate or longer-term entrepreneurial capacities. The litmus test of gentrification through landed possessions was not a litmus test of the abandonment of the business ethic. The quality of the entrepreneurship of these aristocratic-bourgeois business dynasties, either in comparison with that of their non-landed contemporaries or with that of the counterfactual entrepreneurs who might have taken their places if they had withdrawn from business, is beyond ready reckoning. It could equally well be that the British economy was strong enough and growing fast enough to carry some deadwood among these business magnates, or that these business magnates were smart enough businessmen to carry the British economy. One need only look up the Hudson Valley at the rows of great mansions and parks of the Roosevelts, Rockefellers, and Vanderbilts, at the Hearst Castle and estate in California, or at the rural retreats of great German business dynasties like the Krupps, the Hoeschs, or the Siemens, to see that in other economies such manifestations of aristocratic tendencies have not been seen as signs of moral or economic decay. The second main feature of the culture of entrepreneurs, their attitude to leisure, art, sport, and recreation, remains to be examined. Meanwhile, literal landed gentrification emerges as not necessarily a badge of entrepreneurial decadence, but equally and more frequently as a badge of entrepreneurial success and symbol of the penetration of the upper class by cultivated businessmen.

5

Consumption, Culture, and the 'Unenterprising' Businessman

The bicycle theorem holds that if you stop pedalling, you fall off, although this is a delayed reaction if going downhill. The gentrification theorem of economic performance holds that if businessmen become 'detached from the single-minded pursuit of production and profit', they fall off, and sooner or later the economy goes downhill.[1] This is alleged to have been the effect of public schools in particular, strongly abetted by Oxford and Cambridge, but unlike cycling it is not a theory which holds true. Cultural or economic argument which proceeds by analogies drawn from Newtonian physics is doomed to disappointment. Businessmen do not in fact require the perpetual impulse of profit in order to remain in motion. Deviation from the straight and narrow path of the pursuit of profit, through purchase of land, did not unman all the wealthy businessmen who took that course, and did not prevent many of them from fathering great business dynasties. The pseudo-gentrification of much larger groups of businessmen, who in one way and another are said to have become imbued with gentlemanly standards and values, 'aspiring to gentility by copying the education, manners, and behaviour of the gentry', without becoming involved with any considerable landed possessions, presents a more complicated problem.[2] Stripped of several layers of misleading rhetoric and misunderstood history there is a kernel of truth in the notion of a top-down transmission of values and tastes from the landed classes to the non-landed majority of businessmen, and indeed to the middle classes at large, although it is difficult to disentangle that process from the parallel top-down transmission of behaviour from a sophisticated, largely metropolitan, urban bourgeoisie to the new men in the provinces. The contention that pseudo-gentrification of this kind caused businessmen to cease to perform effectively is equally false.

It is a common view that between, roughly, the 1780s and the 1880s there were great changes in the character of the general run of manufacturers, that their rough edges were smoothed away and that in manners, morals, speech,

---

[1] Martin Wiener, *English Culture and the Decline of the Industrial Spirit, 1850–1980* (Cambridge, 1981), 20.

[2] Lawrence Stone and Jeanne C. Fawtier Stone, *An Open Elite?, England, 1540–1880* (Oxford, 1984), 409.

dress, and domestic life they became very like the gentry. There is good foundation for this view, even though the notion that early manufacturers were generically uncouth, unlettered, ignorant, and boorish is grossly exaggerated: no one could pretend that Josiah Wedgwood was uncultured or insensitive, or that the greatest ironfounder of the eighteenth century, John Wilkinson, was uneducated. To attribute changes in manners largely or exclusively to the influence of the gentry and a desire to imitate them is, however, mistaken, the result of a rhetorical trick or a verbal confusion that identifies gentlemanly conduct directly and narrowly with the example of the behaviour of landed gentlemen and landed aristocrats.

There were great changes in gentry and aristocratic manners, also, between the 1780s and 1880s. Most obviously in appearance, in which by the mid-nineteenth century they were generally considered to have become like the upper bourgeoisie (mainly a non-industrial bourgeoisie) in dress, not the other way round, so that it was no longer possible to tell a lord by his everyday, or every evening, clothes, and a squire and his wealthier tenant farmers might well wear similar suits and hats at the agricultural shows. In the eighteenth century the country gentry had quite commonly spoken in the provincial dialects or accents of their regions; by the mid-nineteenth century this had been largely flattened into standard upper-class English. Sir Christopher Sykes of Sledmere, for example, in the 1770s was looking for a tutor for his sons 'who can correct their Yorkshire tones'. Success was limited; one son turned into the hard riding and hard drinking Sir Tatton, who liked to shock London society in the 1850s by speaking broad Yorkshire and wearing his riding boots at smart receptions. By then he was antediluvian, as much subject to banter as Peel with his Lancashire short 'a's.[3] Duelling was perhaps the touchstone of the eighteenth-century gentleman's code, the only acceptable way of upholding honour when a gentleman's integrity was questioned, perhaps over women, perhaps over accusations of cheating at cards. By the 1850s it was gone, finally made illegal in 1852 some years after it had fallen out of favour and become generally regarded as a childish and irresponsible way of settling quarrels; although it should be noted that in 1812 Ellenborough, the Lord Chief Justice, was complaining about the amount of litigation generated by challenges to duels by merchants and tradesmen, arguing that 'really it was high time to stop this spurious chivalry of the counting-house and the counter'.[4]

Moreover it was not only the old-fashioned country squires whose manners could be rude and coarse. Lord John Russell gave an honest description of a

[3] Sledmere MS, Sir Christopher Sykes's Letter Book, 1775–90, Sykes to Revd. W. Cleaver, 15 Sept. 1778; Christopher Sykes, *Four Studies in Loyalty* (1946), 18.
[4] Stone and Stone, *Open Elite?*, 409; O. F. Christie, *The Transition from Aristocracy, 1832–67* (1927), 22–4, 130–4; Boyd Hilton, *The Age of Atonement* (Oxford, 1988), 268.

typical smart London dinner party from his bachelor days during the Regency: 'When the ladies left the dining room,' he wrote,

fresh bottles of port would be brought in, the host would arise and lock the door, and almost every man drank until he was under the table . . . they never joined the ladies again, and a page, towards the end of the drinking, as the men slipped from their seats, would loosen the neck-cloths of the prostrate guests, and it was a regular custom for the valets to come in, carry out their masters, put them in their coaches, and escort them home . . . some of the masters were put into the wrong coaches and carried to the wrong houses . . . much to the astonishment of the wives and other members of the households.[5]

Other accounts said that chamber pots were normally kept in the sideboard, and that the gentlemen were accustomed to relieving themselves on the spot, presumably before they became insensible. Already by the mid-1820s, we are informed, 'heavy drinking had become unfashionable and the gentlemen no longer stayed for hours over their wine before joining the ladies for tea and coffee.'[6] The old habits and orgies had been completely banished from mid-Victorian dining rooms, partly of course as a result of technological changes with the widespread installation of water closets, but mainly because of changes in ideas of politeness and respectability—although some of them crept back among the Marlborough House set in the 1870s.

The manners of gentlefolk were changing and evolving towards the mid-Victorian model of decency, sobriety, and prudery at the very same time as the manufacturers were moving in the same direction, and the apparent gentrification of the manufacturers can scarcely have been a matter of imitating the example set by the pre-Victorian aristocracy and gentry. To account for this by postulating a process of instant emulation without any time lag seems implausible. That would entail the kind of intellectual contortions in which Lawrence Stone tied himself in arguing that from about the middle of the eighteenth century onwards the middle classes sought gentility by copying the education of the gentry, a full half century and more before the schools of the gentry even began to dedicate themselves to the inculcation of gentlemanly values; and when he claimed 'that the great strength of the English landed elite was its success in psychologically co-opting those below them into the status hierarchy of gentility', during the very period in which he detected 'the near total physical isolation of the landed elite from the new industrial base of England's greatness', he implied the success of an incredible conjuring trick which transmitted values across a social and physical chasm between groups which had no contact with each other.[7] A more straightforward explanation is that there was a general reformation of

    [5] Quoted in E. W. Bovill, *English Country Life, 1780–1830* (Oxford, 1962), 108–9.
    [6] Gervas Huxley, *Lady Elizabeth and the Grosvenors. Life in a Whig Family, 1822–39* (Oxford, 1965), 62.   [7] Stone and Stone, *Open Elite?*, 409–12.

manners, affecting many social groups and classes simultaneously: Francis Place certainly affected to believe that this extended to the London artisans, among whom he detected a general onset of sobriety in the 1820s.[8] The reformation of manners did not, of course, just happen spontaneously. It was the work of organized movements, of societies and associations, of writers, preachers, and propagandists, of churches and chapels, of sermons and pamphlets, all of which contributed to the formation of influential opinion and example, which both defined and diffused the Victorian cult of respectability. Some members of the aristocracy and gentry certainly played prominent parts in this movement, but it cannot be maintained that they either initiated or dominated it. If there were dominant groups and individuals, they were the evangelicals, both clerical and lay, moved by the imperative of saving souls, assisted by Dissenters like the Quakers and the newer-fangled Unitarians, who had always combined gentleness of manners with business acumen.[9]

Many of the characteristics of the culture of respectability and domesticity to which industrialists, no less than bankers or professional men, generally conformed by mid-century were properly attributable to what may be termed a process of religiously inspired socialization, and not to gentrification in the sense of mimicry of the landed classes. Insofar as the effects were more than skin-deep, the cultivation of sobriety, thrift, and abstinence should have increased entrepreneurial effectiveness, and certainly not impaired it. At the same time as these behavioural patterns were reinforcing the impulse to save and accumulate, however, many businessmen were developing ways of spending their wealth which might more plausibly be attributed to emulation of the aristocracy and gentry, and which might have acted as diversions from the single-minded pursuit of wealth.

Pride of place among expenditure belongs to the upbringing of children, possibly as the first call on income after meeting the basics of a comfortable subsistence, and certainly as a prime influence on a family's future fortunes. There were, indeed, early instances of wealthy industrialists and merchants giving their sons an aristocratic education, as when the first Sir Robert Peel sent his eldest son to Harrow in 1801 and Christ Church in 1805, or when John Gladstone followed suit some twenty years later, sending William to Eton and Christ Church in the classic aristocratic pattern. These were, however, businessmen engaged in establishing landed families and in arranging for a 'haemorrhage of talent' into public life—where, it can be argued, their

---

[8] Brian Harrison, *Drink and the Victorians: The Temperance Question in England, 1815–72* (1971), 91. Place had a political interest in stressing the presence of the sober and responsible working man.

[9] Boyd Hilton, *The Age of Atonement*, is the best and most recent account of evangelicalism and its impact on society and politics. See also Doreen M. Rosman, *Evangelicals and Culture* (1984), and Elizabeth Isichei, *Victorian Quakers* (Oxford, 1970).

sons did more for the growth of commercial and industrial enterprise than they could ever have done as individual businessmen. Two swallows do not make a summer, and the main flight of businessmen's sons into the public schools did not start for another fifty years, and into the universities later still. Until then most businessmen's sons, if they received any formal education at all, as distinct from serving articles or an apprenticeship, beyond the age of 11 or 12—and some of their daughters—were educated relatively inexpensively in local grammar schools, Dissenting academies, or private-venture establishments such as Hinchcliffe's Academy in Horton House for the Bradford middle classes, which provided an approximation to 'the sound commercial education' which middle-class parents sought, with no classical gentility nonsense. The daughters were more likely, however, to receive at best a more restricted schooling, and the majority were probably taught at home by their mothers or by governesses. The employment of domestics, or near-domestics, to rear and teach their children was likely to be the main sphere of expense on the upbringing of businessmen's children, for the first generation of achievers.[10] Both in point of time and in point of its direct and immediate effects on entrepreneurial performance the expenditure of wealthy businessmen on themselves, their wives, and their households came first. Their education was, in the first place, an education in how to spend their new wealth, a cultural education of the senses.

Virtually all successful businessmen, apart from the complete misers—who were themselves bachelors more often than not—used some of their good fortune to improve, enlarge, and embellish their homes, to give their wives spending money for fashionable clothes and furnishings, to employ staffs of domestics, and to keep horses and carriages. This could be characterized as a form of gentrification, since many of the available models of the architecture and organization of a wealthy lifestyle were provided by the landed classes and could be adapted to urban and suburban living. On the other hand it could also easily be explained as emulation of the style of wealthy merchants or lawyers, who had been setting a pattern of comfortable or opulent living for centuries. The middle course is to say that such expenditure and display were no more than the expected result of affluence, and ranged from neutral to positive in their possible and largely marginal effects on the industrial spirit.

The gradual abandonment of the habit of 'living over the shop' was a matter of health and hygiene as well as of status, and could even be considered as positively non-aristocratic since most landowners lived over their

---

[10] Theodore Koditschek, *Class Formation and Urban-industrial Society. Bradford, 1750–1850* (Cambridge, 1990), 189–95; Leonore Davidoff and Catherine Hall, *Family Fortunes. Men and Women of the English Middle Class, 1780–1850* (1987), 234–40, 289–93; Anthony Howe, *The Cotton Masters, 1830–1860* (Oxford, 1984), 54–61.

estate offices. Such moves were delayed, often until the second half of the nineteenth century, in the mill towns of Lancashire and the West Riding, particularly in the valleys, where big employers built big houses brooding over their mills, allegedly to symbolize the feudal subordination of their workers. City merchants, bankers, and professional men had been making such moves, to the West End and to London's future inner suburbs like Clapham, Dulwich, Hackney, Highgate, or Hampstead, at least since the early eighteenth century; for example, William Morris's father, partner in a discount broker's firm, was following a traditional route in moving from a house in Lombard Street first to Walthamstow and then to a large Georgian mansion on the edge of Epping Forest in a series of steps between 1820 and 1840.[11] In Leeds the move to large villas, set in their own grounds but not in even miniature landed estates, was well under way in the last quarter of the eighteenth century, a matter in the main of the villadom of Little Woodhouse and Woodhouse Lane to the north-west of the centre. These forerunners of Victorian Headingley (which had less grand villas and smaller grounds) were mainly occupied by merchants, presumably woollen merchants: of forty-five villas built before 1815, only four were owned by people describing themselves as industrialists—one dyer, one soap manufacturer, and two tobacco manufacturers—the rest were 'merchants' or 'gentlemen'.[12] Birmingham and Black Country industrialists followed suit in claiming Edgbaston and Tettenhall (two miles from the centre of Wolverhampton) for villadom a generation or more after some of the Leeds upper middle class had migrated up the hill.[13] Sometimes, as at Wightwick Manor, built for the Wolverhampton paint and varnish manufacturer Theodore Mander in the 1880s, these were large houses of exquisite character and William Morris charm but not sitting on landed estates. Large houses with plenty of domestics were certainly emblems of material success, but they were also functional in making the non-business part of life more agreeable and less time-consuming, thus in theory enhancing the productivity of the working day. So too the possession of personal transport combined prestige and convenience. Just as in the late twentieth century the company car is finely graded by rank and status and

---

[11] Charles Harvey and Jon Press, *William Morris. Design and Enterprise in Victorian Britain* (Manchester, 1991), 5–6.

[12] Maurice Beresford, *East End, West End: The Face of Leeds during Urbanisation, 1684–1842* (Thoresby Society, vols. 60 and 61, Leeds, 1988), table 10.1, 308–10, and ch. 10, *passim*.

[13] David Cannadine, *Lords and Landlords. The Aristocracy and the Towns, 1774–1967* (Leicester, 1980), ch. 13; Phillida Ballard, 'A Commercial and Industrial Elite: A Study of Birmingham's Upper Middle Class, 1780–1914' (unpub. Ph.D. thesis, Univ. of Reading, 1984); Mark Girouard, *The Victorian Country House* (New Haven, Conn., and London, 1979), 375–9; Richard Trainor, 'The Gentrification of Victorian and Edwardian Industrialists', in A. L. Beier, David Cannadine, and James M. Rosenheim (eds.), *The First Modern Society* (Cambridge, 1989), 184–92; R. H. Trainor, *Black Country Elites: The Exercise of Authority in an Industrialized Area, 1830–1900* (Oxford, 1993), 70–4.

justified as an essential tool of business efficiency, so Victorian carriages were differentiated by size, function, and elegance, and justified as time-savers; the difference was that the master usually rode to work on a horse, leaving the carriage for the ladies.[14]

Two areas of businessmen's expenditure and consumption are more problematic, both from the point of view of possible gentrification and of possible blunting of entrepreneurial vigour. These were the development of the hunting and shooting bourgeoisie on the one hand, and the art-collecting businessmen on the other, both departures from the thrift and austerity model, both smacking of self-indulgence, and both bearing marks of possible aristocratic derivation. Both contributed to a blurring of the cultural and social distinctions between the old elite and the new wealthy, and to the emergence of a more gentlemanly type of businessman than the stock figure, philistine and anti-blood sports, of the early nineteenth century. Whether they contributed to the emergence of effete and ineffective entrepreneurs is debatable. The Burton brewer, John Gretton, 1st Baron Gretton, for instance is included in the *Dictionary of Business Biography* as a cautionary example of the archetype of reactionary Tory brewer of the inter-war period, lacking in enterprise and resistant to innovation, unworthy successor to his father's business, in part at least because of the time he devoted to hunting at Melton Mowbray.[15] This refers to the twenty years after he became chairman of the brewery in 1908. Yet only a few years earlier, in the 1890s, the great Staffordshire ironmaster and colliery owner, Sir Alfred Hickman—also an inheritor of his father's business—was a most resourceful and successful entrepreneur, rescuing the West Midlands iron and steel industry from the doldrums by emulating 'the Germans in the application of science to industry', while at the same time being one of the leading and most regular members of the Albrighton Hunt.[16]

With the signposts pointing in opposite directions it is difficult to maintain that a partiality for hunting and shooting (or fishing, although that being more of a solitary and individual activity is less well recorded than the other two), although they may have been initially exclusively aristocratic sports, had any particular effect on business virility. Shooting game birds or hares was, indeed, the statutory monopoly of landowners until the Game Reform Act of 1831, since the game laws restricted the privilege to those who owned freehold land worth more than £100 a year (very roughly 800 acres or more when enacted in 1671 by 22 & 23 Charles II, c. 25, declining to about 100 acres just before its repeal).[17] Even after 1831, although anyone

[14] F. M. L. Thompson, *Victorian England: The Horse-Drawn Society* (1970), 15–18.
[15] *DBB*, ii, Gretton.   [16] Trainor, 'Gentrification', 182, 187. *Who Was Who*, i.
[17] P. B. Munsche, *Gentlemen and Poachers. The English Game Laws, 1671–1831* (Cambridge, 1981), 180–1.

could acquire a gun licence on payment of the stamp duty of £3 13s. 6d., it was still difficult to go shooting without being a landowner or knowing a landowner, since the game itself remained in effect the property of the owner of the land on which it happened to live. The obvious course for townsfolk anxious to get among the pheasants and partridges, or the grouse whose slaughter became fashionable rapidly from the 1830s onwards, was to curry favour with old landowners and obtain shooting invitations, or to become new landowners themselves; many businessmen took that path. The even more direct route was to become a shooting tenant, which provided enjoyment of the game without commitment to the wider social or economic implications of becoming a landowner. Until the 1880s it was difficult for an outsider like a city businessman to find any substantial landowner, at any rate in the lowland regions, willing to surrender his own sporting rights, and such shooting leases as there were at this level were usually between neighbouring landowners, where an absentee might let his game to a resident. The grouse moors were rather different, and from the mid-century it was usually possible to rent one, perhaps in harness with the deer stalking, for a season or on a longer lease. After the 1880s the pressure of falling agricultural rents, particularly severe in the great cereal growing regions which were the most hospitable environment for pheasants and partridges, persuaded many landed grandees to pocket their pride and let their shooting wherever they could, with the result that in the 1890s and the Edwardian years rich businessmen were reputed to be the lessees of most of the finest shooting in East Anglia, and the landlords found that shooting rents often produced more than farm rents.[18] The slightly less rich formed syndicates which took shooting leases; already familiar throughout the Home Counties by the turn of the century, these urban-based shooting syndicates of businessmen and professional men developed into the predominant form of lowland shooting organization of the later twentieth century.[19]

Long before agricultural depression opened the countryside to the shooting bourgeoisie in this manner, however, it had been possible to rent smallish acreages from non-gentry landowners, and sporting over a hundred or so acres supplied some energetic rough shooting even if it was too small to provide for the full paraphernalia of game preservation, bird breeding, and grand *battue* slaughter. The Chamberlain and Cadbury sons, for example, did this, although fathers Joseph and George both remained essentially urban industrialists and politicians without rural inclinations.[20] True rough shooting meant grouse moors and deer stalking, tastes which spread beyond strictly localized boundaries only from the 1840s, with the English

---

[18] Pam Barnes, *Norfolk Landowners since 1880* (Norwich, 1993), 22.
[19] John Lowerson, *Sport and the English Middle Classes, 1870–1914* (Manchester, 1993), 38–9.
[20] Ballard, 'A Commercial and Industrial Elite'.

discovery of the Highlands and the development, first, of scheduled coastal steamer services, and then of railways: the LNWR began to run 'grouse specials' from August 1869, the special expresses complete with compartments for the servants, vans for the dogs, and boxes for the horses, designed to take shooting families direct to the moors and glens. The painting by George Earl, in 1893, *Going North, King's Cross Station*, gives a graphic idea of the vast numbers of dogs accompanying shooting, fishing, and golfing passengers.[21]

This new sporting fashion was for the seriously rich, who could afford to take long holidays of several weeks or months; but it caught on with a section of the rich businessmen pretty much in step with its adoption by a section of the English aristocracy. By the 1850s and 1860s the owners and lessees of deer forests in the West Highlands included brewers, a Bass and a Meux, a couple of bankers, a Baring and a Mills, both of the senior partners in the Jardine Matheson trading company, and John Fowler the steam plough maker from Leeds who had acquired the taste when supplying the Duke of Sutherland with the equipment for his gigantic land reclamation scheme at Lairg. That was quite enough to drive one excitable old Scot to declare, in 1866, 'the English squire first drove the poorer Scotch one out of the market and he, in his turn, has been superseded by the millionaires from London, Manchester, and America . . . [in] all our first class deer forests and shootings.' This gross, if understandable, exaggeration was repeated, more graphically, in 1877 by a local man with fifty years' experience as the forester at Blackmount in Caithness: 'For the great part of the kind of sportsmen we have now,' he wrote, 'is cotton manufacturers, coal proprietors, ironmongers, etc., so that the most of our Highland chiefs are gone and many do not know what real sport is except conceit to show themselves marksmen and the less chance for their game the better.'[22] This was still an exaggeration, although by the 1880s the industrial and commercial contingent among the deer-stalking owners and tenants had grown to embrace another brace of brewers, Guinness and Gretton, a number of ironmasters like Crawshay, Guest, and Hickman, Coats and Hermon (of the Horrocks firm, Preston) to represent cotton, Ionides and Loder from among the wealthy merchants, Platt from machine tool making, Allhusen from chemicals, and the leading fashionable Tottenham Court Road furniture dealer and interior decorator, Shoolbred.[23] By the 1870s it was stated that men were ready to pay as much as £2,000 a week for a season's deer stalking,

---

[21] Earl's painting is reproduced in M. Hunter and R. Thorne (eds.), *Change at King's Cross* (1990), title-pages. G. P. Neele, *Railway Reminiscences* (1904), 171, for the 'grouse special'.

[22] Quot. in W. Orr, *Deer Forests, Landlords, and Crofters* (Edinburgh, 1982), 32, 41.

[23] Ibid., App. VII, deer forest owners and tenants, c.1855–1920; the list covers the counties of Ross and Cromarty, and Inverness, only, so that there were certainly many more industrialists and other businessmen with deer forests in the other Highland counties.

presumably with gillies and accommodation thrown in.[24] Despite the deep impression made on the locals by the intrusion of newcomers, deer stalking remained a predominantly aristocratic preserve until 1914, and indeed into the 1920s. Ownership and tenancy of the deer forests was shared between the Scottish aristocracy, if not the old Highland chiefs, and the English aristocracy, with the newcomers commanding not much more than a tenth of the area. They had made their point, however, that they could infiltrate the aristocratic preserves if they wanted, many of them simply as sporting tenants and not as conventional estate owners. As to their credentials as entrepreneurs, their reputations were adequately sheltered by the American millionaires who bought deer forests in the 1870s and 1880s, such as Carnegie, Vanderbilt, and W. L. Winans.

Foxhunting, also, was regarded as an exclusive, aristocratic, sport in the eighteenth and early nineteenth centuries, run by aristocrats and gentry, with members of the local community suffered to join in on moderately equal terms. But hunting was different: there was no legal monopoly, and there was no necessity for participants to own or control any land of their own. All that a townsman needed was to possess or hire a couple of sound horses; leisure; and the means of access to a meet; then, provided his presence was accepted by the local hunt committee, he (or she; the courtesan Skittles was reputedly the best horsewoman and huntress in mid-Victorian England) could go hunting. A great many did. Railways put foxes, even more than pheasants or deer, within reach of the unlanded. But even before railways the hunting townsman and the suburban meet were already attracting increasing attention. Surrey was so much the popular hunting field for Londoners that by the 1820s Croydon was known as 'the Melton of the South' because from it three packs of foxhounds, three of harriers, plus Lord Derby's staghounds, were within easy reach. The Essex Hunt, also, had many Londoners among its members, and relied on the subscriptions of City men for its finances. It was Middlesex and the Old Berkeley Hunt, however, with its convenient meets at Pinner, Harrow, or Watford over into Hertfordshire, which occasioned the classic case in hunting law of Essex v. Capel in 1809, in which the Earl of Essex as local landowner successfully brought an action for trespass against his half-brother, the master of the Old Berkeley, for taking the hunt on to private property after being warned off. This was part of a family feud; and it was also part of the resentment of local landowners and farmers at large fields of strangers careering across their land damaging fences, gates, and crops. The Earl of Essex's counsel argued convincingly 'that Clergymen are descending from their pulpits, Brewers running away from their breweries, tradesmen, clerks and a variety of persons are all occasionally flocking from London . . . [for] no other object

---

[24] *Select Committee on the Game Laws*, BPP 1873, xiii, q. 6637.

than their own amusement' and not, as they pretended, solely and unselfishly to help rid farmers of vermin: a late twentieth-century anti-hunting lobbyist could hardly have put it better.[25]

With the added power of the railways it was not only from London that business and professional people flocked to amuse themselves in the hunting field, although it is true that the great railway influx into the Shires, to the Quorn, the Pytchley, the Cottesmore, or the Fernie, was principally of fashionable Londoners from high society. Although those hunts were physically within easy reach of Birmingham, the social distance created by their exclusive airs was too alarming for most West Midland industrialists, who were more comfortable hunting with the North Warwickshire, the Worcestershire, the South Staffordshire, and above all with the Albrighton and the Albrighton Woodland. The cotton men who hunted rode chiefly with the Cheshire (Engels famously so), the Cheshire Forest in the Wirral, or the North Staffordshire. Strangely, travelling north from Manchester there were no hunts to be found for sixty miles or more, until one reached the Lunesdale and the Coniston. That was easily the largest tract of country in England which was not hunted at all in the nineteenth century, apart from Norfolk and Suffolk. Whereas East Anglia was not hunted because it was the great pheasant country, whose preservers were at war with foxes, Lancashire was not hunted only in part because the countryside of mills and towns was unsuitable, for outside the industrial areas the demand for chasing foxes simply remained too weak to support any packs. On the other side of the Pennines, by contrast, the Barlow, Badsworth, Bramham Moor, York and Ainsty hunts provided blanket coverage of all the great industrial centres from Sheffield through to the north of Leeds; while Tyneside industrialists enjoyed a wide selection from the South Durham, the Braes of Derwent, the Tynedale, the Morpeth, the Haydon, and the North Tyne, without having to venture as far north as the Percy territory, and by the 1880s new men like the Strakers and Joiceys were providing the Masters for some of these hunts.[26] By the beginning of the twentieth century the bankers and manufacturers had taken possession of the hunting field. 'What was once—especially in the pre-railway days—the sport of the landed interest and their tenants', *The Field* observed in 1908, 'has become the sport of the community at large, and in these times two-thirds of every field are businessmen of sorts, while the remaining third is composed of men and women

---

[25] D. C. Itzkowitz, *Peculiar Privilege. A Social History of English Foxhunting, 1753–1885* (Hassocks, 1977), 38–42; R. Carr, *English Foxhunting: A History* (1976), 215–17.

[26] *Baily's Hunting Directory, 1950–51* (1950), with historical notes on each hunt. Edward Joicey was Master of the Haydon, 1886–95, and J. C. Straker was Master of the Tynedale, 1883–1937. In the south-west Sir Gilbert Wills was Master of the Dulverton, 1908–10 (ibid., 110, 135, 205). See also Itzkowitz, *Peculiar Privilege,* 56–60.

who are so well endowed with this world's goods that they have no need to work.'[27]

In 1850, before railways had greatly affected the hunting pattern, there were some 135 packs of foxhounds in England and Wales engaged in regular hunts over hunting countries with well-defined and mutually recognized boundaries, which parcelled out virtually all the territory suitable for the sport. By 1914 there were 178 separate hunts in action, the increase of a third being due almost entirely to the subdivision of former large hunting countries and to more intensive hunting, not to any significant extension of hunting frontiers into previously untouched regions. The more intensive hunting, in turn, was not due to any increase in the numbers of resident landowners or hunting farmers so much as to the influx of business and professional men and their women. A few hunts were abandoned and packs dispersed, because of urban encroachments or rural impoverishment, but with the aid of the motor car and horse boxes the overall increase in hunt numbers continued, reaching 185 before 1939, peaking in the post-war recovery at 200 in 1950, and settling down at 192 in the late 1970s. Foxhunting never caught on in Scotland, which at no time could muster as many as a dozen packs; but in Ireland in the country of 'the Pale' and the south, but not in the north, it was very popular, with 24 packs in 1905–6 and 33 in 1976–7, and Ireland was the source of the most-prized hunters for the English market. Adding in all the other kinds of hunts—harriers, staghounds, draghounds, beagles, and otterhounds—there were 404 hunts in England and Wales in 1912, a total which had declined to 344 in 1935–6 and 341 in 1976–7, the sustained zest for foxhunting being more than countered by steady decline of harriers, and of beagles with their more strenuous demands for rough walking rather than riding.[28] The hunting bourgeoisie had not only developed great staying power but also had become the mainstay of the field, numerically and financially, supporting and subsidizing a few of the great aristocratic names from the past as MFHs in the late twentieth century, but essentially appropriating the hunting traditions, the hunt dinners, and the hunt balls for themselves. The Masters of the late 1970s included the dukes of Beaufort, Buccleuch, and Northumberland, Earl Fitzwilliam, the Earl of Yarborough, and Sir Watkin Williams Wynn, all direct descendants of Victorian Masters; they also included a Sieff, a Vestey, an Arkwright, an Astor, a Dalgety, a Goschen, a Guest, and a MacAlpine, a fair cross-section of new men—and there were no fewer than 61 female MFHs, some of them joint Masters (there had already been 40 in 1950), a fair indication that

[27] Quoted in Carr, Foxhunting, 154–5.
[28] Lowerson, Sport, 32; Baily's Hunting Directory, 1950–51, 5; Baily's Hunting Directory, 1976–7 (1976), 370, statistical summary of hunts in 1905–06, 1935–6, and 1976–7.

women's hunting passions carried them to the top ahead of their penetration of many other former male preserves.[29]

The hunting set was never more than a small fraction of the wealthy middle class as a whole, although it included many of the most prominent manufacturers and money men, and it was no doubt rapidly overtaken in size by the golfing set during the great late Victorian golf boom, as the leading sector of the outdoor middle class. The mushroom growth of golf in England was astonishing: at mid-century there was a single ancient club, the Blackheath, and perhaps a handful of others; by 1914 there were not far short of 1,200 clubs, and, with one or two intermissions, the pace of growth has scarcely slackened since and has clearly accelerated sharply in the closing decades of the twentieth century. Golf in England was far from being exclusively middle class, except perhaps in the early years of its popularity; many of the Edwardian golf courses were municipal, specifically aimed at the clerk and the artisan. On the other hand, the Scottish model from which all derived, although replete with arcane traditions and rules of etiquette, was emphatically not aristocratic, even if the claims to a primitive democracy of the links were spurious. The English craze was essentially a middle-class craze, at first of the middle class on holiday, with seaside courses, and then of businessmen at weekends, and before long on weekdays too, claiming to do more business on the green than in the office, and generating a demand for courses on the fringes of the large commercial and industrial towns. The increasingly elaborate and expensive golf courses and clubhouses could be portrayed as the efforts of syndicates of businessmen to replicate in pseudo-functional form the landscape gardening and country-house building activities of the landed aristocracy and their wealthier brethren who became new landowners, and the social hierarchy of golf clubs, more keenly known to insiders than to non-golfers, could be said to mirror the pecking order of the great country houses. That, however, was pure flattery without a trace of imitation, for there was no aristocratic golf culture to be copied. If businessmen had aristocratic fantasies on the golf courses they were entirely self-induced, although they could have helped in forming a sense of group identity and superiority to non-golfing types.[30]

On the racecourse, in some ways the mirror image of the golf course, matters were different. Horse-racing was emphatically upper-class, aristocratic, and blue-blooded. It was a sport with a large plebeian following and a supporting cast of trainers, bookmakers, and tipsters of very variable respectability, a sport which is said to have had little attraction for the Victorian middle classes. That is understandable in the light of the heavy

---

[29] *Baily's Hunting Directory, 1950–51*, 17–19; *Baily's Hunting Directory, 1976–77*, 371–3.
[30] Lowerson, *Sport*, ch. 5; Roland Quinault, 'Golf and Edwardian Politics', in Negley Harte and Roland Quinault (eds.), *Land and Society in Britain, 1700–1914* (Manchester, 1996), 191–210.

emphasis the mid-Victorian middling middle classes placed on conformity to rules of conduct which held askance the louche reputation of racing and its association with gambling, drinking, and bribery.[31] It is not inconsistent, however, either with racegoing by the richer and less puritanical sections of the middle classes, or with the ownership of racehorses exercising a special fascination for some businessmen. 'The racehorse is now one of the first destinations of the newly acquired wealth of a prosperous financier', it was claimed in 1890, and it was not only bankers who were tempted.[32] One banker who did follow this path was Richard Christopher Naylor, who retired from the Liverpool bank of Leyland & Bullins in 1852 in order to spend more time in yachting, horse racing, and hunting, and who became Master of the Pytchley in 1872. But it was one of the grandsons of the railway contractor, Thomas Brassey, who became the first of the new wealthy to be accepted into the supremely aristocratic governing circle of the racing world, the Jockey Club, in 1898, and to serve as its Senior Steward, in effect the arbiter of the sport, in 1902. And it was the Warrington brewer, William Hall Walker, who became the first racecourse peer when he was created Lord Wavertree in 1919 in return for selling his thoroughbreds and his training establishment to the government, which, on the somewhat misguided prompting of the Army Council, were used to form the nucleus of the National Stud, designed to service future military needs.[33] For businessmen the attractions of owning racehorses were almost the exact opposite of those of making sound investments, except that they offered a reasonably reliable, if extremely expensive, shortcut to acceptance by the racing set without the bother and additional expense of acquiring substantial landed estates. At times when the racing set included a Prince of Wales and his courtiers this was a serious consideration for social climbers. Hence a number of sightings in the 1890s, in the vicinity of Newmarket, Newbury, and similar racing centres, of wealthy businessmen or their heirs with racing stables and training gallops, but no conventional estates: H. L. B. McCalmont (1861–1902), member of the Jockey Club and purchaser of Cheveley Park near Newmarket, great-nephew and principal heir of millionaire stockbroker Hugh McCalmont, was one such.[34]

It is arguable that entrepreneurs who were drawn into the racing world incapacitated themselves for further effective business performance in a

[31] Lowerson, *Sport*, 5, citing Wray Vamplew, *The Turf* (1976); Wray Vamplew, 'Horse-Racing', in Tony Mason (ed.), *Sport in Britain, A Social History* (Cambridge, 1989), 216–18.

[32] Vamplew, 'Horse-Racing', 227, quot. G. H. Strutfield, 'Racing in 1890', *Nineteenth Century*, 27 (1890), 925.

[33] Boase, *Modern English Biography*, vi. 276; 1st Baron Brassey of Apethorpe (1870–1958), *Who Was Who*, v; Vamplew, 'Horse-Racing', 231; William Hall Walker, 3rd son of Sir Andrew Barclay Walker, brewer, was managing director of Peter Walker & Co., brewers.

[34] PRO IR/26/3864, fo. 3847 (Hugh McCalmont, died 1887); H. L. B. McCalmont, *Who Was Who*, i. VCH *Cambridgeshire*, v. 287.

much more decided fashion than those who acquired a taste for hunting or shooting, let alone for golf. It was certainly possible to lose large fortunes more easily on horses than in any other way, save perhaps in casinos. A classic early twentieth-century case of a monumental crash through reckless betting came from the old order, when the Marquess of Breadalbane practically bankrupted the family with his racing debts, causing most of the immense coast-to-coast Scottish estates to be sold off, large blocks in 1921 and more after his death in 1922.[35] In the business world of the inter-war years it was established folklore that slow horses, fast cars, and fast women were the usual temptations which dissipated business fortunes. In effect that restated in twentieth-century idiom the mid-Victorian, Smilesian, precepts that self-indulgence could lead to ruin, and that thrift, austerity, and abstinence were the keys to worldly success. In many ways the significance of the emergence of the outdoor bourgeoisie, the hunting, shooting, racing, or golfing sets which were developing strongly from the 1850s onwards, lay in their wilful and unashamed deviation from the abstinence model, rather than in any assessment of the extent to which their pleasures and indulgences derived from aristocratic and gentry examples. Given the cultural and intellectual dominance of the abstinence model with its evangelical and Dissenting credentials as the key to understanding early nineteenth-century businessmen, it is understandable that early examples of pleasure-seeking or sport-loving businessmen should have been regarded as deviants, lured away from the paths of entrepreneurial righteousness by the siren voices of an antipathetic, anti-work, aristocratic culture. When it became apparent, however, that pleasure-seeking and sport-loving businessmen were extremely numerous, and that it was not at all abnormal for them to fail to conform to a pattern which divided their lives strictly between work, domestic family life, and virtuous public service to church, chapel, or civic community, then it also became perverse to persist in regarding them, as aberrants whose culture betrayed or negated some abstract entrepreneurial ideal.[36] The more straightforward reading of the evidence is that there were cultural divisions within the ranks of entrepreneurs, some were against blood sports and some were in favour, some regarded gambling as sinful while others saw it as a kind of application of business methods to leisure interests, some regarded strong drink as a temptation of the devil and others saw it as a useful and pleasant social, and business, lubricant. These divisions, once one steps outside the strict tests of the acquisition of landed estates, had no more than a tenuous connection with any process of gentrification, and these different varieties of businessmen did not correlate in any obvious way

[35] *Estates Gazette,* 1 Jan. 1921, 31 Dec. 1921.
[36] The 'entrepreneurial ideal' and its mid-Victorian triumph is classically defined in Harold Perkin, *The Origins of Modern English Society, 1780–1880* (1969), esp. pp. 273–90.

with entrepreneurial success or failure. The hunting Rothschilds, the polo-playing Cowdrays, the deer stalking Basses from Burton, were entre-preneurial successes; but it is impossible to say whether they were more, or less, successful than the non-hunting, non-shooting, John Rylands, William Lever, or John Ellerman.

Businessmen divided themselves into hearties and non-hearties according to their personal taste for hunting and shooting and other country pursuits, if these came within their resources, rather than as a reflection of their atti-tudes to the landed classes. In much the same way different lines of cleavage developed within the wealthy bourgeoisie between the philistines and the aes-thetes for a variety of financial, social, and artistic reasons which had little to do with emulation of the aristocracy. There is a strong impression, it is true, that art collecting, connoisseurship, and patronage were aristocratic pas-times, and that the new rich, particularly the provincial manufacturers, were ignorant, scornful, and dismissive of the world of art as frivolous, wasteful, and unproductive. This literary tradition, resting firmly on the intellectual arrogance of Jeremy Bentham, Matthew Arnold, John Ruskin, and William Morris, is as memorable and as misleading as all great cultural state-ments. It was a view which had no place for an early industrialist like Josiah Wedgwood, whose keen appreciation of the commercial value of good art did not proceed from ignorance or contempt for cultivated taste. All the same, it is true that patronage of living artists, at least to the extent of com-missioning family portraits and, in the eighteenth century, pictures of fam-ily groups with their favourite animals in romantic parkland poses, was a typical activity of landed families: it was part of the process of creating the cultural identity of a family of substance and continuity, laying down a col-lection of family portraits as one might also lay down collections of family silver or family muniments. It is also true that many, perhaps most, country houses and town houses came to house collections of art treasures, ranging all the way from accumulations of bric-a-brac and indifferent copies, up to great collections later to be recognized as of world importance. Most of these were the fruits of generations of accumulation of the spoils of youth from the Grand Tour and the loot of conquests in India and the East, assem-bled haphazardly, without direction, and with the minimum of artistic knowledge. Only a few were put together purposefully, with discrimination and serious knowledge, by wealthy individuals consumed with the collect-ing passion and well served by the advice of experts and agents. Among these few several were simply acquired en bloc, as when the aftermath of the French Revolution presented opportunities for buying the collections of dis-tressed or decapitated French royalty and nobles by the shipload, at knock-down prices. Thus the Duke of Bridgewater bought the bulk of the Orleans collection, sold by Philippe Égalité, much of which was instantly resold at a considerable profit while the best pictures were divided between Bridgewater's son-in-law and co-heir, Lord Stafford, his nephew, Lord Gower and the nephew's father-in-law, the Earl of Carlisle.[37]

There was, however, nothing inherently or exclusively aristocratic about these things. Collecting was a function of wealth, and there was a long tradition of mercantile wealth going into both patronage and collecting, a tradition fashioned by Italian and Dutch merchant princes, but one not lacking in English examples. The stockbroker Julius Angerstein who donated his collection of pictures to form the nucleus of the National Gallery was an early nineteenth-century instance. Manufacturers have been arbitrarily excluded from this tradition by the device of erecting an ideal type dedicated to the pursuit of profit and material utility, to whom art and culture were the wasteful and selfish indulgences of the idle rich, and then declaring that any manufacturer who strayed from this ideal had been seduced and corrupted by the lure of aristocratic luxury and decadence. Some colour is lent to this view by the opinion of some historians that 'most of the manufacturers were ill-educated, coarse and rough, with an extremely limited range of ideas', and by the arguments of second-rate intellectuals like Samuel Laing, the early Victorian travel writer and social critic, that art and high culture, painting, sculpture, and opera, were unproductive and useless, flourished in the unwholesome aristocratic and pre-industrial climate of Bavaria, Italy, or Sweden (interestingly, not in Norway, which had a one-class peasant society with no aristocrats, and no art), and had no reputable place in the free, capitalist, and progressive air of Britain.[38] Added confirmation is apparently provided by the behaviour of those northern industrialists who set out to present a softer and more cultured image to the world, by acquiring bad copies of old masters from the dealers who were already active in Manchester and Leeds in the early 1800s, in direct imitation of the gentry. Yet by the 1840s a group of industrialists had emerged which was both independent in its attitude to works of art and unaffected in its economic drive by its relations with artists.

It is misleading to single out the industrialists for special attention, were it not for the fact that it is specifically the entrepreneurial thrust of manufacturers which has been called in question. In reality it was the upper middle-class elites of the major provincial towns, or more precisely a cross-section of those elites comprising merchants, bankers, and professional men as well as industrialists, who made the moves which gave the lie to metropolitan taunts that they were nothing but uncultured money-grubbing philistines. High culture came to the new industrial towns in the 1820s, its arrival

[37] Gervas Huxley, *Lady Elizabeth and the Grosvenors* (Oxford, 1965), 60.
[38] Janet Wolff and J. Seed (eds.), *The Culture of Capital: Art, Power, and the Nineteenth-century Middle Class* (Manchester, 1988), introduction, p. 5; B. Porter, '"Monstrous Vandalism": Capitalism and Philistinism in the Works of Samuel Laing, 1780–1868, *Albion*, 23 (1991), 253–68.

marked by such events as the establishment of the Royal Manchester Institution in 1823, and the vogue for 'polytechnic exhibitions' where pictures were publicly displayed along with collections of useful and educational objects, a fashion which saw such exhibitions in Manchester, Leeds, Sheffield, Newcastle, and the Potteries in the 1830s, and many more places besides in the 1840s.[39] The agents of this developing interest, and in many ways the driving force behind it, were the new model art dealers, experts specializing in pictures and no longer handling a diverse jumble of books, coins, clocks, furniture, and odds and ends as well, who seem to have first come on the scene in Manchester when Vittore Zanetti set up business in 1804 as a framer of pictures and mirrors, and quickly branched out into importing and selling paintings. The key figure was Thomas Agnew, who came to Manchester in 1817, took over Zanetti's business in 1828, and over the following forty years used the Manchester base to make Agnews into one of the leading dealers on the national and international art market. The appearance of Agnew, and a few other skilled dealers of similar breed, in provincial centres implied a pre-existing or at least clearly incipient market for art, of a sort. What Agnew and his like did was to wean the provincial buyers from their taste for old masters, which were all too often fakes, or by overpriced minor artists, and educate them in the delights of buying British, that is works by living British artists. This tactic made sound commercial sense for the dealers, promising to stimulate more sales and commissions, and it tended to create a distinction between the collecting criteria of metropolitan and provincial buyers, confirming their independence of one another.[40]

Art production and selling methods adapted to the growth in the overall size of the art market, and artists increasingly went in for speculative painting, producing works in advance of any firm buying orders and selling them through exhibitions, a process which enabled them to assert the autonomy of artistic expression and its independence from the dictates of patronage, although if they wished to make a living they still had to pay heed to what the market wanted. Nevertheless the traditional method of dealing in which a patron commissioned a painting on a specified subject, and possibly meddled in its execution, also survived; this provides clearer evidence of the middle-class involvement with the art world. Thus, Ford Madox Brown's great painting, *Work*, which figures on the dust jackets of dozens of books on Victorian social history, was commissioned by the Leeds stockbroker, Thomas Plint, who gave instructions that the painting was to include the figures of Carlyle and Kingsley, and a 'a quiet, earnest *holy*-looking' lady

[39] J. Seed, 'Commerce and the Liberal Arts: The Political Economy of Art in Manchester, 1775–1860', in Wolff and Seed, *Culture of Capital*, 55; T. Kusamitsu, 'Great Exhibitions Before 1851', *History Workshop*, 9 (1980), 70–89.   [40] Seed, 'Commerce and the Liberal Arts', 53–5.

distributing tracts. *Work* was more than ten years in the painting, and Plint died before it was finished in 1865; but he had left his mark on a picture famous for its portrayal of the physical power and force of manual labour, and not apparently related to its capitalist origins in a provincial industrial town (the scene of *Work* is Hampstead High Street), although that mark was somewhat discordant since his tract-distributing lady stands uneasily and impotently on the sidelines while the central figure of the navvy drinks large quantities of beer.[41]

In much the same way a rather less renowned painting, Daniel Gabriel Rossetti's *Venus Verticordia*, was influenced by its commissioner, a leading Bradford stuff merchant and exporter, John Mitchell, who was alarmed by the disturbing nakedness of the girl holding a menacing little dart, and insisted that Rossetti screen it a little with an armful of honeysuckle.[42] By way of contrast, the Manchester engineering company owner, Thomas Fairbairn, who commissioned Holman Hunt's painting *The Awakening Conscience*, was apparently not in the least upset by the picture's subject, that of a kept woman starting up from her lover's lap on realizing her sin and the irrevocable loss of her chastity, merely asking Hunt after the finished work had been handed over if he would repaint the expression on the girl's face. Fairbairn was either sufficiently insensitive to the picture's message or sufficiently impressed by Holman Hunt's talent to order a second picture from him ten years later, a resounding affirmation of family values called *The Children's Holiday* showing Fairbairn's wife and a handful of his younger children having tea in the garden. Since in the interval he had purchased an earlier Holman Hunt, *Valentine Rescuing Sylvia from Proteus*, in which Sylvia is saved in the nick of time from attempted rape, the likelihood is that Fairbairn both admired Hunt and wished to possess a group of paintings reflecting on different aspects of illicit and legitimate sexual unions. Whether he hung these three pictures together, to tell a moral story, is not recorded: his wife might not have cared to be placed next to a mistress. His appreciation of Holman Hunt certainly extended to buying more of his work, and finally to commissioning a portrait of himself.[43]

These few examples suggest that the new rich, at any rate the provincial new rich, had decided, independent, and individual views when they commissioned works of art, views which were not hidebound by conventional ideas of respectability and which were not influenced by any reference to contemporary fashions among aristocratic art patrons. The aristocrats were likely to be more degenerate than the industrialists, collecting nudes indiscriminately like

[41] Caroline Arscott, 'Employer, Husband, Spectator: Thomas Fairbairn's Commission of the *Awakening Conscience*', in Wolff and Seed, *Culture of Capital*, 160–2.

[42] M. Hardman, *Ruskin and Bradford: An Experiment in Victorian Cultural History* (Manchester, 1986), 34, 232–7.   [43] Arscott, 'Employer, Husband, Spectator,' esp. pp. 165–6.

the Earl of Wemyss who was said to have 'a particular rage for naked beauties . . . the lecherous Old Dog is not likely to send a Venus or a Cupid begging'; although the largest and most expensive piece of respectable
Victorian erotic art, Edwin Long's *Babylonian Marriage Market*, was in fact
commissioned by the Lancashire cotton master, Edward Hermon.[44] The
impression that the new rich had a partiality for the pre-Raphaelites is confirmed by the evidence of the much more numerous purchases they made at
exhibitions and through art dealers. Burne-Jones, for example, sold his
paintings chiefly in that way (his stained glass and his tapestries were more
likely to be commissioned), and it is thought that he sold more of them in
his native Birmingham, perhaps helped by local loyalty, than he did in the
more aristocratic London art market. Snobbish art historians have assumed
'that uncultured northern industrialists took a particular liking to pre-
Raphaelite pictures, blind to their failings', and have explained this liking
with supercilious condescension. A typical example comes from Quentin
Bell in 1982:

From the very first these painters found their market among those whom contemporaries would have considered an ignorant and philistine clientele, the 'self-made'
men and manufacturers of the North. . . . The advantage from the Pre-Raphaelite
point of view, of this kind of client, was that he would have been relatively uneducated. He would not have known enough to know that for a cultivated public, Pre-
Raphaelite painting was full of faults.[45]

Less offensive explanations are available. It might be that the new rich, if
they decided to enter the art world at all, were particularly attracted to the
work of contemporary, living, artists because they could identify with them
as being new men themselves, modern, up-to-date, more relevant than dead
painters, dealing with subjects drawn from contemporary life; or it could
have been that contemporary art was generally cheaper and more reliable
than the old masters on the market, not being so liable to fakes, forgeries,
and second-rate imitations. It may be that adherence to the modern caused
a shift in the allegiance of the new wealthy from pre-Raphaelites and British
artists to the Impressionists, around the turn of the century. The evidence is
inconclusive, but quite apart from the exceptional collection put together by
Samuel Courtauld (1876–1947) it seems possible that more Impressionists
were sold to Glasgow businessmen, for instance, in the years just before

[44] Ibid., 161; Janet Wolff, 'The Culture of Separate Spheres', in ead. and Seed, *Culture of Capital*, 130. The *Babylonian Marriage Market*, painted in 1875, was sold by Hermon and subsequently and bizarrely became part of the foundation collection of Royal Holloway College for Ladies, purchased in 1882: J. Chapel, *Victorian Taste: The Complete Catalogue of Paintings at Royal Holloway College* (1982), 108–09.

[45] Quentin Bell, *A New and Noble School: The Pre-Raphaelites* (1982), quot. by Arscott, 'Without Distinction of Party', 135.

1914, thanks to the salesmanship of the persuasive and well-connected dealer Alexander Reid, than were sold in London.[46]

The lines of division among art patrons and collectors between the aristocracy and gentry who owned old masters and family portraits, and the industrialists and other members of the provincial upper middle class who owned moderns and contemporaries, were plain to see at the exhibitions mounted in several provincial centres in the 1830s and 1840s for the enlightenment and moral improvement of the working classes. These were exhibitions of pictures loaned by their owners, and almost invariably the Italian, Flemish, Dutch, and German pictures were owned by local landed families, while the business and professional men supplied the modern British paintings. The lists of local business and professional men who loaned pictures from their private collections, in Leeds, Manchester, Wigan, Bolton, Oldham, Preston, Bradford, Birmingham, and elsewhere, were both impressively long and broad in their occupational composition. In all these towns merchants, bankers, merchant-manufacturers, textile manufacturers, ironmasters, cotton masters, engine and machine makers, brass founders, flax spinners, surgeons, physicians, lawyers, wine merchants, tea merchants, booksellers, and music teachers figure among the picture owners. Out of a list of some sixty Victorian new men who were noted art collectors, compiled from the lists of these exhibitions and from entries in the *Dictionary of Business Biography*, no more than a handful collected old masters or pre-1800 paintings; all the rest went in for contemporaries. The exceptions included Samuel Cunliffe-Lister, 1st Lord Masham, who concentrated on Reynolds, Romney, and Gainsborough; Charles Morrison, the wealthiest new man of the century, who mixed Rembrandt with Turner; Samuel Montagu, 1st Lord Swaythling, who mixed Turner with Reynolds and Morland; and Alfred Beit, who favoured seventeenth-century Dutch and Spanish pictures. It may have been significant that these men also went in for the acquisition of country houses and estates, although so too did collectors of Turners like the shipping magnate Sir Donald Currie, and collectors of pre-Raphaelites like the banker George Rae.[47] The members of the urban elites who became art lovers doubtless remained a minority, and quite possibly the great majority was, and remained, unrepentantly philistine or at least indifferent: but the numbers of art collectors had become so numerous by mid-century that this had plainly emerged as an activity characteristic of a group within the industrial and commercial middle class, and not simply the hobby of a few eccentric individuals.

[46] Ex inf. Dr Alastair Reid, Girton College, Cambridge. See also Dianne Sachko Macleod, *Art and the Victorian Middle Class* (Cambridge, 1996), 403, 437.

[47] *DBB* all entries for businessmen who died before 1914 who are noticed as having 'noted' art collections; Howe, *Cotton Masters*, 296–7; Hardman, *Bradford*, 48–9, 53–5, 212–14; Arscott, 'Without Distinction of Party,' 141–2; Seed, 'Commerce and the Liberal Arts', 64–5.

It was an activity, it has been said, which in the hands of the business elites gave 'art a social use value' which distinguished it, commendably, from 'the social redundancy of aristocratic collections'.[48] That is more questionable. Certainly the public exhibitions in the major provincial towns, which culminated in the great Art Treasures Exhibition in Manchester in 1857—an exhibition of international importance, larger and of higher quality than anything previously staged in Britain, which attracted one and a half million visitors, including many who made special journeys from the Continent—were mounted chiefly with didactic and morally improving ends in mind. The argument was that art would help to civilize the workingman and woman: the exhibition would be an uplifting alternative to the public house, and exposure to the elevating influence of pictures of high quality would weaken or extinguish the appetite for coarse and mindless sensual pleasures, and might improve the awareness of textile workers of the commercial importance of good design.[49] There may well have been these utilitarian and moral justifications for making art publicly accessible to the working classes, even if the expected effects on their morals and general behaviour were not readily apparent. But it does not at all follow that either the aristocratic or the businessmen owners of the pictures which were loaned to such exhibitions had similar utilitarian or moral motives for acquiring their pictures in the first place. That an exhibition simply 'brought art out of the private interior of the aristocrat and into the public sphere', a private interior where it had its place for a variety of non-instrumental reasons, was just as likely to have been true of the businessman collector.[50]

The motives of the businessman collector were no doubt as private and personal as those of the aristocrats, as well as being part of a group or subgroup cultural imperative. Some businessmen treated art as a commodity and judged pictures purely as investments, an attitude carried to extremes in the twentieth century when Alan Bond, in 1989, paid twice as much for Van Gogh's *Irises* as he did for his 1,000-acre estate in Oxfordshire, acting on an expert opinion that it is the most valuable picture in the world: he had to resell both within a year as his fortune melted away.[51] Others—such as Henry McConnel, 'the greatest cotton spinner in the world' in the early nineteenth century, Sir Andrew Walker, the Liverpool brewer who gave the Art Gallery to the city in 1877, Henry Tate and Samuel Courtauld of later Gallery bequests, or in the 1990s Andrew Lloyd Webber and 'sensation' Saatchi—have paid top prices in their time in building up renowned collections, without therefore regarding them as simple investments. Some did indeed devote their efforts to building up local galleries, open to the public, putting 'their

---

[48] Howe, *Cotton Masters*, 299.
[49] Seed, 'Commerce and the Liberal Arts', 71–2; Howe, *Cotton Masters*, 299–300.
[50] Seed, 'Commerce and the Liberal Arts', 71.   [51] *The Times*, 4 Nov. 1993.

faith in the value of culture within the urban community, in a way unknown to land-hungry merchant aristocrats'.[52] Private collectors, keeping their pictures in their own homes and occasionally lending them to exhibitions, may well have had less public-spirited motives. Some land-hungry cotton masters, like Edward Hermon 'a lavish patron of contemporary artists' including Edwin Long and the builder of Wyfold Court near Henley with its huge picture gallery, managed to accumulate pictures, country houses, and land, as did several of the new rich from other industries such as Armstrong at Cragside, Bolckow at Marton Hall near Middlesbrough, or Ismay at Dawpool in Cheshire.[53] For many collectors the dominant motive was display, the desire to impress friends and neighbours and to satisfy the impulse to collect objects—Harry Panmure Gordon (1837–1902), a London stockbroker, besides being well known as a breeder of collies had the best collection of carriages in the world. Edmund Potter, a Manchester calico printer, told the Select Committee on Schools of Art in 1864: 'I believe that the largest support to modern painting has really been given in Manchester. I believe the purchases made of paintings and works of Art in the last twenty or thirty years, have been larger in the Manchester district than in any district in the country.' He added that the motive for buying pictures was a love of display rather than a love of art, commenting that 'I believe it is a fact that whenever there is a very successful period in trade it is a good time for the sale of pictures'.[54] Businessmen could also satisfy their desires for display more economically through collecting pictures than through acquiring country houses and landed estates. Hermon's great collection was sold in 1881 for £37,000 and the notable collection of Thomas Taylor of Wigan, cotton master (who had also purchased an Oxfordshire estate and served as High Sheriff of that county in 1863) was sold for £34,500 in 1883, amounts possibly larger than the prices paid for the acquisitions but mere fractions of the sums spent in acquiring land. One of the largest art sales of the century, that of the collection of the railway engineer of the Forth Bridge, Sir John Fowler, realized £66,000 at Christies in the 1890s, a tithe of what the 'notoriously rapacious' Fowler had laid out in purchasing 57,000 acres in Ross-shire in 1865–7. While the best art collection in the whole North-East was assembled by James Leathart (1820–95), the salaried manager of the lead manufacturing firm of Locke, Blackett & Co, whose salary was raised to £600 a year in 1874: already in 1873 the *Athenaeum* had praised his collection of pre-Raphaelites which included a portrait of his wife by Rossetti and of himself by Ford Madox Brown. He had, admittedly, married a daughter of the soap maker

[52] Howe, *Cotton Masters*, 296.
[53] Girouard, *Victorian Country House*, 425, 412, 403; *DBB* for art collections of Bolckow and Ismay.
[54] Edmund Potter, *Report of Select Committee on Schools of Art*, BPP 1864 (446), 135, 127, quoted in Seed, 'Commerce and the Liberal Arts', 65, 77.

Thomas Hedley, but they had sixteen children to care for, and when he died in 1895 he left no more than £14,924, and no land. The motives of business-men collectors differed from those of aristocratic collectors perhaps only in the absence of the spur of a family tradition or the urge to create one: most of the businessmen's collections, on the death of the collector, seem either to have been bequeathed to a local gallery, or to have been dispersed at sales.[55] The cultural autonomy of the business elite, however, clearly established by the middle of the nineteenth century, derived from the distinctive composition of their collections and their superior appreciation of living artists, not from any deep-seated differences in the instrumentality or self-justification which they applied to their ownership of pictures.

The cultural education of successful businessmen, which shaped their tastes, sensibilities, and interests, largely determined how they spent their wealth and thus, by derivation, provided much of the motivation for their con-tinued pursuit of more wealth. It clearly did not produce a single, homoge-neous type. It enabled important sections of the business elite to cut free from the apron strings of the aristocracy and gentry, and to assert their autonomy, most clearly in the field of art, but also to some extent in the hunting field and the shooting grounds; it did this at the cost of dividing the business elite, and indeed the upper middle class more generally, into differ-ent and in some degree antagonistic fractions. The hunting set and the artis-tic set probably had little in common, but the really significant divide was between those sets on the one side, and on the other the section of the upper middle class which kept faith with the Evangelical and Dissenting precepts against blood sports, against self-indulgence and personal extravagance, against wasteful and unproductive activities. A 'puritanical' wing of this kind survived in good voice until 1914, and only crumbled gradually in the inter-war years. It tended to decry the other branches of the business elite as renegades who had been seduced by aristocratic ways and who had fallen for the temptations of luxury and frivolity. The mistake of some historians has been to take this at face value, and to assume that the 'puritans' were the good entrepreneurs. The 'sinners' in this story committed their own sins without being led astray by wicked aristocrats, and they seem to have been at least as successful as the 'puritans' at making lots of money.

[55] DBB for Fowler, Hermon, and Leathart; Howe, *Cotton Masters*, 253, 261, 300, for Taylor. An extensive treatment of Victorian collectors, and of the disposal of their collections after death, is in Macleod, *Art and the Victorian Middle Class*, esp. the Appendix, 379–489.

6

Gentlemanly Values, Education, and the Industrial Spirit

The wealthy entrepreneurs of late Victorian Britain, while clearly part of the upper middle class, did not put on a convincing display of class or group solidarity. Some were only too anxious to lose their identity and escape from their social origins by becoming as like the traditional landed classes as possible, through possessions, marriages, and lifestyle. Most, however, proclaimed their social or cultural autonomy, but they asserted this independence in a great variety of ways which criss-crossed the group with internal divisions that expressed divergent, sometimes conflicting, values and interests. The great fissure was the prolongation into the ranks of successful businessmen of the church–chapel divide, putting the abstemious sheep with their Nonconformist consciences on one side, proclaiming their lack of contamination by aristocratic or gentry vices, and the indulgent goats with their unapologetic pursuit of material pleasures on the other. There was a pronounced tendency for individual sheep, when they grew rich, to turn into goats. The goats complicated the issue by splitting into different, and to some extent competing, herds. The grandest were the aristocratic bourgeoisie with their country estates, their sporting estates, their grandiose new country houses, and their great businesses; the larger flocks were composed of the hunting bourgeoisie, the shooting bourgeoisie, the racing set, the golfing set, and the art patrons and collectors, flocks with some overlapping membership but also capable of disapproving of each other quite sharply. These divisions did not appear to be reflected in any way in the money-making capabilities of the business class as a whole, although the puritanical sheep were prone to claim that they were the only true possessors of the work ethic and the entrepreneurial spirit. The existence of the divisions, however, made it difficult to believe that all businessmen shared a common culture. Unity and coherence were restored, or more exactly were for the first time created, in this fragmented grouping, it has been claimed, by the development of a common education experience for businessmen, the public school system, a system which had the unfortunate, or maybe the intended, effect of practically killing off the industrial spirit.[1]

[1] Martin Wiener, *English Culture and the Decline of the Industrial Spirit, 1850–1980* (Cambridge, 1981) 16.

The supposedly anti-industrial and anti-business attitudes instilled by the public schools lie close to the heart of the cultural explanations which historians have offered for British economic decline, to which the alleged indifference to business enterprise fostered by universities comes a close second. Corelli Barnett, whose *Audit of War* is an impassioned, intemperate, and somewhat misleading exposition of the sorry state and technological backwardness of the British economy revealed by its performance in the Second World War, is very clear about this. In the Victorian public schools of the late nineteenth and early twentieth centuries, he claims, 'the sons of engineers, merchants, and manufacturers were emasculated into gentlemen. Here the children of wealth were taught that the pursuit of wealth was vulgar, ignoble, and unknightly, not to say the mark of the cad and the bounder: and that the more estimable career lay in "public service" '.[2] Martin Wiener is equally certain about the anti-business influence of public schools, but more hesitant about the timing and extent of their direct impact on the sons of businessmen, although he does finally maintain that

The public schools gradually relaxed their entrance barriers. Boys from commercial and industrial families, however, were admitted only if they disavowed their backgrounds and their class. However many businessmen's sons entered, few future businessmen emerged from these schools, and those who did were 'civilized'; that is, detached from the single-minded pursuit of production and profit.[3]

Wiener attaches this closely to his gentrification thesis by portraying the public schools and their ethos as essentially aristocratic, a stance also adopted by Lawrence Stone.[4] There are thus two separate questions to examine: were the public schools, particularly after the mid-Victorian reforms, aristocratic institutions? and did the public schools, whether aristocratic or not, exercise the baleful and pernicious anti-business influences that have been asserted?

It was indisputably aristocratic to go to Eton and Christ Church, or Eton and Trinity College Cambridge: these were the recognized routes for the sons of peers and wealth landed gentry, they were so in 1900, had been so in 1800, and were still so in 1950. It has been maintained, with good justification, that Eton was the only genuinely aristocratic public school.[5] Even that opinion may, on some definitions, be misleading, for it rests on the fact that the overwhelming majority of the titled aristocracy, something like two-thirds of them, alike in the 1950s and in the 1870s, had been educated at Eton, with no more than 10 to 15 per cent going to also-ran Harrow. Rubinstein's most recent work, however, shows that no more than one-third

---

[2] Corelli Barnett, *Audit of War* (1986), 221.   [3] Wiener, *English Culture*, 20.

[4] Lawrence Stone and Jeanne C. Fawtier Stone, *An Open Elite? England, 1540–1880* (Oxford, 1984), 409.

[5] W. D. Rubinstein, *Elites and the Wealthy in Modern British History* (Brighton, 1987) 181.

of the fathers of Eton boys were landowners, at any point in the nineteenth century.[6] The school patronized by the majority of the landed aristocracy thus did not rely on the landed aristocracy to supply the majority of its pupils. The image of Eton, and of Harrow, as the schools of first choice for the well-born, wealthy, and socially ambitious cannot be destroyed by statistical analysis, and it is likely that a high proportion of the non-landed fathers of boys at both schools were themselves allied to the landed aristocracy or gentry either by blood, in cadet and younger sons' lines, or by profession in the church or army. If the aristocratic reputation of Eton, and probably of Harrow as well, should be allowed to survive in the face of the figures, the same kind of analysis of the status and occupation of schoolboys' fathers places the other seven Clarendon schools clearly on the far side of the aristocratic fence. If it was true of such old foundations as Winchester and Rugby, Charterhouse and Shrewsbury, that they attracted no more than a sprinkling of the sons of the lesser gentry and an occasional sprig of the aristocracy, it was even more true of the new Victorian public schools like Cheltenham, Marlborough, Radley, or Wellington that they were scarcely ever patronized by the landed classes themselves; although they were by close allies, who were sometimes kith and kin, from the church, army, and the law.[7]

The key could be found in the example of Haileybury, converted from an East India Company training college for its servants into an 'open' public school catering above all for the Indian Civil Service and the Colonial Service. And it could be found in Matthew Arnold's celebrated comment to the Taunton Commission on endowed grammar schools, in 1868:

So we have amongst us the spectacle of a middle class cut in two, in a way unexampled anywhere else; of a professional class brought up on the first plane, with fine and governing qualities, but without the idea of science; while that immense business class which is becoming so important a power in all countries, on which the future so much depends and which in the leading schools is, in England, brought up on the second plane, cut off from the aristocracy and the professions, and without governing qualities.[8]

---

[6] W. D. Rubinstein, *Capitalism, Culture and Decline in Britain, 1750–1990* (1993), table 3.4. The text, p. 119, states that the percentage of landed fathers of boys at Rugby declined to only 2.6 per cent in the 1895/1900 cohort, whereas table 3.4 has a figure of 13 per cent of landed fathers for 1895/1900. Harold Perkin, *The Rise of Professional Society: England since 1880* (1989), 71, has a similar finding, that 81 per cent of the great landowners in the period 1880–99 had been to Eton, and only 18 per cent to all the other Clarendon schools put together.

[7] The old Catholic landed families sent their sons to Downside or Ampleforth. Rubinstein, *Capitalism, Culture*, table 3.4, analyses samples of entrants and their fathers for three dates, 1840, 1870, and 1895/1900, for Winchester, Rugby, St Paul's, Cheltenham, Dulwich, and Mill Hill, as well as for Eton and Harrow.

[8] Quoted in Perkin, *Professional Society*, 83, but misdated 1869.

Matthew Arnold was rather misleading in suggesting that there was a complete educational separation between the professional and the business classes, but entirely right in implying that the great weight of demand which sustained the schools of 'the first plane', that is the growing number of public schools and the reformed grammar schools, came from the professional class. The Victorian public schools were for the sons of professional men, not for the sons of the gentry. To a limited, but increasing, extent they were also for the sons of businessmen; but the first and most important point demonstrated by Rubinstein's analysis of the family backgrounds of boys attending Eton, Harrow, Rugby, Winchester, Cheltenham, Dulwich, St Paul's, and Mill Hill in the nineteenth century is that, as between the three categories of landowners, professional men, and businessmen, the largest single group of fathers was in every case that of the professional men, frequently as at Winchester, Cheltenham, or St Paul's forming the clear majority of fathers, with the one exception of Mill Hill, one of the leading Dissenting (Congregational) boarding schools on the public school model, where the great majority of boys consistently came from business families.[9]

On this kind of evidence the great Victorian public school cult, regardless of whether it affected businessmen or not, had very little to do with gentrification in the sense of adopting or imitating the schooling of the landed classes, and a great deal to do with professionalization in the sense of establishing and replicating the schooling of the professional class. Harold Perkin, conceding (1989) that public schools did propagate anti-industrial attitudes, draws the conclusion that these were not aristocratic in origin but 'were in fact the newly emergent social values of the reforming schoolmasters and dons whose disdain for industry and trade stemmed from their conviction that professional service was in every way superior both to endowed idleness and to what they regarded as "money grabbing" '.[10] This is much nearer the mark than his previous (1969) view that the reformed public schools 'embraced the new entrepreneurial ideal and its morality and instilled them into the sons of the aristocracy and gentry'.[11] Even the revised version, however, does not leave a great deal of room for the fact that the prime purpose of Thomas Arnold at Rugby, Charles Vaughan at Harrow, and all their followers and imitators as reforming headmasters, was not to provide an education tailored to the requirements of the professions, but to educate Christian gentlemen and to instil the idea of service. A Victorian public school, it was maintained, could turn virtually anyone into a gentleman through its magic of muscular Christianity, team games, strict and largely self-policed discipline, internal self-government, and group loyalty. For fathers the main advantage of a public school education may well

---

[9] Rubinstein, *Capitalism, Culture*, table 3.4.   [10] Perkin, *Professional Society*, 119.
[11] Id., *The Origins of Modern English Society, 1780–1880* (1969), 298.

have been that it fitted their sons for honourable and well-paid careers; but it did that more by slotting them into a particular social network than by equipping them with any special intellectual or vocational skills. For mothers the benefits of a public school education for their sons narrowed down to the single one that it made them into gentlemen, members of a newly defined social class and possessors of a stamp of approval which was instantly recognized by other mothers, with marriageable daughters, as proof of eligibility.

The public school, in the business of making gentlemen, was therefore closely identified with a form of gentrification, and even though the gentlemanly ideal which it cultivated was distinctive and far removed from the original landed gentry model with its emphasis on birth, breeding, and honour, that was nevertheless the model from which it ultimately derived. Hence in the context of a discussion of the significance of gentrification it would be misleading to try to sweep the public schools under the carpet, and it is necessary to examine their impact on businessmen and their effect on entrepreneurial vigour. The question is partly a matter of numbers, partly one of the quality and suitability of the education.

No one has ever pretended that the education offered at Victorian public schools actively encouraged or stimulated the development of entrepreneurial or business skills and abilities. The normal academic criticism has been that their concentration on the classics and neglect of modern or 'useful' subjects such as mathematics, natural science, modern languages, or English literature, not only failed to provide any preparation for business life but also was a positive discouragement to the choice of careers in business. That may indeed have been so, but the criticism is misdirected, because it exaggerates the influence of what went on in the classroom as distinct from the rest of the school ethos, because it misconstrues the extent to which the academic curriculum was intended to be a preparation for any specific careers, non-business or business, and because it attributes excessive importance to formal schooling as the formative and determining influence as distinct from the educative influences of family, friends, and peer groups. Much of this can be demonstrated from the non-business angle, that of the professions which provided the bulk of the support for the great expansion of Victorian public schools and the most important outlet for their product. It is, indeed, remarkable that the unreformed public schools, long before the days of Thomas Arnold and the other reforming headmasters, had already become firmly established favourites with the older professions in church, law, medicine, and the civil service. These schools were notorious for their incompetence, corruption, indiscipline, and absence of teaching, among many other deficiencies. Yet in a sample of professional men born between 1790 and 1810, whose careers were sufficiently distinguished to attain entries in Boase's *Modern English Biography*, almost a third attended public

schools, whose education had practically nothing to offer them, a proportion only slightly smaller than that of those whose secondary schooling had
been at the academies and grammar schools with reputations for efficient
and 'relevant' teaching.[12]

This finding confirms that neither the content nor the quality of the
teaching at the unreformed public schools was of much relevance to career
choices and prospects. The public schools mattered partly because of their
supposed character-forming magic, but mainly because they gave access to
the ancient universities; and for the high-achieving professionals that was
clearly important, since two-thirds of the group went on to university. This
remained true, in a less straightforward way, of the reformed schools and,
with one or two exceptions, of the new schools of the mid- and late-
Victorian expansion. The teaching became more competent and professional, and perhaps more interesting with a switch from rote learning of
Latin and Greek grammar to the translation and reading of classical literature. This may have been a fine way of training the intellect, but it was not
self-evident that the classics were a necessary or an ideal preparation for
entering the professions. A classical education was indeed made to function
as precisely that, the royal route into the professions, not for intrinsically
important educational or vocational reasons, but because the teachers and
administrators arranged matters that way. In other words, entry requirements were based on the qualities that the classics might provide rather than
on the knowledge or skills which might be appropriate for particular professions or jobs. Thus, the continued emphasis on the classics in the public
schools was attuned to ease of entry to Oxbridge, and the Civil Service
entry examinations were constructed so that they particularly suited those
who had read Greats. Any specific training, and the acquisition of useful
knowledge appropriate to the duties of a home civil servant, a member of
the diplomatic service, the colonial service, or the ICS, came after entry and,
until after the Second World War, was largely picked up on the job just as in
any trade. Other professions followed broadly the same pattern, with training for the law, medicine, or the church taking place after university or after
a first degree in a non-vocational discipline. The army and the navy did take
a different course, with naval boys usually skipping public school and going
direct to Dartmouth, and army boys generally missing out university, particularly if they went to one of the new specialist army public schools like
Wellington, which catered specially for the sons of army officers, or to a
public school with a specialized army division alongside its mainstream
classics division, which most of the larger public schools established in the

---

[12] Sample of the first 100 entries of business and professional men (excluding clergy, military, political, and literary men) in F. Boase, *Modern English Biography*, 3 vols. (Truro, 1892–1901), vol. i.

second half of the nineteenth century, the 'army side' having a curriculum which bore a slightly closer relationship to the professional requirements of a military career than the traditional classics regime, by including rather more maths and cadet training.

The essential point is that a public school education, as far as academic studies or the development of thinking processes are concerned, was not a form of job training or an investment in producing a one-purpose piece of human capital. In principle, at least, it was concerned with developing what would now be called transferable skills, which is what the theory of a liberal education, as opposed to a practical education or vocational training, was supposed to be about. It is true that neither the public schoolboys nor their parents expected much to be learnt at a Victorian public school, and the low esteem in which classroom work was held was only gradually displaced in the inter-war years; but to the extent that anything was learnt it did not automatically disqualify the boy for a non-professional career, for instance in business. A nodding acquaintance with Homer or Cicero, after all, was of no more obvious direct use to a district magistrate in darkest Africa than to a millowner in darkest England. Outside the classroom the main thrust of the public school in character-formation and the making of gentlemen may well have tilted the balance in an anti-business, or at least anti-industrial, direction, although the influence of the peer group in schools where boys with businessmen fathers were in a minority was probably more decisive. The widely attested influence of the Victorian public school in instilling a sense of responsibility and public service, regarded as the antithesis of the pursuit of profit, remains, however, problematic. The intense competitiveness of organized games and the central place they occupied seemed to have more to do with the values of loyalty and the team spirit than with disinterested public service; and loyalty and team spirit were not alien to the culture of the most successful Victorian family firms any more than they are to the most highly praised Japanese firms in the 1990s. Harold Perkin emphasizes that the public schools and universities were 'only incidentally anti-industrial', being dedicated to education for public service. Defenders of public schools and classical education not unnaturally put the case rather more positively: 'For children of superior intellect', it was asserted in 1904, 'a classical education undoubtedly affords the best means of training, especially if they are going into business, or purpose to make practical or theoretical science their life's work.' The most recent historian of education agrees with this favourable view, remarking of the introduction of natural science into the teaching in the late nineteenth century, and the swelling encouragement of games and athleticism that: 'The games playing made boys fit, of virile physique, developed qualities of character, self confidence and leadership, encouraged sociability and team working to achieve goals and discouraged bookishness—all qualities attractive to business and industry'.[13] In any case a businessman moderately well-versed in the teachings of popular political economy did not need to wait for the arrival of Thatcherism to argue that the pursuit of profit was a public service, perhaps the most essential type of public service, since it was bound up with the creation of wealth and jobs.

The image of the Victorian public school is one of cold baths, games fields, prefects, fags, anti-intellectualism, and cold chapels, which has generally been portrayed, perhaps quite correctly, as an unpromising specification for a nursery of future entrepreneurs; although for reasons unexplained it has been equally widely accepted as a description of a highly suitable nursery for future statesmen and imperial governors. Nevertheless, the capacity of the combined force of the classics and the public school ethos to kill off the industrial spirit has been much exaggerated. Not only did some businessmen send their sons to public schools, where the intention could have been to make them into trade-despising gentlemen, or could just as well have been to equip younger sons for whom there was no room in the family business for alternative careers; but also, more tellingly, some of the old boys went into business, and it was not unknown for a few of those to do rather well, like Samuel Jones Loyd, Lord Overstone, Eton and Trinity College Cambridge, wealthiest and perhaps most successful of all Victorian bankers.

The numbers were small, but from the middle of the century onwards not so small as to be insignificant. In the early nineteenth century it was very uncommon for successful businessmen to have been at a public school, less than 5 per cent of those businessmen, mainly from the world of finance, who secured an entry in Boase's *Modern English Biography*; but then very few of that cohort of businessmen who were of school age before 1830 had any secondary education of any kind.[14] Thereafter the numbers of public school-educated businessmen rose, but all the available studies indicate that the proportion remained low before 1914, and did not become a clear majority of the leading figures in industry until after 1945. Different groups of businessmen have been counted and analysed by different researchers, so that the overall picture is impressionistic and incomplete rather than precise and systematic. Still, all the findings point in the same direction. Charlotte Erickson pioneered the study of the social origins and education of British industrialists, in the hosiery and steel industries, more than thirty years ago, and showed that while the steel men were several cuts above the hosiers in social standing, wealth, and education, no

---

[13] Perkin, *Professional Society*, 370; T. Pellatt, *Public Schools and Public Opinion* (1904), 78; Michael Sanderson, *Education and Economic Decline in Britain, 1870 to the 1990s* (Cambridge, 1999), 42. [14] Source as in n. 12.

more than 16 per cent of them, before 1900, were public school products. Tony Howe, examining the early Victorian cotton masters, found that about 15 per cent of them went to public schools (and much the same percentage to university). Hartmut Berghoff, in the largest scale investigation yet conducted, identified the schooling of more than 750 businessmen from Birmingham, Bristol, and Manchester, active between 1870 and 1914, and established that 18 per cent of them had been to a public school. Bill Rubinstein, looking at the origins and education of 226 chairmen of the largest British industrial companies who have held their positions in the twentieth century, showed that the proportion who went to a public school moved from 32 per cent for the chairmen who reached the top between 1900 and 1919, to 54 per cent for the 1940–59 cohort.[15] It should be noted that at the time Charlotte Erickson was writing, in the 1950s, a public school education for late Victorian and early twentieth-century business leaders was assumed to be a sign of economic and social success, and to provide a presumption of efficient and intelligent management; while by the time of Howe, Berghoff, and Rubinstein, in the 1980s, the assumption was that a business leader with a public school education was likely to be conservative, unenterprising, and inefficient. These figures can be supplemented by the analysis of groups of more rarified and generally more famous businessmen, those interesting enough to be included in the *Dictionary of Business Biography*, and those sufficiently notable—usually by virtue of prominence in local or national political life and not simply in business—to have secured an entry in *Who's Who*. In the *Dictionary* group about 20 per cent of those born between 1840 and 1869, and thus in their entrepreneurial prime roughly between 1880 and 1914, went to public school. Samples drawn from *Who Was Who* indicate that about 25 per cent of those who died between 1897 and 1916, who were at their most active in business in a comparable pre-1914 period, were educated at public schools; a proportion which increased to 30 per cent of those who died between 1916 and 1928, and finally topped 50 per cent with the crop of 1961–70.[16]

These are not measures of identical groups, and in particular some refer to all businessmen, and others to industrialists alone, excluding the financial and commercial sectors. The convergence of the measures, however, is

[15] C. Erickson, *British Industrialists: Steel and Hosiery, 1850–1950* (Cambridge, 1959), 30–5, 110–14; table 10, steel men in office 1875–95, 16 per cent, and 1905–25, 31 per cent, had been at public schools; A. C. Howe, *Cotton Masters*, 55–7; H. Berghoff, 'Public Schools; and the Decline of the British Economy, 1870–1914', *Past & Present*, 129 (1990), 148–67; Rubinstein, *Elites and the Wealthy in Modern British History*, 196.

[16] Y. Cassis analysed all entries in vols. i–iv of the *DBB* of those born between 1840 and 1869, and found that 20.6 per cent had been to public school: cited in Berghoff, 'Public Schools', n. 19. *Who Was Who*, i, ii, and vi, sample of all B surnames in each volume.

striking. The general conclusion is inescapable. At no time before 1945 did the long arm of the public schools reach very far into the boardrooms of British industry. It is, therefore, absurd to saddle the public schools with a major share of responsibility for what is claimed to have been the generally lacklustre performance of the British economy before 1945, and especially absurd to claim that the onset of economic decline between 1870 and 1914 could have been caused by their pernicious anti-industrial influence. There simply were not enough public school boys in charge of businesses for their managerial and entrepreneurial performance, whether good or bad, to have had any decisive impact one way or the other. As it happens the small band of public school products among the pre-1914 business leaders included such figures as Gilchrist Thomas, the inventor of the basic process for making steel, Sir James Chance, the glass maker for the Crystal Palace, Michael Bass, the Burton brewer, Sir Thomas Boord, the London distiller, and John Crosfield, the Warrington soapmaker: men such as these do not seem to have been inferior in industrial spirit, or in actual achievement, to the non-public school majority of businessmen.

Once the public school men had taken control of the major part of British business it might be worth testing for links between a public school education and the troubles of the British economy since 1945, but such a foreshortened time-span completely destroys the apocalyptic appeal of the gentrification thesis, which relies for its effect on the proposition that British society never came to terms with industrial and entrepreneurial values and has been in economic decline since 1850, not on the unexciting observation that the British economy has underperformed since the 1960s. Martin Wiener convinced himself that the public school types were far more prominent in British industry before 1914 than was in fact the case through a not uncommon misunderstanding of the meaning of statistics. Looking at the work done in analysing career patterns from information in the published registers of public school old boys, he correctly observed that 'virtually all the leading public schools were sending more and more of their boys into the business world' between 1850 and 1914, citing figures from Marlborough, Merchant Taylors, and Clifton which show an increase in the fraction of school leavers going into business from less than 10 per cent to 25 per cent or more in that period.[17] Such figures establish that there was a significant growth in the business product of public schools, but they should not be taken as a measure of the significance of that product in relation to the total supply of businessmen.

Wiener, indeed, gets into a Catch-22 muddle over public schools. The economy was damaged, it is claimed, because the public schools turned their students away from industry; if, nevertheless, some public school boys

[17] Wiener, *English Culture*, 138, quot. W. J. Reader, *Professional Men* (1966), 212–13.

did go into industry the economy was damaged even more, because these are claimed, almost by definition, to have been boys of inferior intelligence and ability to their fellow-classmates who did not go into industry; and finally the economy took an even more severe beating because the public schools creamed all the best talents in the country, leaving only the also-rans to manage the bulk of the business sector.[18] There could be no winners in such a nightmare world. The entrepreneur or managing director who had not been to public school was handicapped because the selective system determined that he was of inferior ability, while the businessman who had been to public school was handicapped because his education had unfitted him for effective business, making him anti-industrial and teaching him to regard the profit motive with disdain. Victorian Oxbridge came in for similar criticisms: the older universities neglected science and technology; their atmosphere and their teaching nurtured contempt for business; and they alienated such businessmen's offspring as came their way from feeling any pride in their origins and from any inclination to follow in their father's footsteps. Luckily for the economy, so the argument runs, the universities' effects were less dire than those of the public schools, simply because the universities remained more isolated from the world of industry and thus had more limited opportunities for inflicting serious damage.[19]

There is a grain of truth in these points, perhaps two grains. But the separation between Oxbridge and industry was greatly exaggerated. Until the 1880s Oxford's contacts with business were indeed exceedingly slender, with both a tiny intake of the sons of businessmen and a tiny output of graduates who went into business, but that was hardly surprising since it was well understood that the university 'was virtually a training college for the clergy and little else', and the only obvious reason for businessmen to show any interest was to find a conversion course for one of their otherwise unemployable sons.[20] After the 1880s the isolation was steadily eroded, so that in the years just before 1914 more than a quarter of Oxford and nearly one-fifth of Cambridge undergraduates were the sons of businessmen, and around 15 per cent of the annual output of graduates from both Oxford and Cambridge were entering industry. For Cambridge this assimilation of business people might be attributed to the university's eager adoption of industrially relevant science and engineering subjects from 1875 onwards: by 1914 Cambridge was probably the world leader in physics, it was very strong in chemistry and engineering, and it was the home of Marshallian economics. In contrast, Oxford lagged far behind in all the 'industrial' sciences, although not in medical science, and its appeal to the business world would have to be explained not in terms of the industrial relevance of its

---

[18] Wiener, *English Culture*, 138.   [19] Ibid., 22–4.
[20] M. Sanderson, *The Universities and British Industry, 1850–1970* (1972), 50.

teaching, but perhaps in terms of the rise of the school of Modern History, which was at this period locked in its struggle for supremacy and on its way to replacing Greats as the 'queen of the Arts'. Reba Soffer has recently shown that the brightest of the History graduates had no contempt for industry, and that more went into business than into the church before 1914, while in the 1920s more entered business than either the law or the church. The percentages following careers in business and industry were markedly higher than those for all graduates, approaching one-quarter of the History graduates compared with the 15 per cent of all graduates— although the main destinations of the History graduates continued to be the public service and the education sector, and the historians in business were very likely to have done a spell in public service before starting on business careers, or to perform some form of public duty while holding their business posts.[21]

It might be possible to construct an argument showing that History graduates were better suited or more favourably disposed towards industry than Classics graduates had been in the days when Greats dominated, or at least that they were less unsuited, but internecine disciplinary disputes are in fact irrelevant to any explanation of the increase in the number of graduate businessmen. Before the days of the polyversities no university degree in any subject, with the possible exception of Divinity, was a job ticket in the sense of being a job-specific vocational training: all were branches of the Newmanite tree of a liberal education concerned with the development of the intellect, though some branches had a better opinion of themselves than others and the natural sciences, having thrown off any association with the classics, were accustomed to thinking that they were not in the same 'useless knowledge' bracket as the arts. On the practical level, the newly established University Appointments Boards in both Oxford and Cambridge found that the demand from big businesses like Shell, Brunner, Mond (the forerunner of ICI), and the major railway companies, was for Oxbridge graduates in geology, chemistry, or engineering, not for classicists or historians, who were left to their own devices if they wished to place themselves in industry.[22] These, both classicists and historians, certainly contributed as much as the scientists to the rising proportion of business leaders who were graduates: 10 to 15 per cent in the early 1900s, a quarter in the inter-war years, a third in the 1940s and 1950s, and two-thirds by the 1960s—Oxbridge graduates consistently dominated the field: 10 per cent in the 1900s (all from Oxford), one-fifth in the inter-war period and in the

[21] Reba N. Soffer, *Discipline and Power: The University, History, and the Making of an English Elite, 1870–1930* (Stanford, Calif, 1994), 198–203, and figs. 7–12. This is an analysis of the careers of all History graduates from the leading History colleges, Balliol and King's College Cambridge, 1882–1929; a stringent test since these were regarded as the most 'academic' and 'public service orientated' colleges.   [22] Sanderson, *Universities and British Industry*, 56–9.

1940s and 1950s, and 45 per cent in the 1960s (with Cambridge providing almost twice as many as Oxford after 1919).[23] The increase, however, was probably due as much to business adjusting itself to take what the universities had to offer, as to the universities adapting themselves to the needs of industry through introducing more practical courses: it is notable that while most of the new civic universities did introduce such practical courses, and frequently established reputations as leaders in particular areas of industrial technology—as brewing in Birmingham, metallurgy in Sheffield, mining in Newcastle, or leather in Leeds—their graduates rarely reached the top positions in industry as company chairmen. This was symptomatic of one of the failings of British industry since the First World War, that technicians, even university-educated technicians, were regarded as useful, especially for research in science-based industries, but not of managerial calibre. Graduate recruitment to industry, it seems, was influenced by the Oxbridge style, perhaps of clear thinking and clear expression, perhaps of social ease and effortless superiority, rather than by any appreciation of the expertise contained in an Oxbridge degree.

The civic universities founded in the second half of the nineteenth century did indeed send a high proportion of their graduates into industry, ranging in the early 1900s from Birmingham's one-quarter, through Manchester's and Bristol's one-third, to Newcastle's half or more, and on the whole these seem to have been themselves the sons of well-to-do businessmen—although these universities did also recruit students from both professional and skilled working-class families, and may have converted some of them into businessmen. Scottish universities, however, were not business-orientated, and smaller proportions of their graduates went into business than did from Oxbridge: 8 per cent of Glasgow graduates in the late 1890s, and barely 2 per cent of Aberdeen's in the 1900s.[24] The question whether a university education turned the sons of businessmen away from business is, however, most often posed only in the context of Oxford and Cambridge, the assumption being that neither the civic nor the Scottish universities had any inbuilt contempt for trade (although they definitely were not unsuccessful in converting businessmen's sons into public servants or professional men). Michael Sanderson is convinced that in spite of the impressive performance of Cambridge in moving graduates into industry

[23] Rubinstein, *Elites and the Wealthy*, 200, table 7.14. 'Business leaders' in this context were the chairmen of the largest industrial companies (excluding bankers, shipowners, and iron and steel manufacturers), taken from Philip Stanworth and Anthony Giddens, 'An Economic Elite: Company Chairmen', in eid. (eds.), *Elites and Power in British Society* (Cambridge, 1974), 81–101. More detailed figures for Oxford and Cambridge graduates entering business careers, in several sub-periods between 1850 and 1914, are cited in Sanderson, *Education and Economic Decline*, 52; they are similar to those in the text.

[24] Sanderson, *Universities and British Industry*, 100–1, 174, 177.

from the 1900s onwards, and the less impressive but still considerable similar achievement of Oxford, 'there is evidence from both universities that they tended to move sons of businessmen away from a business career, in Oxford this being reinforced in some colleges by a strong public service or professional ethic', the latter remark being a coded way of saying that Balliol had made the civil service virtually into its private fief. The only direct evidence offered for this conclusion, however, is a speech by a scientist, John Perry, at Oxford in 1903 in which he attacked Oxford for failing to establish links with industry, which he said

was especially dangerous for the country at large because Oxford was taking middle-class boys who ought to be succeeding their fathers in industrial management: 'their factories are so badly managed . . . They are what I call unskilled workmen, that is unskilled owners of works and it is Oxford which is to blame for their unskilfullness . . . she has always ostentatiously held herself aloof from manufactures and commerce'.[25]

The invective is splendid; but what it appears to say is that businessmen's sons went to Oxford and returned to their father's businesses without any adequate or relevant training, not that they vanished from the world of manufactures and commerce. Maybe it would have been better for the health and efficiency of manufactures and commerce if they had vanished.

Bill Rubinstein, on the other hand, has recently concluded 'that public school entrants, in their own later careers, regularly followed in their fathers' footsteps: the sons of professional men normally took up a professional career, the sons of businessmen, in the majority of cases, themselves became businessmen'. And although he has fewer data on the destinations of university entrants who were the sons of businessmen, he is confident that university education, also, did not produce any significant 'haemorrhage of talent' away from business life.[26] There were few career changes between father and son, and the small seepage of businessmen's sons out of finance or industry was more than counterbalanced by the drift of sons of professional men into industry. This finding is a sharp and lethal instrument for puncturing the claims of Corelli Barnett and Martin Wiener that the sons of businessmen were 'emasculated into gentlemen' by the public schools and turned against the world of business and all its works, which they were taught to regard as sordid. More than that, the finding suggests a possible explanation of the low level of business input or output from public schools or universities before the last quarter of the nineteenth century, and its rise thereafter, which is linked to changes in the structure of business and not to the pursuit of gentrification, or to changes in the character or content of the education on offer.

[25] Ibid., *Universities and British Industry*, 60, 37.
[26] Rubinstein, *Capitalism, Culture*, 119–24, 137–9.

Throughout the Victorian years family firms and partnerships continued to be the dominant forms of business organization, and in a family business there was as a rule no room for more than one son (or sometimes son-in-law) to make a living while preparing to take over from his father. The chosen son was normally the eldest, but could perfectly well be a younger son thought to have particular aptitude for the business. The other sons, who were not destined to enter the family business, might be educated, if it could be afforded, with the professions in view, not because of any anti-business prejudices but from the strongly pro-business motive of protecting the family firm from the potentially crippling burden of trying to support excessive numbers of functionally superfluous sons. In this way the public schools and the universities, acting as a high road into the professions and especially into the rapidly expanding imperial and home civil services, can be seen as a necessary instrument for safeguarding what may be loosely termed a form of 'business primogeniture' that was essential for the financial health and entrepreneurial vigour of the family firm. It is true that in one of the very few studies of the question of succession in family firms Mary Rose reaches the opposite conclusion, that 'formal provision for succession in the family firm was by no means common', and that recruitment of men of ability from outside the family was often the key to maintaining continuity and entrepreneurial vigour.[27] The resolution of these conflicting views is most likely to be found in the diversity of business histories. The characteristic form of business organization remained the family firm or partnership into the twentieth century, but many such firms, perhaps the majority, were not sufficiently successful or sufficiently large for continuation in the same ownership for several generations to be practicable, so that on the death of the owner it was necessary to withdraw capital from the business to provide for the widow and children, this being accomplished by finding a purchaser from outside the family. Other family firms, however, were sufficiently prosperous to support both widows and second and third generation members of the family as owners of a continuing family concern. Recruiting men of ability and appropriate experience from outside the family in order to maintain continuity was possible within the limits of familiarity with the industry, the locality, and most advantageously within the circle of the family's acquaintance. Outside those limits it remained very difficult for anyone without previous connections with the family and its type of business to gain an entry into industry, and this was the main reason why few sons of professional men made careers in business. The world of business ignored or rejected them, since it offered few openings,

---

[27] Mary B. Rose, 'Beyond Buddenbrooks: The Family Firm and the Management of Succession in Nineteenth-century Britain', in J. Brown and ead. (eds.), *Entrepreneurship, Networks and Modern Business* (Manchester, 1993), 127–43.

regardless of whether their upbringing and education had led them to disdain business.

The most important change in this situation, beginning to have some effect from the later decades of the nineteenth century, was in business organization, not in education. The corporate form was more and more widely adopted, and concurrently many firms grew in size and developed elaborate and institutionalized managerial structures, developments which weakened the grip of the family on the firm by diluting both financial and managerial control. As firms grew larger and more impersonal, and as ownership became separated from management, it became at once more possible and more necessary for strangers with no previous history of involvement in business to enter industry, and to do so with reasonable prospects of becoming managing directors or company chairmen on individual merit, assisted perhaps by the possession of an old school tie. This was the essential context for the growth, marked from the early twentieth century onwards, in the relative importance of business careers for the products of public schools and the older universities. The idea that the public schools and universities were damagingly anti-business and anti-industrial in their influence almost needs to be stood on its head: it was business and industry which were anti-public school and anti-university, although it would be less tendentious to say that for sound organizational reasons business and industry remained largely aloof from the traditional institutions of elite education. Rapprochement came also for sound organizational reasons, and had been under way for some time before the educational system, particularly the public school part of it, made any serious moves to be more positively industry-friendly in what it offered. Although some natural science was introduced quite rapidly from the 1860s onwards, it was scarcely designed to equip its recipients for a life in industry, and the teaching was widely regarded in the business world as being too theoretical and remote from actual practice.[28] Even when schools made positive efforts to be more industry-friendly the introduction of subjects like 'business studies' into the curriculum was neither useful nor encouraging to future businessmen; and the business parents were probably most impressed by the shift in general emphasis from games to academic achievement, to which most public schools succumbed in the 1950s.

The numbers game is by itself sufficient to exonerate the public schools and universities from direct responsibility for any economic decline in Britain before 1914, and from any major share of responsibility for poor performance before 1945, simply because their graduates did not occupy

---

[28] D. C. Coleman, 'Gentlemen and Players', *Economic History Review*, 2nd ser., 28 (1973), 92–116, esp. pp. 112–13; Sidney Pollard, *Britain's Prime and Britain's Decline. The British Economy, 1870–1914* (1989), 173.

the commanding heights in industry until after 1945.[29] The indirect responsibility, however, might have been large, for the reformed grammar schools of the second half of the nineteenth century modelled themselves closely on the public schools in the matter of the central place of the classics, and the business leaders of the time were twice as likely to have been grammar school boys as public school boys.[30] The case for the dire influence of the public schools seems to have returned by the back door, since the received view is that the classics nurtured cultured but ineffectual businessmen, ill-equipped to stand up to their more appropriately educated, thrusting, and resourceful foreign competitors. That case rests substantially on an unfavourable comparison of the supposedly amateurish and uncompetitive British with the apparently vastly superior German entrepreneurs in the period of Germany's headlong industrial growth after 1870, and on the assumption that the German superiority had something to do with an education system which featured the *Realschulen*, secondary schools that rejected the classics and were strong on modern subjects and technology, and at the tertiary level the *Technische Hochschulen*, which by the 1890s had become fully-fledged technical universities. This is a neat argument, but a mistaken one. It turns out that the leading German businessmen preferred to send their sons to the *Gymnasium*—roughly equivalent to grammar schools—where they themselves had been educated, and moreover that the *Gymnasium*, besides carrying a great deal more social prestige than the *Realschule*, was far more starchily anti-modern and far more wedded to a strictly classical syllabus than any English grammar school or public school by the 1870s. Similarly the *Technische Hochschulen*, although on the whole superior in their facilities and their standards to the civic universities and the rather later polytechnics which were their English equivalents, were decidedly inferior in status to the old-established German universities, which remained fiercely loyal to their humanist traditions. The sons of successful businessmen went to universities to mingle with the old elites of the land, the army, and the law, while the *Technische Hochschulen* turned out technicians and chemists rather than entrepreneurs.[31]

For those who cared to look outside Britain it was obvious that classical education of the grammar school type did not necessarily have any harmful consequences for the economy or for the vigour and robustness of entrepreneurs. While the German experience gives the classics a clean bill of

[29] Hartmut Berghoff, 'Public Schools and the Decline of the British Economy, 1870–1914', *Past & Present*, 129 (1990), 156; Rubinstein, *Capitalism, Culture*, 113.

[30] Berghoff, 'Public Schools', 154 and table i. D. J. Jeremy, 'Anatomy of the British Business Elite, 1860–1980', *Business History*, 26 (1984), 3–23, esp. table 5.

[31] Berghoff, 'Public Schools', 154 n. 15; S. Pollard, 'Reflections on Entrepreneurship and Culture in European Societies', *Transaction of the Royal Historical Society*, 5th ser., 40 (1990), 156–7; Pollard, *Britain's Prime*, 149–52, 169–71.

health in this respect, it does not prove that English grammar schools, public schools, or universities were ideal seed beds for raising strong new entrepreneurial stock. It remained true that until after the Second World War the schools did not do much to adapt their teaching or their general ethos to the needs of business, and then it was the decline and disappearance of jobs in the Indian Civil Service, the Indian army, and the colonial service which gave a clear signal that survival meant strengthening the alternatives to 'public service' as the objects of elite education. Although technology and engineering, especially at the research level, were increasingly well looked after from the 1880s in the universities, old (at least in Cambridge) as well as new, it also remained true until the 1970s that the universities paid little attention to enterprise and business management as possible fields for academic enquiry and for teaching. That was understandable. Not only is it difficult for the academic mind to grasp the idea that business management might be a definable and describable academic discipline, but also even when that has been grasped it has not proved easy to devise a syllabus of reliable practical utility for businessmen. It has perhaps been too readily assumed that the Americans solved that problem in the 1950s, by adapting and formalizing the mathematically based management techniques developed for operational purposes during the Second World War, and using these as the foundation of studies in the graduate business schools that proliferated in the USA in the 1950s and 1960s. The MBAs who graduated from these schools were extremely successful, especially in middle management, and were widely hailed as the key to the international dominance of American industry. The British educational system was extremely sluggish in following suit, and was about thirty years behind the American in establishing specialized business schools and in producing homegrown MBAs—Oxford, when it gets round to establishing one, will be more than forty years behind. It could be that at this point, roughly between 1950 and 1980, the British universities failed to succour industry as well as they might have done, and that the failure was due to the predominantly anti-vocational, Newmanite, prejudices of the university establishment, attitudes closely parallelled, it might be said, by the technological and pure science, non-managerial, values of university engineers and natural scientists.

That, however, is too bleak a picture. The universities were in these years quietly increasing their output of accountants, without the fanfare of proclaiming new departures, and the accountants were insinuating themselves and their cost-benefit concepts into the management of business. In any case, at the very moment when Britain was beginning to catch up with America in providing business schools it seemed that American industry was being overtaken by Japanese; one prominent feature of the Japanese system of 'lean production' which appeared to be at the heart of their industrial success was that it was not the brainchild of business schools, of which there are very few in Japan, since an academic management education is considered irrelevant. Japanese firms, we are told, 'recruit university-educated people because they know they are capable and intelligent', but are not particularly concerned with what students learn at university.[32] In 1999 the prospect of Japanese industrial supremacy looks more uncertain than it did five years ago, but even in America it has been admitted that business schools cannot teach entrepreneurship. Perhaps if Oxford waits long enough it will find that Newman is back in fashion, that business schools if not altogether redundant are just for middle management, and that entrepreneurs require well-trained minds plus experience on the job. They also require an ability to see and exploit fresh opportunities for new products, new markets, or new techniques, an ability which cannot be imbibed from textbooks or taught in management courses.

Corelli Barnett slammed into the 'practical men', the men without scientific or technical education who learnt their trade in the firm and on the shop floor, as the men responsible for Britain's industrial decline from the 1870s through to the post-1945 years. They were the type of men who had previously led British industry to world domination, and this earlier success had entrenched the type so firmly in business culture that it was impervious to any need to adapt to the increasingly theoretical, science-based, and sophisticated nature of industrial and business operations.[33] Echoing this view and improving on it, Martin Wiener claimed that successful 'practical men' 'found their main task in life to be ensuring that they and their heirs behave like leisured landed gentry rather than like the successful innovators they had once been', thus contributing as much to industrial decline as their rivals and opposite numbers on company boards, the 'educated amateurs' who had been gentrified at public schools into abjuring any competitive, innovatory, or aggressive behaviour.[34] Now, in the 1990s, 'practical men' are back in the vanguard of successful business leaders, with the considerable difference from the Victorian and pre-1945 versions that today's practical men need to be highly educated before they are capable of translating the requirements and prospects of a particular industry and a particular firm within it into the best possible technical and business practice.

In the interval between the 1870s and the 1990s both the 'educated amateurs', the businessmen who were the products of public schools and universities, and the 'practical men' who had no elite schooling and no university education, have been held responsible for a poor economic performance that has failed to match that of Britain's international competitors.

[32] R. R. Locke, 'Education and Entrepreneurship: A Historian's View,' in Brown and Rose (eds.), *Entrepreneurship*, 73–4.

[33] Barnett, *Audit of War*, 94–7, 100, 209.   [34] Wiener, *English Culture*, 139.

That is pathetic as a contribution to serious discussion, since it amounts to saying that pretty well everyone who has been involved in running businesses has been inefficient and incompetent. That highlights the inherent absurdity of the whole thesis linking economic decline to the gentrification of businessmen, for that thesis must rest on the assumption that the great majority of businessmen succumbed to the baleful influence of a gentry culture and became unenterprising, without allowing for the possibility that outsiders uncontaminated with such a cultural virus might have stepped on to the stage and exploited the opportunities which the effete were letting fall from their grasp. Even if the entire population had been affected by the cultural malaise—as, it has been alleged, hyper class-conscious Britain indeed was—disease-free foreigners might be expected to have staked their claims to the rich pickings that British businessmen were too feeble to take for themselves. That, indeed, is exactly what has happened, from Singer sewing machines in the mid-nineteenth century, through Hoover, Ford, and General Motors in the inter-war period, to Sony, Toyota, Nissan, and Honda in the 1980s. This, however, has been a two-way process, with British-owned and managed concerns popping up in the USA, France, and Germany, suggesting that all advanced economies from time to time have entrepreneurial gaps, and benefit from imports of chief executives as well as of capital. The fact that the British economy has for long been open and receptive to such imports, but that they have not occurred on any overwhelming scale, also suggests that native British entrepreneurial deficiencies have not been so widespread and so calamitous as the pessimists would like to think.

If British businessmen have in fact become increasingly feeble since some indeterminate point in the past—as the onset of decadence virtually every decade from the 1850s to the 1960s has its advocates—the culprit cannot have been the educational system of public schools and the universities, so often seen as the great vehicle for the propagation and dissemination of gentry values and anti-business and anti-industrial attitudes, because it has simply not had the leverage to wield such awesome influence. It has not turned the sons of businessmen against their fathers' occupations, except to a marginal extent; and it supplied no more than a minority of the leading business figures until after the Second World War. A very different picture can be painted if responsibility for Britain's economic performance is laid at the feet of the state and governments, where a large share undoubtedly belongs especially since the First World War when government found responsibility for the economy thrust upon it. Until after 1979 the great majority of cabinet ministers, most of them Conservatives since they were in power for most of the time, were products of this educational system, and quite narrowly the alumni of Eton, Harrow, and Oxbridge, while almost all the civil service mandarins were Oxbridge folk, presumably all busy dispensing, consciously or unconsciously, the anti-industrial prejudices they were supposed to have imbibed.[35] The role of the state in causing, or managing, economic decline is a separate question. Meanwhile, some leading businessmen at least must have avoided contamination by the debilitating influences to which they are alleged to have been exposed, since if they had not been successful in running their own businesses against the prevailing tide of decline it would have been passing strange to call them in to tell everyone else how to conduct their affairs more effectively, in schools, the health service, local government, the universities, and the civil service.[36] And thus, in the businessman's revenge, unable to meddle directly with the public schools because they are beyond the reach of government financial control, they have clobbered the universities in the name of a plausible but mistaken theory and a piece of distorted and misleading history. It is not a course of action which is likely to rekindle the industrial spirit or encourage economic growth.

[35] For cabinet ministers (before 1955), see W. L. Guttsman, *The British Political Elite* (1963), ch. 4, tables i, ix, xii, xv, and diagram A. For top civil servants (permanent under-secretaries, 1880–1970) see Rubinstein, *Elites and the Wealthy*, tables 7.7 and 7.11.

[36] Richard Greenbury, a grammar school boy and chairman and chief executive of Marks & Spencer (which he subsequently steered into deep commercial trouble), was a Thatcher favourite for prescribing new strategies for civil service departments; while Lord Rothschild, Eton and Christ Church, was called in to sort out the Research Councils.

7

Conclusion: The Rise and Fall of Cultural Explanations of Economic Performance

Gentrification has been around for a very long time as a typical, probably *the* typical, outward expression of the upward social mobility of the wealthy in Britain. Leaving aside any question of the purely cultural gentrification of education, manners, and style, for centuries there has been a continuous process of literal, territorial, gentrification, sustained by a substantial flow of new money into landed estates and country houses, attested alike by contemporaries and historians. Recent revisionist attempts to deny this have foundered on the rocks of their own evidence. Lawrence Stone rounded off his great work of identifying and counting the owners of large country houses in three selected counties by concluding that:

During the whole 340-year period covered by this study there were only 137 men of business who bought their way into the elite in our three counties. They only amount to 6 per cent of all owners, and only a third of all purchasers, the bulk of the latter being men enriched by public office or the law. The real story of the English elite is not the symbiosis of land and business, but of land and the professions, just as in the rest of Europe.[1]

A more likely interpretation of the figures on which this resounding conclusion rests suggests that something closer to one-third than to one-twentieth of the owners of the Stones' houses in 1880 were men of business or the descendants of men of business, the end result of 340 years of gentrification.[2]

Until historians came along in the 1950s and 1960s no one thought of calling this flow of new wealth into land a 'haemorrhage of talent' or of capital, from productive into unproductive employment, for to

---

[1] Lawrence Stone and Jeanne C. Fawtier Stone, *An Open Elite? England, 1540–1880* (Oxford, 1984), 403.
[2] Ibid., table 6.2 (unpaginated). This shows that over the whole period 1579–1879 there were 157 (not 137) men of business as purchasers. The main point, however, is that while over the period 1579–1879 there may have been a total of 2,246 individuals who were or had been owners of the houses in the study—of which total 157 is indeed only 6.9 per cent—there were not 2,246 houses in the study but at the peak, in 1879, 460 houses. An unknown number of business purchasers were transients who did not have descendants among the owners alive in 1879, but not far short of one-third of those 460 houses were owned, in 1879, by business purchasers or descendants of earlier business purchasers, many of them of course long since fully assimilated into the ranks of the landed aristocracy and gentry. There is a similar critique of the Stones' '6 per cent conclusion' in Eileen Spring, 'Businessmen and Landowners Re-engaged', *Historical Research*, 72 (1999), 86–7.

contemporaries the process seemed a laudable way of marking entrepreneurial success and achievement which obviously had no deleterious effects
on an economy which continued to flourish and grow. Cobden, it is true, in
the 1850s viewed the gentrification of the millowners with its pervasive,
servile, and pernicious pseudo-aristocratic values, as a kind of social and
political haemorrhage of talent which had lured its victims away from the
true path of free trade and radicalism into political passivity and betrayal of
their class identity; but he did not see it as a sign of entrepreneurial failure
in a business sense.[3] Not until the British economy was perceived to be in
decline and people cast around for scapegoats to blame for this did anyone
begin to argue seriously that what had once been regarded as marks of
success were in fact causes of failure. The story of this reversal of attitudes
is a compelling illustration of the fallibility of cultural explanations of
economic performance, and of the influence of contemporary opinions on
historical scholarship.

For as long as Britain led the world in technology, the proliferation of new
capital and consumer goods, industrial production, international trade and
shipping, and international finance there was no good reason to worry
about the vitality of her entrepreneurs, the state of the British economy or
the vigour of its performance, apart from worries about cyclical fluctuations
and their causes. There was indeed growing concern about some of the
social consequences of economic developments, concern which was to swell
by the 1840s and 1850s into a school of thought which regarded industrialization itself as a catastrophe. G. R. Porter's *Progress of the Nation* (1836,
revised edition, 1847) was a sustained, statistical, hymn in praise of the
achievements and advances since the beginning of the century in manufactures, mining, commerce, transport, and in consumption; but it acknow-
ledged there were problems, the chief of which in Porter's view was the
woeful state of 'public education'. His assumption was that with the political will to provide for popular education already evident in 1839, the public
revenues and the economy which supported them were quite strong enough
to produce the necessary resources.[4] There was also concern, vigorously
expressed until the 1840s and only becoming muted thereafter, that some
sections of the British economy were too weak to withstand unrestricted
foreign competition: some of these, notably agriculture, but also shipping,
and the timber trade, were large, economically important, and politically
powerful sectors of the economy, while others like the silk and the glove
industries were economically almost insignificant but equally
shrill in their proclamations of weakness. All of these were regarded, by free

---

[3] See above pp. 12–15.
[4] G. R. Porter, *The Progress of the Nation* (revised edn., 1847), preface, xxii–xxiii. Given the persistent inadequacy of educational provisions in Britain one concludes that the political will has
never been firm enough to outweigh arguments about lack of resources.

traders rather then by themselves, as vested interests whose lack of effort and innovation was due to commercial policies which sheltered them from any need to become competitive, rather than to any entrepreneurial failure. Before the 1870s the only contemporary hint of entrepreneurial frailty came from the maverick free market ideologue, Samuel Laing, and then only indirectly. Laing, in his defence of philistinism and complete rejection of the utility of high culture and learning as incompatible with business enterprise, and his belief that in Britain 'there is no feeling for the fine arts, no foundation for them, no esteem for them' so that her businessmen were not diverted from the unremitting pursuit of profit, was presumably unaware that as he was writing many of the most successful business leaders in Manchester, the West Riding, Birmingham, and Glasgow were taking to collecting pictures, patronizing artists, cultivating concerts, and endowing libraries and museums. Nevertheless, he was implicitly asserting that many of Britain's most successful entrepreneurs were becoming weak and effete in the 1840s and 1850s because they were eschewing philistinism and succumbing to the cultural embrace.[5]

To be sure, there was some feeling, already being voiced in the 1830s and 1840s, that in comparison with the exuberantly optimistic enterprise and infectious, even intemperate, enthusiasm for innovations and gadgetry of American businessmen, the British—workers as well as industrialists, perhaps especially workers—were cautious, conservative, and traditionalist, wary of new methods, new technology, and new products.[6] Such observations, however, scarcely amounted to criticisms of British entrepreneurial spirit, and did not deny the overwhelming British domination of technological advances and their commercial adoption in the previous half century and more. One uneasy reflection on the Great Exhibition of 1851, otherwise a celebration of British industrial supremacy, was that the Americans had outstripped the British in the quality and range of agricultural machinery. By 1867 the British chemist Lyon Playfair reported on the Paris Exhibition of that year that 'our country had shown little inventiveness and made little progress in the peaceful arts of industry since 1862' and was being overtaken in the development of ever more complicated and self-acting machinery by the French and Germans, not to mention the Americans, a deficiency which he attribute to a lack of technical education, but not to entrepreneurial sloth.[7]

[5] B. Porter, '"Monstrous Vandalism": Capitalism and Philistinism in the Works of Samuel Laing, 1780–1868', *Albion*, 23 (1991), 265, quoting Laing, *Notes of a Traveller, on the Social and Political State of France, Prussia, Switzerland, Italy and other Parts of Europe* (1842), 485. See above p. 77.

[6] e.g. de Tocqueville in 1831, J. S. Buckingham in 1841, cited in H. J. Habakkuk, *American and British Technology in the 19th Century* (Cambridge, 1962), 112, 114.

[7] Asa Briggs, *Victorian Things* (1988), 21–2.

Some far-sighted observers had foreseen as early as the 1830s and 1840s that the USA would before long overtake Britain economically and probably become the world's leading economic power. Cobden, visiting America in 1835, had looked out across the great central plain from the summit of the Alleghanies and remarked: 'Here will one day be the head-quarters of agricultural and manufacturing industry; here will one day centre the civilization, the wealth, the power of the entire world,' an opinion confirmed on his second visit to the United States in 1858 when he was greatly impressed by the material progress made since 1835, attributing it in effect to the motive power of emulation: 'It is the universal hope of rising in the social scale,' he told Bright, 'which is the key to much of the superiority that is visible in this country.' *The Economist*, soon after its establishment, had prophesied that 'the superiority of the United States to England is ultimately as certain as the next eclipse'.[8] Such forecasts, however, related to the sheer size of the United States and its natural resources, and the easily foreseeable growth in its population, which meant that its total output, consumption, and wealth would before long surpass Britain's, and were in no way forecasts of faltering or deficient British economic performance. It was not until other countries, specifically Germany and the United States, were seen to be out-competing Britain in the markets for several products, as well as surpassing Britain in total output of basic industrial materials like coal, iron and steel, and chemicals, that the more hot-headed of contemporaries and the less level-headed historians who followed them began to talk of Britain's decline and attribute it to shortcomings in entrepreneurial performance.

This happened with the great fall in prices and profits in the 1880s and 1890s, and the emergence of potentially great new industries in electricity, telecommunications, inorganic chemicals, and motor vehicles in which Britain was decidedly not in the lead. The sense of failure and inferiority was epitomised in E. E. Williams's book *Made in Germany* published in 1896. He painted an alarmist picture of German industrial superiority and flagging British competitiveness which created panic among some contemporaries and coloured later historians' views of the whole 1870–1914 period. Describing German advances in textiles, chemicals, printing, and musical instruments—Britain had dominated the 'mass' production of pianos hitherto, to the great profit of Henry Fowler Broadwood (1811–93) and his 5,000–acre estate of Lyne in Surrey—Williams sent a chilling message to the middle classes. 'Roam the house over, and the fateful mark [giving nation of origin, required by the 1887 Merchandise Marks Act] will greet you at every turn, from the piano in your drawing room to the mug on

---

[8] Morley, *Life of Cobden*, 31, 688. *The Economist*, quot. in Asa Briggs, *The Age of Improvement* (1959), 400.

the kitchen dresser, blazoned through though it be with the legend *A Present from Margate*.' Explaining the German penetration of the British market with goods the British were accustomed to produce themselves Williams commented: 'It is all very well to run an old-established business; but you must diligently and continuously be striving to bring its methods up to date. And this is what English manufacturers fail to recognise.' Thus was the stage set for a belief in the decline of Britain and its attribution to entrepreneurial failure because of a culture of complacency and conservatism.[9]

Other commentators followed Williams's lead. One in the *Contemporary Review* in 1900, having observed that 'German goods are not only rising in value, but they oust English manufactures in every market in the world', concluded that 'the serious decline of England as a great industrial centre has begun . . . the giant is visibly exhausted, and is slackening speed . . . Nations, like man, have their exits and their entrances. England was the first to develop the "great industry", she will be the first to lose it.'[10] To a more sophisticated generation which is growing accustomed to the products of globalization the contemporary reaction of the pre-1914 generation to *Made in Germany* may seem out of proportion, even hysterical. After all if one roams round the house in the late 1990s one is likely to find 'Made in China' on almost any household appliance from a mobile phone to a folding pushchair, without concluding that China has leapt into pole position in high technology and manufacturing industry. Late twentieth-century China is taking advantage of borrowed technology, cheap and dexterous labour, and the eagerness of well-established western companies to 'outsource' the production of some of their components and the manufacture of some of their branded products. Late nineteenth-century Germany was admittedly using indigenously generated technological advances alongside borrowed technology and relatively low labour costs, but in essence was simply exhibiting the results of what later economists would term the 'convergence' of advanced economies, and in retrospect was not threatening to push Britain into an economic decline, or even to halt the continuing increase in her per capita income, let alone to reduce her to an impoverished, deindustrialized, wasteland.

Convergence, however, if they had known the term, was exactly what many late Victorian journalists and politicians feared and found unacceptable, since it implied that Britain was ceasing to be the world's leading economic power and was on the way to being simply one among a group of

---

[9] Quot. by Harold James, 'The German Experience and the Myth of British Cultural Exceptionalism', in Bruce Collins and Keith Robbins (eds.), *British Culture and Economic Decline* (1990), 94.

[10] W. Clarke, 'The Social Future of England', *Contemporary Review*, 77 (1900), quot. by Barry Supple, 'Fear of Failing: Economic History and the Decline of Britain', in Peter Clarke and Clive Trebilcock (eds.), *Understanding Decline* (Cambridge, 1997), 13–14.

more or less equals in per capita terms, which in turn signified that Britain was becoming weaker than larger and more populous countries in terms of total production and wealth, and therefore was in danger of declining as a Great Power. The shock of ceasing to be the leading power produced a search for scapegoats, as well as schemes to halt and reverse the decline under Joseph Chamberlain's banners of Imperial Preference and Tariff Reform. The scapegoats were found in the industries which were failing to adopt the latest technology; steel, chemicals, cotton, electrical goods, and coal mining were singled out as the principal culprits. The producers tended to blame unfair competition and restrictive labour practices. Commentators tended to blame the entrepreneurs, for being conservative, lethargic, averse to innovations, untutored and uninterested in technology and science, and ill-prepared to face international competition.

Thus were born, in the 1890s, the twin concepts of British economic decline and entrepreneurial failure which have been around ever since. Both have become powerful and persistent myths which have coloured, and continue to colour, much thinking about twentieth-century Britain by politicians, civil servants, educators, journalists, economists, and economic historians, and their perceptions in turn have been strong influences on policy decisions. Like all good myths these rest on a certain amount of real experience and evidence, whose significance has however become distorted and exaggerated until a travesty of the truth prevails. It is quite true that in several important branches of manufacturing industry late Victorian and Edwardian Britain was no longer in the lead either in total output or in new technology, and with a few significant exceptions such as television, earth-moving machinery, aero engines, or clockwork radios, that has continued to be so throughout the twentieth century. It is equally true that throughout this period it has been easy to find examples of incompetent, ignorant, and lethargic entrepreneurs and managers who have been indifferent to, or actively resistant to, the adoption of new methods in their firms. In all likelihood examples of such poor performers could be found in pre-1880 industries in Britain, and in any of the much praised post-1880 advanced economies of the United States, Germany, or, post-1945, Japan, since otherwise there would scarcely have been many business failures and bankruptcies in the paragon economies. Neither of these observations, however, establishes that Britain has been in economic decline ever since the 1880s, or that Britain has experienced a general, collective, and persistent attack of entrepreneurial failure.

It has been repeatedly demonstrated that over the whole period from the 1880s to the 1990s the British economy has grown, in terms of Gross National Product and of income per capita, and moreover has grown consistently at average annual rates not significantly different from those of the century and more before the 1880s. The accepted measures of growth rates, excluding the years of the two World Wars, are that 'British Gross Domestic Product grew at about 2 per cent annually between 1873 and 1913, at a little over 2 per cent between 1924 and 1937, and at almost 3 per cent between 1951 and 1973.'[11] The remainder of the decade of the 1970s, 1973–9, saw a disastrous and unprecedented fall in the growth rate to almost nothing, an experience with dramatic effects on perceptions and subsequent government policies, but taking the period 1960–79 as a whole the British growth rate was sustained at a little over 2 per cent annually, as it was also in the period 1979–89 when supposedly radical new pro-enterprise policies were adopted.[12] In the first half of the nineteenth century the annual growth rate had been between 2 and 3 per cent, but had begun to decline from 1860 onwards; while in the hundred years before 1800 it had probably been well below 1 per cent until starting to increase in the 1780s.[13] Thus in the long run, over the last two hundred years, Britain has sustained a remarkably stable rate of economic growth, never very high in terms of international comparisons, and never very low either, and clearly not indicative of either decline or failure.

This broadly constant growth curve is the product of the divergent experiences of different sectors of the economy, the prolonged decline of the agricultural sector for one thing, and more importantly the decline since the 1950s in the contribution of industry, both extractive and manufacturing, to the Gross National Product, and the rise in relative importance of the service sector. This has provided a cue for one draconian solution of the problem of 'British decline', Professor Rubinstein's iconoclastic argument that Britain never was an industrial economy, never embraced industrialism, but always was essentially a commercial and financial economy (akin to the seventeenth-century Dutch economy), and hence that there is no 'loss of industrial spirit' to explain.[14] Such a courageous and decisive cutting of a Gordian knot which has puzzled generations of politicians, journalists, and historians, commands admiration more than assent. It rests on the somewhat fragile foundation of Rubinstein's demonstration that more extremely large individual fortunes have consistently been made in banking, finance, and commerce than in industry, by men whose businesses operated from London addresses rather than addresses in provincial industrial centres. This observation may tell us little more than that lucky openings for abnormal profits were more numerous in banking, finance, and commerce than in

---

[11] Supple, 'Fear of Failing', 10.

[12] Simon Szreter, 'British Economic Decline and Human Resources,' in Clarke and Trebilcock, *Understanding Decline*, 96.

[13] N. C. R. Crafts, 'The Eighteenth Century: A Survey', in Roderick Floud and Donald McCloskey, *The Economic History of Britain since 1700*, 2 vols. (Cambridge, 1981), i, 2; R. C. Floud, 'Britain 1860–1914: A Survey', ii, 7.

[14] W. D. Rubinstein, *Capitalism Culture and Decline in Britain, 1750–1990* (1993), *passim*.

industry, and that industry was more strongly competitive than the other sectors, thus limiting the possibilities of individual aggrandisement. It tells us nothing about the aggregate amount of personal wealth generated in the different sectors, nor about the relative importance of the sectors. Indeed, when all analyses of the sectoral distribution of British national income show that the industrial sector (extractive and manufacturing) has been consistently larger than the commercial and financial sector ever since 1688, and has been easily the single largest sector of the economy from the 1820s, when agriculture was dethroned from its previously dominant position, to the 1970s, it would seem hard to sustain the view that Britain has never been an industrial economy.[15] The people who honoured Arkwright and Peel, Stephenson and Brunel, treasured the Rocket and the Great Eastern, and celebrated their technological prowess in the Great Exhibition, had every reason to be called 'The First Industrial Nation', and their pride in later industrial achievements from turbines to jet engines, from Flying Scotsman to QE II, from Forth Bridge to Severn Bridge, abundantly confirmed their acceptance of industrialism.

Simple denial of the existence of a British industrial economy does not, therefore, satisfactorily dispose of the question of decline. If any well-informed person is obliged to concede that there has been no absolute decline in British economic performance, and that the living standards of ordinary citizens have risen dramatically in the twentieth century, especially since 1945, this has not stopped many commentators, historians, and politicians wringing their hands over Britain's decline relative to other countries. The fact that Britain had been overtaken by the United States before 1914 in national income and in income per head, a superiority decisively reinforced as a result of the First World War, did not arouse any strong feeling that this was a consequence of British economic weakness which potentially could be reversed by a more dynamic and efficient performance; that is at least until the 1940s when British purchasing agents visiting American aircraft and munitions factories became convinced not merely of the superiority of American productivity but also of the comparative inefficiency of British production methods and the deficiencies of British industrial managers. To be overtaken by Germany was a different matter, and even though in the crucial measure of income per head, which measures living standards, Britain remained ahead until the 1960s, Britain was dropping steadily behind in Gross National Product before 1914, which measures the country's economic muscle, and this was freely ascribed to entrepreneurial failure at the time and by historians when they turned their minds to the subject in the 1960s.[16]

---

[15] Phyllis Deane and W. A. Cole, *British Economic Growth, 1688–1959* (Cambridge, 1962), 156, 161, 166–7, 175, 178, 180–1.

[16] Figures for real national income per capita for USA, Britain, France, West Germany, and Japan, for 1950–91, in Harold Perkin, *The Third Revolution* (1996), table 1.1. The development

Initially the favourite explanation for entrepreneurial failure in the thirty years before 1914 was the education system or lack of it in comparison with the much-praised German one, which it was claimed produced an abundant supply of science and technology graduates sensitive to the opportunities for adopting new technologies and starting new industries.[17] The strength of British trade unions and their restrictive practices, however, gave entrepreneurial failure a close race in the favoured explanations of poor performance before 1914. By way of contrast, in the inter-war period there was not so much talk of British economic decline, since although the United States was clearly forging ahead in the 1920s and confirming her position as the world's major economic power, the economies of the other countries which had fought in the First World War were in varying degrees of trouble, and in the 1930s particularly the British economy outshone them all.[18] Instead of economic decline and general entrepreneurial failure attention in Britain was focused on the problems of long-term unemployment, over valuation of sterling, institutional restraints on domestic investment, and the predicament—admittedly substantially composed of obstinate and stupid managers—of the declining industrial giants like coal and cotton. During the Second World War, and in the astonishing post-1945 recovery, the performance of the economy was widely thought to have been most impressive, far removed from decline and decadence. Then in the 1960s the German, Japanese, and French economies began to overtake the British not merely in total GNP but also in GNP per head, the British economy faltered and was held to have contracted 'the British disease', and the end of Empire added to the woes of the governing class. The labels 'Made in England' and 'Made in Britain' came to be associated with old-fashioned design, poor quality, and unreliability, and a mood of pessimism and despair descended on many of the chattering classes.

The result was that economic historians went off to look for deep-seated causes of the malaise of the economy in the supposedly critical climacteric of 1870 to 1914, while some of the less academic intelligentsia looked for long-term causes of decline in British institutions and culture. The first wave of historians to return from inspecting the records of British economic performance between 1870 and 1914 reported discoveries of inefficiency and incompetence which confirmed the opinions of the late Victorian and Edwardian economic journalists. Their conclusions on the decisive

from the 1960s of the debate on entrepreneurial failure and relative decline in the rate of economic growth is admirably treated in Peter Payne's essay, 'Entrepreneurship and British Economic Decline', in Collins and Robbins, *British Culture and Economic Decline*, 25–58.

[17] e.g. F. A. McKenzie, *The American Invaders* (1902); A. Shadwell, *Industrial Efficiency*, 2 vols. (1906); or Herbert Gray and Samuel Turner, *Eclipse or Empire?* (1916), cited by Payne, 'Entrepreneurship and British Economic Decline', 42.

[18] David Landes, *The Unbound Prometheus* (Cambridge, 1969), 391.

contribution of entrepreneurial failure to this outcome were most forcefully and persuasively expressed by Derek Aldcroft in his 1964 article on 'The Entrepreneur and the British Economy, 1870–1914'.[19] Entrepreneurial sluggishness and lethargy, dogged attachment to traditional and obsolete machinery and technology, and an indifference or outright hostility to science and research matched only by an arrogant neglect of the needs of export customers, were among the chief features revealed in this analysis of decline. In explaining why entrepreneurs had all of a sudden become so unentrepreneurial and so incapable in the pursuit of profits there was some dalliance with the notion that preceding success and affluence bred apathy and indolence towards business and enthusiasm for landed estates and gentry status, but Aldcroft veered away from this approach towards a cultural interpretation in favour of placing prime emphasis on deficiencies in technical education, the disadvantages of an early start in industrialization, the imperfections of British financial institutions, the drawbacks of a business structure dominated by small, generally family, firms, and the sheer traditionalism of the British people.

Aldcroft's classic article ended, however, with the classic academic ploy of admitting that 'much further research is required into the history of individual firms and industries before a final judgment can be passed.'[20] In due course a second wave of historians descended on the records of individual firms, and industries, and emerged proclaiming that by and large business records contained no evidence of entrepreneurial failure and on the contrary showed that entrepreneurs made sensible and rational decisions in the context of the market conditions, the labour and capital costs, and the technology appropriate to those conditions. This body of work was summarized by L. G. Sandberg in 1981, who concluded that

it is unfavourable to the hypothesis of 'entrepreneurial failure'. While some examples of 'technological backwardness' and other types of failure have been found . . . it is not established that the failure rate was any higher than in other countries, including the United States and Germany, during the same period [1870–1914] or than in Britain during earlier periods. Much less has it been shown that British 'entrepreneurial failures' in this period exceeded those in Germany and America by so much that they can materially have contributed to Britain's relative economic decline.[21]

---

[19] D. H. Aldcroft, 'The Entrepreneur and the British Economy, 1870–1914', *Economic History Review* 2nd ser., 17 (1964), 113–34.   [20] Ibid., 134.

[21] L. G. Sandberg, 'The Entrepreneur and Technological Change,' in Roderick Floud and Donald McCloskey (eds.), *The Economic History of Britain since 1700*, 2 vols. (Cambridge, 1981), ii, 119. The robust and influential refutation of the notion of entrepreneurial failure pre-1914 is in Donald McCloskey, 'Did Victorian Britain Fail?', *Economic History Review* 2nd ser., 23 (1970), 446–59, and, on one of the key industries, his book *Economic Maturity and Entrepreneurial Decline: British Iron and Steel, 1870–1913* (Cambridge, Mass., 1973).

With a deft movement of the goalposts entrepreneurial failure re-entered serious discourse later in the 1980s, notably in the work of Bernard Elbaum and William Lazonick in which the evidence of the entrepreneurial failure of British businessmen is that they failed 'to confront institutional constraints innovatively'.[22] This defined entrepreneurial failure as the failure of businessmen to have the imagination, vision, and daring or recklessness to jettison established and profitable methods of organization and production in favour of radically different and possibly more profitable methods; this was something very different from the previously accepted definitions, although it was admittedly attractive in according prime importance to more dynamically enterprising qualities than those of simple business competence. Peter Payne, in his 1990 survey of 'Entrepreneurship and British Economic Decline', while inclined to accept some of the force of the Elbaum and Lazonick view, concludes that the chief reasons for the British economy performing below expectation, especially since 1945, lie not in entrepreneurial failure but

first, [in] the inability of the British educational system to supply suitably trained middle management skills, applied scientists, production engineers and cost accountants; and second, [in] a labour force reluctant to accept and accommodate to change, the inevitable consequences of unimaginative labour-management relations over past decades . . .[23]

Under the impact of the dire performance of the British economy, particularly of the industrial sector, in the 1970s, when relative decline threatened to turn into absolute decline at the time of the three-day week, the debate about decline and entrepreneurial ineptitude spilled over from the comparatively dispassionate investigations of the academics into the partisan and polemical world of contemporary analysts, media pundits, journalist-historians, and thinking-politicians, all eager to provide instant diagnoses of the 'British disease' and prescriptions for its cure. In their haste to find deep-seated causes and to peddle their nostrums the findings of the careful scholarly work on the performance of the economy between 1870 and 1914, and the complexities of assessing the contributions of entrepreneurs and managers to that performance, were ignored or brushed aside. This was unfortunate, for even a nodding acquaintance with the historians' findings would have convinced even the most impetuous of the new radical brigade that there were considerable difficulties in advancing interpretations of British 'decline' which predicated causes that were operative before 1914, let alone before 1870.

[22] Bernard Elbaum and William Lazonick (eds.), *The Decline of the British Economy* (Oxford, 1986), 2.   [23] Payne, 'Entrepreneurship and British Economic Decline', 46.

Thus, ignoring this obstacle to grand theorizing about Britain's fall from mid-Victorian grace, the 'British disease' which hitherto, in the 1960s, had been pictured in terms of wretched industrial relations, excessive trade union power, low labour productivity, and poor and unreliable quality of manufactured goods, was redefined as primarily the outcome of incompetent and inefficient management, and lack of vigorous enterprise, which in turn were reflections of an ingrained anti-business, anti-enterprise culture. Anthony Sampson's *Anatomy of Britain* (1962) had paved the way for a cultural explanation of the 'British disease' by depicting the ruling elites in church and state, in Conservative and Labour parties, in civil service and universities, in trade unions and big business, as old-fashioned, ill-informed, class-ridden, out of touch with the modern world of high technology, and incapable of halting Britain's slide towards second class status. The cultural explanation of Britain's predicament was developed during the 1970s by journalists like Tom Nairn, columnist-historians like Corelli Barnett, economists like G. C. Allen, and politicians like Keith Joseph, who announced in 1975 that

Britain never really internalized capitalist values, if the truth be known . . . For four centuries the rich man's aim was to get away from the background of trade—later industry—in which he had made his wealth and power. Rich and powerful people founded landed-gentry families; the capitalist's son was educated not in capitalist values but against them, in favour of the older values of army, church, upper civil service, professions, and landowning.[24]

Just so. For a front-bench Tory to turn against the values of army, church, professions, and landowning was in itself a cultural revolution, a foretaste of the unleashing of the full Thatcherite fury at all enemies of the enterprise culture.

It was also an identification of gentrification as the engine of the anti-business culture and hence a foretaste as well of the full-blooded exposure of aristocratic and gentry culture as being responsible for the decline of the industrial spirit since 1850 in Martin Wiener's 1981 book. That, *English Culture and the Decline of the Industrial Spirit, 1850–1980*, became a cult book of the 1980s, in business schools, think tanks, and newspaper offices, as well as in government circles, and its message was influential in policy-making in the Thatcher government, not least towards the universities, which were regarded as the chief seedbeds of the anti-business attitudes. At least, since even a radicalized Conservative government dedicated to the benign rule of market forces could not have the face or force to attempt to

---

[24] Sir Keith Joseph, *Reversing the Trend: A Critical Re-Appraisal of Conservative Economic and Social Policies* (1975), 60; G. C. Allen, *The British Disease* (1976); articles in the weeklies by Nairn (1970, 1979) and Corelli Barnett (1975), cited in Raven, 'British History and the Enterprise Culture', 186, 189.

curb the propensity of the wealthy to acquire the symbols of gentrification, land and country houses, or to interfere with the public schools, which in the Wiener view were prime culprits in inculcating anti-business values, the universities, which were vulnerable to government control because of their financial dependence on taxpayers' money, had perforce to be paraded as the main anti-business villains. In the process of emasculating the universities and undermining their standing as world-class centres of excellence Keith Joseph, by now Secretary of State for Education, admonished the universities in 1985 'to be concerned with attitudes to the world outside higher education, and in particular to industry and commerce, and to beware of "anti-business" snobbery. The entrepreneurial spirit is essential for the maintenance and improvement of employment'.[25]

This, from a government which had just managed to wipe out nearly one-third of manufacturing industry and double the number of the unemployed, through its interest rate, taxation, budgetary, and exchange rate measures, was little short of brazen effrontery. It was not Wiener's fault that his thesis was believed and acted upon by doctrinaire politicians to whom it was a godsend in furnishing respectable intellectual and historical support for their free market, monetarist, ideology and its accompanying enterprise culture mantra. His mistake was to construct his thesis on the unreliable foundations of selective quotations from literary sources and an unfortunate belief that history started in 1850: gentrification, emulation of gentry manners and values, and denunciation and denigration of businessmen—merchants rather than industrialists, since there were few of those before the early nineteenth century—in contemporary literature had been going on for centuries before 1850, and it would be perverse in the extreme to claim to detect evidence of faltering or declining industrial (or entrepreneurial) spirit in those years of the making of 'the first industrial nation'. Moreover the insularity of the Wiener thesis precluded mention of the fact that Germany's much lauded industrial vigour in the second half of the nineteenth century was accompanied by criticisms and denunciations of the crass materialism of businessmen by the German intelligentsia and literary community every bit as vehement as anything Wiener discovered in his English sources.[26]

[25] Quot. by Keith Robbins, 'British Culture versus British Industry', in Collins and Robbins (eds.), *British Culture and Economic Decline*, 3.

[26] There is an excellent guide to the extensive critical outpouring occasioned by Wiener's book in Raven, 'British History and the Enterprise Culture'. The most potent exposés of the bias in the selection of literary sources, and of the anti-business elements in German nineteenth-century literature, are to be found in Neil McKendrick, ' "Gentlemen and Players" Revisited: The Gentlemanly Ideal, The Business Ideal and the Professional Ideal in English Literary Culture', in id. and R. B. Outhwaite (eds.), *Business Life and Public Policy; Essays in honour of D. C. Coleman* (Cambridge, 1986); J. M. Winter, 'Bernard Shaw, Bertold Brecht and the Businessman in Literature', ibid.; and Harold James, 'The German Experience and the Myth of British Cultural Exceptionalism', in Collins and Robbins, *British Culture and Economic Decline*.

For a while the Wiener diagnosis was endorsed, and embraced, by some seriously professional if not historically alert scholars, such as Ralph Dahrendorf in his 1982 book *On Britain*, in which one chapter is devoted to 'The Vanishing of the Industrial Spirit'; and David Marquand, a serious historian if not an economic historian, who regurgitated a substantial part of Wiener in condensed form for readers of *The Times* as soon as the book was published, affirming

that one of the main reasons for Britain's failure to keep pace with competing econ-omies is that, for more than a century our elite culture has been anti-entrepreneurial, anti-industrial and, in a professional sense, anti-productive—esteeming the tasteful consumption of wealth, but disparaging its creation and creators. In that culture, talking and writing have consistently ranked higher than making or selling; know-ledge without obvious utility higher than knowledge with it. Hence the paradox of an industrial society rich in Nobel prize winners, but starved of technological inno-vation; rich in talented civil servants but starved of trained managers; rich in theo-rists of the business cycle, but starved of thrusting businessmen. And hence, of course, the creeping de-industrialization which now threatens to turn the relative economic decline of the last 100 years into absolute decline.[27]

This was little short of *traison des clercs* for one who lived by writing which imparted knowledge without obvious utility. Quite soon, however, criti-cisms and refutations had replaced endorsements in the academic journals and university textbooks; and in politics within a couple of years Mrs Thatcher had latched on to 'Victorian Values' as a key plank in her Party's platform, values which, however imperfectly understood as actual historical expressions of the beliefs and standards of any specific set of Victorians, were decidedly thought to include self-help and enterprise, thrift and pru-dence, values not closely associated with the gentry culture which Wiener thought was becoming increasingly dominant at the time, but consistent with a thriving industrial spirit which he had argued was declining.[28]

Very sensibly Martin Wiener did not continue with depictions of the decline of the industrial spirit or attempt to defend his version of English culture from the criticisms and attacks which it excited, but instead re-established his credentials as a distinguished historian by cultivating a completely different set of interests in crime and punishment in late Victorian Britain. Correlli Barnett, whose historical diagnoses of British decline were if anything even more important than Martin Wiener's in influencing the opinions and pol-icies of right-wing intellectuals and thinking politicians in the 1970s and 1980s, was not so prudent, and in his sustained efforts to pin down the rea-sons for British decline inadvertently revealed the essentially subjective,

[27] *The Times*, 3 Sept. 1981, 10, quot. in McKendrick, ' "Gentlemen and Players" Revisited', 101.

[28] James Walvin, *Victorian Values* (1987) and T. C. Smout (ed.), *Victorian Values*, Proceedings of the British Academy, 78 (Oxford, 1992) provide the best introduction to this subject.

polemical, and ever-changing nature of the cultural explanations.[29] Correlli Barnett started his career as a military historian, with his 1963 history of French, German, and British First World War generals and admirals, *The Swordbearers*. While announcing that 'the theme of this book is the decisive effect of individual human character on history', he also claimed that the war revealed 'French economic and social obsolescence . . . [and] British industrial decay', and his main conclusion was not that particular individuals like Jellicoe had a decisive influence on the course of events, but that the naval defeat at Jutland (as he chose to regard it) was due to the deficiences of Britsh naval equipment, themselves a reflection of 'the general obsolescence of British technology before 1914'. Indeed, moving a long way from the original intention of showing the impact of individuals on events, Barnett foreshadowed exposures of systemic weaknesses in the fabric of British society going much deeper than mere military and naval shortcomings. 'The social and intellectual values of industrial society never ousted those of the aristocracy' among the officer corps, he announced; and more sweeping still he concluded that:

The general British decadence had the same roots as the defeat at Jutland—the propogation of social and emotional values unrelated to the hard facts of power and survival. The superiority of the gentleman over the industrialist was accepted, as was that of the arts over science, of status, right and tradition over function . . . The children of the middle classes, who in Germany emerged as the new type of industrial leader, in Britain went off to rule the Indians . . . There was thus nothing accidental . . . in what happened at Jutland, nor in what happened in the forty-odd years after Jutland. It was part of a vast process of dissolution that began about 1870.[30]

In 1972, with *The Collapse of British Power*, he moved a stage beyond military failings towards a more general theory of persistent weaknesses in British political and commercial leadership before 1939 as being responsible for Britain's decline as a Great Power. The argument now was that a predominant streak of ruthless hardness in the national character was necessary if Great Power status was to be sustained, and that this had been disastrously eroded by the combination of public schools and Christianity. 'The public school was the instrument that turned the *arriviste* middle classes into "gentlemen", in whose scale of snobbery imperial or public service or the professions were the only careers for brilliant men,' he maintained; while 'by 1870 evangelical Christianity, like a clove of spiritual garlic, had permeated British life' with dire effects on ruthlessness and

[29] For assessments of the influence of Correlli Barnett's views see Rubinstein, *Capitalism, Culture and Decline*, 18–19; Peter Clarke, 'Keynes, New Jerusalem, and British Decline', in Clarke and Trebilcock, *Understanding Decline*, 145, 151–3; David Cannadine, 'Apocalypse When?', ibid., 276–7.   [30] Correlli Barnett, *The Swordbearers* (1963), Author's Preface and pp. 181–8.

enterprise.[31] By 1975, as a columnist, he was trying out this general theory of weakness and decline, by following the fashionable trend away from ascribing most of Britain's ills to overmighty trade unions and ungovernable workers towards arguing that 'the English disease is not the novelty of the past 10 or even 20 years . . . but a phenomenon dating back more than a century' to the pernicious influence of Dr Arnold on the public school ethos.[32] This article was a prelude to his full-scale historical account of the descent of Britain, *The Audit of War* (1986), which became one of the most influential books of the 1980s. *The Audit of War* is concerned largely with the Second World War and the alleged technological backwardness, incompetence, and inefficiency of the British war economy and arms industries in comparison with the German, and with the aftermath of the war.

The origins of this backwardness, however, are firmly anchored in Dr Arnold, the Victorian public schools and their indoctrination of the sons of engineers, merchants, and manufacturers with anti-business values in the process of turning them out as Christian gentlemen, and in the Victorian nonconformist chapels which taught the working classes to disparage material comfort and possessions in favour of rewards in the next world.[33] No matter that this observation sat uneasily with the shortsighted self-interest of workers pursuing higher wages without reference to competitiveness or productivity, for Barnett was mainly concerned to explain the post-1945 decline of Britain from world power status to fourteenth place in the league table of the world's industrial nations in terms of the spread of a dependency culture and the rise of the nanny state. This, he argued, was because Britain had thrown away the opportunity of reconstruction and modernization at the end of the Second World War and instead had set up a welfare state which had turned the British people into 'a segregated, subliterate, unskilled, unhealthy and institutionalised proletariat hanging on the nipple of state maternalism'.[34] The wartime planning of the welfare state he managed to ascribe to a coterie of wishy-washy Christians—Beveridge at their head [who was not a Christian], William Temple [archbishop of Canterbury], Hugh Dalton [an atheist whose father had been an Anglican dean], Harold Laski [a Jew], and others—who hatched the blueprints while everyone else was preoccupied with winning the war; and their paternalistic Christianity was traced back to the assumed humanitarian collectivism of Victorian Christianity. This historical linking of Victorian values, the alleged paternalism of the Victorian poor law, and the Christian gentleman ideal of Victorian public schools with the origins of the post-1945 welfare state was

---

[31] Correlli Barnett, *The Collapse of British Power* (1972), 23, 43, 96.
[32] Id., 'Obsolence—and Dr Arnold', *Sunday Telegraph*, 26 Jan. 1975, quot. by Wiener, *English Culture*, 3.   [33] Id., *The Audit of War* (1986), 213–33.
[34] Ibid., 304.

highly contrived and superficial.[35] In effect Corelli Barnett was unsuccessfully trying to splice together as cultural explanations of an assumed century of decline the gentry culture and its assumed anti-business values, the dependency culture and its assumed anti-work values, and welfarism and its assumed ruinous costliness.

In further pursuit of the reasons for Britain's failure to grasp the opportunity of modernizing her industrial structure and production methods at the end of the Second World War, in 1995 Correlli Barnett produced *The Lost Victory*. This was a recapitulation and extension of *The Audit of War*. The deeply damaging, ruinously expensive, and inherently vain pursuit of the New Jerusalem of the welfare state remained the prime cause of Britain's poor performance, coupled with the overstretch of attempting to sustain a world role that was beyond her resources—ironically in the early 1990s this was known, approvingly, as 'punching above one's weight' by members of the anti-welfare state party. The new departure was to add to these causes of the allegedly wasted years of 1945–50 the insidious and pernicious influence of Keynes and Keynesian economics. The ending of mass unemployment, Barnett argued, was one of the key elements of the vision of New Jerusalem; Keynes had provided the theory for attaining full employment, and post-war governments pledged themselves to achieve full employment through Keynesian manipulation of aggregate demand; experience had shown 'the pervasive harm of full employment' which sucked up taxpayers' money, fuelled inflation, and diverted attention from the real structural and managerial problems of the economy, 'which could not be cured, only temporarily masked, by turning up the Keynesian burner under the economy as a whole'.[36]

By the 1990s it was of course quite normal in right-wing and monetarist circles to dance on Keynes's grave and proclaim the errors and fallacies of Keynesian economics, not uncommonly, as in Correlli Barnett's case, misunderstanding and misquoting Keynes in the process. In the context of the present discussion of cultural explanations of Britain's economic performance, however, the significant feature of *The Lost Victory* is the shift in emphasis away from deep-seated, long-term, and essentially socio-cultural causes (soft-centred, social-conscience, Christianity and ingrained working-class anti-capitalism) and towards 'false' economic theory, essentially the work of one influential individual. There are many common threads in these four books, notably the reiterated denunciations of public schools and

---

[35] See esp. José Harris, 'Enterprise and Welfare States: A Comparative Perspective', *TRHS*, 5th ser., 40 (1990), esp. pp. 183–191; and id., 'Victorian Values and the Founders of the Welfare State', in Smout (ed.), *Victorian Values*, esp. pp. 166–8, 181.

[36] Quotations from Correlli Barnett, *The Lost Victory* (1995) in Peter Clarke, 'Keynes, New Jerusalem, and British Decline', 145–6, 151; Clarke's chapter shows that Barnett's interpretation, and criticisms, of Keynes are based on a series of misunderstandings of the documentary evidence.

evangelical Christianity, and it is possible, even if not probable, that one out of the troop of Barnett Mark 1, Mark 2, Mark 3, or Mark 4 is a credible and verifiable explanation of the 'decline of Britain', should it be admitted that the relative decline of Britain in the last one hundred, or the last fifty, years has been greater than it need or ought to have been in the light of the resources, talents, and opportunities available to the British economy. The key feature, however, is not the 'truth' of any one explanation, but the demonstration of the ease with which different versions of cultural and ideological explanations of the same set of developments can be aired, influenced by the current intellectual-political opinions and preoccupations of the moment.

The erratic, inconsistent, and subjective nature of these cultural interpretations is even more starkly revealed by the way in which the appeal to 'Victorian values' can lead in the Correlli Barnett version directly to the vain pursuit of the new Jerusalem, the nanny state, the dependency culture, and catastrophic economic decline, and in the Margaret Thatcher version to the reinstatement of the virtues of prudence, thrift, self-help, and the enterprise culture, renewed vigorous economic growth and the complete antithesis of the nanny state.[37] Similarly, while the admired 'enterprise culture' of Victorians dedicated to self-help and self-improvement could lead some devotees to great feats of entrepreneurial dynamism and individual achievement which propelled the economy ever onward and upward, other devotees chose to demonstrate their achievement by ploughing back their material rewards into the physical and educational manifestations of the gentry culture which propelled the economy ever downward. In truth, culture is a fickle guide, so flexible, anxious to please, and so easily moulded to suit any one of a range of preconceptions, that it is unwise for historians to trust it beyond the limits of independent corroboration from other types of more objective witnesses. As for gentrification, it is clear that it has occurred over the last two centuries and more, and is currently still occurring. It has taken several forms, and those which are purely a question of education, manners, and lifestyle are scarcely amenable to definitive measurement, although the strong impression is that at least they have had no overwhelming anti-industrial or anti-business effects. Landed gentrification, the 'basic' form, can be measured, albeit not perfectly; over the centuries the appetite of new men for land has varied not so much in intensity as in the quantities of land to which individuals have aspired, as the motives for its acquisition have shifted since the 1880s from ambitions to join the old-established landed elite to indulgence in personal desires for country living, country sports, and local status. At no point, however, would it appear to have had any pronounced effects on the performance of the national economy or on the overall economic

---

[37] Harris, 'Victorian Values', 166.

performance of the gentrified new men, being in some hands an incentive to accumulative efforts and in others a disincentive, while on balance it is seen to have been a derivative of individual achievement and aspiration more than a determinant of economic advance or decline.

New Men of Wealth and the Purchase of Landed Estates

1. MILLIONAIRES DYING BETWEEN 1809 AND 1893

Crawshay, Richard, 1739–1810, ironmaster; grandson William II, 1788–1867, bought Caversham Park, Oxfordshire, 1,500 acres, £3,175 p.a. (1873).

Rundell, Philip, 1754–1827, goldsmith, (childless); nephew Joseph Neeld bought Grittleton, Wilts., estate, worth £11,260 (1856).

Peel, Sir Robert, 1750–1830, cottontot, bought Tamworth, Staffs.; in all 9,923 acres, worth £24,532 p.a. (1878).

Hollond, William, d. 1836, EIC servant; eldest son inherited, and enlarged by purchase, Benhall, Suffolk; in all 4,243 acres, worth £6,071 p.a. (1878).

Rothschild, Nathan M., 1777–1836, banker, purchased Gunnersbury Park, Middx., worth £4,782 p.a. (1884).

Arkwright, Richard, 1755–1843, cottontot, purchased Hampton Court, Hereford, 10,559 acres, worth £14,972 p.a. (1878).

Denison William J., 1770–1849, banker, purchased Denbies, Surrey, and East Riding estate; in all, including subsequent purchases by nephew, 52,655 acres, worth £67,876 p.a. (1878).

Cubitt, Thomas, 1788–1855, builder, purchased Denbies, Surrey; 6,789 acres worth, £8,509 p.a. (1883).

Morrison, James, 1789–1857, merchant banker, purchased Basildon Park, Berks.; Scottish grouse moors and deer forest; in all 74,518 acres, worth £29,369 p.a. (1878).

Miles, Philip J., d. 1846, Bristol merchant, purchased Leigh Court, Somerset, and Kingsweston, Glos.; in all *c.* 8,600 acres, worth *c.* £15, 900 p.a. (1878).

Goldsmid, Sir Isaac L., 1778–1859, bullion broker, purchased St John's Lodge, Regent's Park, and Wick House, nr. Brighton; eldest son purchased Rendcomb Park, Glos.; in all 7,120 acres, worth £31,501 p.a. (1878).

Dunbar, Duncan, 1804–62, shipowner, childless; built London town house, Porchester Terrace; *no country estate.*

Baird, William, 1796–1864, ironmaster, purchased Elie House, Fife, 3,575 acres, worth £8,815 p.a. (1878).

Gurney, Hudson, 1775–1864, banker, purchased Keswick Hall, Norfolk, 6,864 acres, worth £8,965 p.a. (1878).

Thornton, Richard, 1776–1865, Baltic merchant, underwriter, purchased Cannon Hilll, Merton, Surrey, with *c.* 136 acres, childless; nephew owned Streatham Hall, Exeter, with land worth £1,684 p.a. (1878).

Crawshay, William, 1788–1867, ironmaster; see Crawshay, Richard, 1739–1810. This Crawshay purchased Caversham, Oxon.

Eyres, Samuel, 1793–1868, woollen manufacturer; sole heiress purchased Dumbleton Hall, Glos; in all 4,183 acres, worth £6,274 p.a. (1883).

Guinness, Sir Benjamin L., 1798–1868, brewer, purchased Ashford, Co. Galway; in all 23, 885 acres, worth £10,966 p.a. (1878).

Scott, Samuel, 1807–69, banker; father, Sir Samuel, purchased Sundridge Park, Kent; he, younger son, added to it—800 acres, worth £4,050 p.a. (1883)—Scott family estates extended to 60,723 acres, worth £9,802 p.a. by 1883.,

Fielden, Thomas, 1791–1869, cottontot, purchased Greenbank, Caton Green, Lancs., childless; heirs were three nephews; one purchased Grimston Park, Yorks W.R., 3,379 acres, worth £9,000 P.A. (1878), another purchased Nutfield Priory, Surrey, and Beachamwell, Norfolk, in all 5,224 acres, worth £5,708n p.a. (1878).

Forman, William H., 1794–1869, ironmaster, childless; heir, nephew, Alexander Henry Browne, purchased Spindleston, Bamburgh, and Callaly Castle, Alnwick, Northumberland; in all 5,797 acres, worth £7,162 p.a. (1883).

Brassey, Thomas, 1805–70, railway contractor; eldest son, Thomas, purchased Normanhurst, Sussex, 3,617 acres, worth £4,102 p.a. (1873); second son, Henry Arthur, purchased Preston Hall, Kent, 4,061 acres, worth £11,253 p.a. (1883); third son, Albert, purchased Heythrop House, Oxon., 4,275 acres, worth £5,100 p.a. (1883).

Loder, Giles, 1786–1871, Russia merchant, purchased small estate in Wilts., worth £1,870 p.a. (1871); eldest son purchased Whittlebury, Northants, in all 10,241 acres, worth £11,527 p.a. (1883).

Baxter, Sir David, 1793–1872, linen manufacturer, purchased Kilmaron Castle, Fife, and Kincaldrum, Forfar; in all 4,248 acres, worth £3,906 p.a. (1878).

Baring, Thomas, 1800–73, banker, purchased Norman's Court, Hants., 8,673, acres, worth £6,886 p.a. (1878).

Wright, Francis, 1806–73, ironmaster, rebuilt Osmaston Manor, Derbyshire, and extended family estate to 6,000 acres, worth £12,052 p.a. (1873).

Glyn, George C., 1797–1873, (Lord Wolverton) banker, purchased Stanmore property (356 acres), and Iwerne Minster, Dorset (completed by eldest son), c.3,500 acres, worth £3,957 p.a. (1888).

Rothschild, Baron Mayer A., 1818–74, banker, purchased Mentmore, Bucks., 4,500 acres, worth £9,289 p.a. (1877).

Langworthy, Edward R., 1796–1874, cottontot, childless; fortune divided between wife, brother, and 14 nephews and nieces; *no country estate.*

Love, Joseph, 1795–1875, colliery owner, childless, purchased and built Mount Beaulah, Co. Durham (later, known as Springwell House, then as St Leonard's School), c. 150 acres; *no country estate.*

Rothschild, Sir Anthony N., 1810–76, banker, purchased Aston Clinton, Bucks., extended house, twice, built model village.

Baird, James, 1802–76, ironmaster, purchased Cambusdoon, Ayr., 20,000 acres, Inverie House, Knoydart, 60,000 acres, Auchendrane and Muirkirk, Ayr.; in all 85,578 acres, worth £14,800 p.a. (1878).

Heywood, John P. 1803–77, banker, purchased Cloverley, Salop, 4,049 acres, worth £7,048 p.a. (1878).

de Stern, Viscount David, 1807–77, banker, purchased Bolney, Sussex, 601 acres, worth £709 p.a. (1877); eldest son purchased Hengrave Hall, Suffolk.

Goldsmid, Sir Francis H., 1808–78, bullion broker, purchased Rendcomb Park, Glos.; see his father, Goldsmid, Sir Isaac L., 1778–1859.

Penn, John, 1805–78, naval engineering, lived at The Cedars, Lee, Kent, fortune divided equally among 4 sons and 2 daughters; *no country estate.*

West, Richard T., 1813–78, East India merchant, purchased Streatham Hall, nr. Exeter, worth £1,684 p.a. (1878).

Rothschild, Lionel N., 1808–79, banker, purchased Tring Park, Herts., Halton, Bucks., etc.; in all 15,378 acres, worth £28,901 p.a. (1878).

Mills, John R., 1797–1879, silk manufacturer, purchased Kingswood Lodge, Kent, Clermont, Norfolk, and inherited father's purchases, Tolmers, Herts., etc.; in all 15,756 acres, worth £21,261 p.a. (1878).

Crawshay, Robert T., 1817–79, ironmaster, son of William Crawshay (d. 1867).

Williams, John M., 1813–80, copper smelter, purchased Pengreep, Cornwall; father (d. 1858) purchased Caerhays Castle, Cornwall; in all 8,125 acres, worth £13,392 p.a. (1878).

Wrigley, Thomas, 1806–80, paper & cotton manufacturer, purchased small estate nr. Bury, Lancs., worth £1,555 p.a. (1880), and Wansfell House, Windermere.

Mackenzie, Edward, 1811–80, civil engineering, purchased Fawley Court, Bucks.; in all 25,851 acres, worth £21,595 p.a. (1878).

Jardine, Andrew, 1812–81, China merchant, purchased Lanrich Castle, Perth, and nearly 10,000 acres in Dumfries; in all 12,659 acres, worth £8,230 P.A. (1878).

Wise, Francis, 1797–1881, distiller, purchased Angrove, Co. Cork; in all 21,248 acres, worth £11,314 p.a. (1878).

Loyd, Samuel J., Baron Overstone, 1796–1883, banker; father (d. 1858) purchased Lockinge, Berks., 20,536 acres, worth £26,512 p.a. (1878), given to his daughter in 1858; he purchased Overstone Park, Northants and other estates, in all 30,849 acres, worth £58,098 p.a. (1878).

Wythes, George, 1811–83, railway contractor, purchased Copt Hall, Essex; in all 5,857 acres, worth £20,098 p.a. (1878).

Meux, Sir Henry, 1817–83, brewer, purchased Theobalds, Herts.; in all 14,747 acres, worth £21,718 p.a. (1878).

Coats, Thomas, 1809–83, sewing thread manufacturer, purchased Auchendrane House, on river Doon, Ayr.; son James (d. 1912) purchased more estates in Scotland.

Bass, Michael T., 1799–1884, brewer, purchased Rangemore Hall, Staffs., c. 1,000 acres, worth £1,864 p.a. (1884).

Watney, James, 1800–84, brewer, purchased Haling Park, Croydon, Surrey; in all 2,295 acres, worth £4,249 p.a. (1883).

Foster, William, 1821–84, worsted manufacturer; father, of Black Dyke Mills (d. 1879), purchased Hornby Castle, Lancs, in 1861; in all 12,725 acres, worth £9,098 p.a. (1883).

Fletcher, James, 1807–85, foreign merchant, purchased Woolton Hall, Liverpool, Rosehaugh, Avoch,the Black Isle, and Letham Grange, Arbroath; in all 14,298 acres, worth £14,178 p.a. (1883).

Arthur, James, 1819–85, clothing, shirtmaker, *no country estate.*

Watney, James, 1832–86, brewer, son of James Watney, 1800–84; leased Fannich deer forest, Ross; son Vernon J. Watney purchsed Cornbury Park, Oxon, in 1900, c. 5,000 acres, worth £6,239 p.a. in 1883.

Hodgson, William, 1803–86, barrister, son of sugar refiner Thomas Hodgson; inherited from bachelor brother John (d. 1882), who purchased Gilston Park, Herts., in 1852, 2,091 acres, worth £3,248 p.a. (1883); he purchased land in Cumberland, worth £3,698 p.a. (1886). A bachelor, all estate inherited by nephew, Edward Salvin Bowlby (d. 1902).

de Stern, baron Herman, 1815–87, financier, *no country estate*.

McCalmont, Hugh, 1809–87, stockbroker, purchased, and built, Abbeylands, Co. Antrim, c.148 acres, worth £438 p.a. (1873); childless, great-nephew Harry L. B. McCalmont inherited, and purchased, Cheveley Park, nr. Newmarket, Cambs., c.1890.

Miller, Sir William, 1809–87, Russia merchant, purchased Manderston estate, Duns, Berwick, 961 acres, worth £2,969 p.a. (1873), and built house; rebuilt by his son, 1901–5.

Rylands, John, 1801–88, cottontot, purchased, and built, Longford Hall, Stretford, Lancs., in 1857, 207 acres, near his mills, childless.

Glyn, George C., 2nd Lord Wolverton, 1824–88, banker, eldest son of 1st Lord Wolverton, 1797–1873; completed purchase of Iwerne Minster, and built house, 1877–82.

Pearce, Sir William, 1833–88, shipbuilder, town house in Piccadilly, *no country estate*.

Hardy, Sir John, 1809–88, ironmaster, son of John Hardy, ironmaster (d. 1855), who purchased Staffordshire estate, worth £2,361 (1855); added to Dunstall estate, Staffs., 2,338 acres, worth £5,618 p.a. (1883); other sons of John Hardy (d. 1855) were Charles (d. 1867), purchased Chilham Castle, Kent, 3,249 acres, worth £4,500 p.a. (1883); and Gathorne, purchased Hemsted Park, Staplehurst, Kent, 5,188 acres, worth £6,426 p.a. (1883).

Fielden, Samuel, 1814–89, cottontot, nephew of Thomas Fielden, 1791–1869, purchased Crowborough Warren, Sussex.

Clayton, Nathaniel, 1811–90, agricultural engineer, purchased Waddington, Lincs., 350 acres, worth £410, and Withcall, Lincs., c.2,600 acres; heirs were two grandsons, instructed to purchase estates—Nathaniel Clayton Cockburn did so at Harmston, Lincs.

Allhusen, Christian, 1806–90, chemical manufacturer, purchased Stoke Court and Mount Alexander, Bucks.; 515 acres, worth £1,169 p.a. (1890).

Smith, William Henry, 1825–91, newsagent, purchased Greenlands, Henley, Bucks., estate in Suffolk, and Silverton and Moretonhampstead, Devon; in all 15,690 acres, worth £15,213 p.a. (1891).

Bullough, John, 1837–91, machinery manufacturer, purchased Meggernie Castle, Perth, 32,000 acres, and Kinloch Castle, Rhum.

Chapman, David B., 1799–1891, banker, purchased Downshire House, Roehampton, *no country estate*, but seventh son, Horace Edward Chapman, purchased Donhead estate, Wilts.

Brassey, Henry A., 1840–91, railway contractor, son of Thomas Brassey, 1805–70; purchased Preston Hall, Aylesford, Kent.

Hills, Frank C., 1808–92, chemical manufacturer, purchased Redleaf, Penshurst, Kent, 1,672 acres, worth £3,263 p.a. (1892), and other land worth £1,461 p.a. (1892).

Thompson, Samuel H., 1807–92, banker, purchased Thingwall Hall, Lancs., 30 acres, worth £487 p.a., and surrounding land worth £516 p.a. (1892).

Walker, Sir Andrew B., 1824–93, brewer, purchased Osmaston, Derby, 3,400 acres, from Francis Wright (d. 1873), and small Gateacre estate, nr. Liverpool, in all worth £4,845 p.a. (1893).

Peckover, Algernon, 1803–93, banker, son of Jonathan Peckover, banker, of Wisbech; Algernon lived at Sibalds Holme House, Wisbech St Peters, Isle of Ely, which he may have purchased himself, 3,391 acres, worth £6,111 p.a. (1893).

A total of 74 millionaires, in terms of personalty at death, who were not hereditary landowners, died between 1809 and 1893. Of these, 7 did not acquire any country estate, and a further 7 acquired a 'house in the country' with little land attached.

Source

All millionaires listed in W. D. Rubinstein, 'British Millionaires, 1809–1949', *Bulletin of the Institute of Historical Research*, 48 (1974), App., pp. 206–10, which includes information on values of personalty left at death, not included here.

The individuals in this listing, as in those in R. Britton's listing cited below, are arranged in chronological order of date of death, and this arrangement has been preserved in this Appendix and in Appendices 2, 3, and 4 (i) (b).

Source of information on land purchases

PRO, IR26, Legacy and Succession Duty Registers—especially Succession Duty from its imposition in 1853 to replacement by Harcourt's Death Duties in 1894.

Return of Owners of Land, 1873, Parl. Papers: C. 1097 (1875), England and Wales; C. 899 (1874), Scotland; C. 1492 (1876), Ireland.

J. Bateman, *The Great Landowners of Great Britain and Ireland* (1878 edn. and 1883 edn.), R. Britton, 'Wealthy Scots, 1876–1913', *Bulletin of the Institute of Historical Research,* 58 (1985), 78–94.

Abbreviations

(1873)=information from *Return of Owners of Land.*
(1878)=information from Bateman (1878 edn,).
(1883)=information from Bateman (1883 edn.).
(other dates)=information from IR26.

Scottish Millionaires Dying Between 1876 and 1893 Not in
W. D. Rubinstein's List

Jardine, Andrew, 1813–82, China merchant, £1,370,976, merchant and
landowner, son of David Jardine, d. 1856, farmer.

Coats, Thomas, 1811–84, sewing thread manufacturer, £1,308,734, thread manufacturer, no land, son of James Coats, thread manufactuer, d. 1857, worth
£6,740.

Miller, Sir William, 1810–88, merchant and railway director, £1,023,389, merchant and landowner, son of James Miller, merchant, d. 1855.

Source

R. Britton, 'Wealthy Scots, 1876–1913', *Bulletin of the Institute of Historical
Research*, 58 (1985), 78–94.

2. MILLIONAIRES DYING BETWEEN 1894 AND 1914

Page, Henry, 1813–94, maltster, not traced.

Greenall, Sir Gilbert, 1806–94, brewer, purchased Walton Hall, Cheshire, and
Tilstone House, Tarporley, Cheshire; Master of Belvoir Hunt.

Robinson, John Peter, 1837–95, retailer, lived in Hornsey Lane, Middx.

Cunliffe, Roger, 1824–95, bill discounter, purchased country house, Tyrrells Wood,
Surrey.

Booth, Sir Charles, 1812–96, distiller, purchased country house, Netherfield, Ware,
Herts.

Goldsmid, Sir Julian, 1838–96, financier, purchased country house, Somerhill, Tonbridge, Kent.

Bibby, James J., 1813–97, shipowner, purchased Hardwicke Grange, Salop, 1868,
Sansaw, Clive, Salop, and house on Windermere.

Heywood-Lonsdale, Arthur P. 1835–97, banker, purchased Shavington and Cloverley,
Salop.

Gray, Sir William, 1823–98, shipbuilder, residence: The Cottage, Greatham, West
Hartlepool.

de Rothschild, Baron Ferdinand, 1839–98, banker, purchased, and built, Waddesdon,
Bucks.

Mills, Charles H., Baron Hillingdon, 1830–98, banker, purchased country house,
The Wildernesse, Sevenoaks, Kent; Hillingdon Park, Uxbridge; Camelford
House, Park Lane.

Davies, Edward, 1852–98, colliery owner, not traced.

Ratcliff, Richard, 1830–98, brewer, purchased Walton, Derby, 1,687 acres, in
1878, and Rangemore Hall, Derby, from Michael Bass.

Lea, Charles W., 1827–98, condiment manufacturer, not traced.

Muntz, George F., 1822–98, metal manufacturer, purchased Umberslade,
Warwickshire, 2,486 acres, worth £3,948 p.a. (1873).

Beddington, Maurice, 1821–98, clothier, purchased The Limes, Carshalton, Surrey; London town house, Westbourne Terrace.

Isaacson, Frederick W., 1831–98, colliery owner, etc., London town house, Upper Grosvenor Street.

Gretton, John, 1833–99, brewer, purchased Stapleford Park, Leics., and Scottish sporting estate.

Foster, William Orme, 1814–99, ironmaster, purchased Apley Park, Salop, in 1868 for £550,000, 8,547 acres, worth £17,850 p.a. (1878), and Camolin Park, Co. Wexford, 9,724 acres, worth £4,686 p.a. (1878); in all 21,062 acres, worth £28,426 p.a. (1878).

Raphael, Henry L., 1832–99, stockbroker, banker, purchased country house, The Cottage, nr. Newmarket.

Tate, Sir Henry, 1819–99, sugar refiner, purchased house in country, Park Hill, Streatham.

Ismay, Thomas H., 1838–99, shipowner, purchased, and built, Dawpool, Cheshire, 1877.

Nixon, John, 1815–99, colliery owner, purchased large grouse moors.

Sutton, William R., 1836–1900, carrier, purchased country house, Sunnydene, Sydenham, Surrey.

Smith, Samuel G., 1822–1900, banker, purchased country house, Sacombe, Ware, Herts.

Armstrong, William G., 1st Lord Armstrong, 1810–1900, arms manufacturer, purchased, and built, Cragside, Northumberland, and Bamburgh Castle, Northumberland; in all 10,000 acres.

Cunliffe-Brooks, Sir William, 1819–1900, banker, purchased Barlow Hall, nr. Manchester, Glen Tanar, Aberdeen, and Aboyne Castle, Aberdeen, in 1888, from Marquess of Huntly.

Craig, James, 1828–1900, distiller, purchased Craigavon, Co. Down.

Lewis Samuel, 1837–1901, money lender, London town house, Grosvenor Square.

Cook, Sir Francis, 1817–1901, warehouseman, purchased country house, Doughty House, Richmond; and Montserrat Palace, Cintra, Portugal.

Stern, James, 1836–1901, banker, London town house, Carlton House Terrace.

McCalmont, Henry L. B., 1861–1902, stockbroker, Cheveley Park, nr. Newmarket, and London town house, Grosvenor Place.

Ralli, Stephen A., 1829–1902, foreign merchant, London town house, Park Lane.

Maple, Sir John B., 1845–1903, furniture retailer, purchased Childwickbury, Herts.—later sold to Jack Barnato Joel.

Palmer, Samuel, 1820–1903, biscuit manufacturer, purchased house, Northcourt, Hampstead.

Raphael, Edward L., 1831–1903, banker, purchased country house, Iden Manor, Staplehurst, Kent.

Sebag-Montefiore, Sir Joseph, 1822–1903, banker, purchased country house, East Cliffe Lodge, Ramsgate.

Brook, Edward, 1826–1904, sewing thread manufacturer, purchased Hoddam Castle, Dumfries, in 1878, and Kinmount, Dumfries.

Charrington, Spencer, 1818–1904, brewer, purchased country house, Hunsdon House, nr. Ware, Herts.

Thomasson, John P., 1841–1904, cottontot, purchased country house, Woodside, nr. Bolton, Lancs.

Denison-Beckett, Edmund, 1st Lord Grimthorpe, 1816–1905 barrister, banker, purchased Batchwood, St Albans, Herts, 3,400 acres.

Cook, Wyndham F., 1860–1905, warehouseman, London town house, Cadogan Square; racing yacht; art collection.

Jardine, Sir Robert, 1825–1905, China merchant, purchased Castlemilk, Lockerbie, Dumfries, and Lanrick Castle, Perthshire.

Tennant, Sir Charles, 1823–1906, chemical manufacturer, purchased The Glen, Innerleithen, 5,200 acres.

Smith, Thomas V., 1825–1906, distiller, purchased Ardtonish, Argyll, 12,000 acres.

Walker, Vyell E., 1838–1906, brewer, purchased Arnos Grove, Southgate, famous classical house.

Loeffler, Johann C. L., 1832–1906, engineer, London town house in Campden Hill Road.

Herring, George, 1835–1906, financier, purchased Putteridge, Luton, Beds., and Bridge House, Maidenhead.

Hatfield, Gilliat, 1834–1906, snuff manufacturer, purchased Morden Hall, Surrey, in 1866, 310 acres, worth £1,177 p.a. (1873), and Hatfield House, York WR, 626 acres, worth £906 p.a. (1873).

Steinkopf, Edward, 1841–1906, mineral water (Apollinaris) purchased Lyndhurst estate, Haywards Heath, Sussex; London town house, Berkeley Square.

Raphael, George C., 1837–1906, banker, purchased country house, Castle Hill, Englefield Green, 33 acres.

Sturdy, William, 1832–1906, stockbroker, purchased Pax Hill Park, Lindfield, Sussex.

Clark, Stewart, 1830–1907, sewing thread manufacturer, purchased Dundas Castle, Linlithgow, and Cairdhu, Co. Antrim.

Whiteley, William,1832–1907, department store owner, left £1 million to endow Whiteley Village, Cobham, Surrey, for old people.

Blackwell, Thomas F., 1838–1907, condiments manufacturer, purchased country house, The Cedars, Harrow Weald.

Schillizzi, John S., 1840–1908, foreign merchant, purchased country house, Red Court, Haslemere, Surrey, in 1897.

Bischoffsheim, Henry L., 1829–1908, financier, purchased country houses, Warren House, Stanmore, Middx, Buckland House, Berks., The Severals, Newmarket; and London town house, Bute House, South Audley Street.

Wood, James M., 1841–1908, shipowner, residence, The Towers, Ullet Road, Liverpool.

Bass, Michael A., 1st Baron Burton, 1837–1908, brewer, purchased Rangemore, Burton, Derby, 2,400 acres.

Lithgow, William T., 1854–1908, shipbuilder, purchased Drums, Landbank, Clyde; Ormsary estate, Knapdale, Argyll, in 1902.

Morrison, Charles, 1817–1909, warehouseman, purchased large estates in Berks. and Scotland; Basildon Park, Berks.; Islay, Argyll.

Wills, Sir Frederick, 1838–1909, tobacco manufacturer, purchased Northmoor, Dulverton. Somerset, 1,500 acres, and house in Bournemouth.

Currie, Sir Donald, 1825–1909, shipowner, purchased Garth, Aberfeldy, and Glen Lyon estate.

Mond, Ludwig, 1839–1909, chemical manufacturer, purchased Winnington Hall, Northwich, Cheshire, and large estate at Combe Bank, Sevenoaks, Kent.

Salting, George, 1836–1909, Australian sheep, flat in St James's Street; major art collector.

Wills, Sir Edward P., 1834–1910, tobacco manufacturer, purchased Hazelwood, Stoke Bishop, nr. Bristol, and Clapton Manor.

Schroder, Sir John H. W., 1825–1910, banker, purchased country house, The Dell, Englefield Green, Surrey.

Scott, Sir Walter, 1826–1910, railway contractor, purchased country house, Beauclere, Riding Mill, Northumberland.

Agnew, Sir William, 1825–1910, art dealer, London town house, Great Stanhope Street.

Butler, Charles, 1821–1910, insurance broker, purchased country house, Warren Wood, Hatfield, Herts.

Silver, Henry, 1828–1910, not traced.

Foster, John, 1833–1910, worsted manufacturer, purchased Combe Park, Whitchurch, Oxon.; Master of South Herefordshire Hunt; father (1821–84) owned 10,841 acres, Lancs., and 1,884 acres, York, WR.

Hickman, Sir Alfred, 1830–1910, ironmaster, purchased, and built, Wightwick, nr. Wolverhampton.

Wills, Henry O., 1828–1911, tobacco manufacturer, purchased Cotham Park, Bristol.

Wills, William H., 1st Lord Winterstoke, 1830–1911 tobacco manufacturer purchased Blagdon, Somerset, and Combe Lodge, Somerset.

Savill, Walter, 1837–1911, shipowner, purchased The Finches and Kenwards Farm, Lindfield, Sussex, becoming 1 of 6 principal landowners in the parish of 5,739 acres.

Dunkels, Anton, 1846–1911, diamond merchant, London town house, Hyde Park Gardens.

Sofer-Whitburn, Charles J., 1835–1911, banker, purchased Addington Manor, nr. Maidstone, Kent; London town house, Ennismore Gardens.

Quilter, Sir William C., 1841–1911, stockbroker, purchased Bawdsey Manor, Woodbridge, Suffolk.

Montagu, Samuel, 1st Lord Swaythling, 1832–1911, banker, purchased South Stoneham House, Hants, 1,200 acres, and Townhill Park, Hants; London town house, Kensington Palace Gardens.

Kitson, James, 1st Lord Airedale, 1835–1911 locomotive manufacturer, purchased Gledhow Hall, Leeds (built for Jeremiah Dixon, clothier, 1766–7).

Aird, Sir John, 1833–1911, engineering contractor, purchased Wilton Park, Beaconsfield, Bucks., and Highcliffe Castle, Hants; London town house, Hyde Park Terrace, with private theatre.

Coats, James, 1841–1912, sewing thread manufacturer and landowner (Britton), son of Thomas Coats, d. 1883, sewing thread manufacturer.

Furness, Christopher, 1st Lord Furness, 1852–1912, shipowner, purchased Grantley
    Hall, Ripon, York WR, and Tunstall Court, West Hartlepool; in all 30,000
    acres, London town house, Grosvenor Square.

Stern, Sydney J., 1st Lord Wandsworth, 1845–1912, banker, purchased Hengrave
    Hall, Suffolk, London town house, Great Stanhope Street.

Coats, Archibald, 1840–1912, sewing thread manufacturer and landowner (Britton),
    son of Sir Peter Coats, d. 1890, sewing thread manufacturer.

Dunn, Sir William 1833–1912, banker, S. African retailer, purchased country house,
    The Retreat, Lakenheath, Suffolk.

Cruddas, William D., 1831–1912, shipbuilder, purchased Haughton Castle,
    Humshaugh, Northumberland.

Vivian, William G., 1827–1912, colliery owner, copper smelter, purchased Clyne
    Castle, Blackpyll, Glamorgan.

Coats, Peter, 1842–1913, sewing thread manufacturer, purchased Garthland Place,
    Paisley, and Whitney Court, Herefordshire, where chief landowner of parish of
    1,513 acres.

Coats, Sir James, 1834–1913, sewing thread manufacturer, purchased Auchendrane,
    Ayr, London town house, Charles Street, Berkeley Square.

Weir, William, 1826–1913, ironmaster, purchased a dozen estates in Ayrshire.

McEwan, William, 1827–1913, brewer, London town house, Berkeley Square.

Fry, Joseph S., 1826–1913, chocolate manufacturer, house in Union Street, Bristol.

Fenwick, George J., 1821–1913, banker, purchased Pelton, Co. Durham, and Crag
    Head, Bournemouth.

Raphael, Louis E., 1853–1914, banker, London town house, Connaught Place.

A total of 96 millionaires, in terms of personalty at death, who were not hereditary landowners, died between 1894 and 1914. Of these, 50 acquired country
estates; 26 acquired country houses with little land attached; 10 had London town
houses (excluding those with London town houses plus country estates or country
houses); 6 had plain houses; 4 have not been traced.

Source.

All millionaires listed in W. D. Rubinstein, 'British Millionaires, 1809–1949',
Bulletin of the Institute of Historical Research, 48 (1974), 206–10, which includes
information on value of personalty left at death, not repeated here.

*Source of information on country house, country estate, and London town house
purchases and leases*

Who Was Who, i (1897–1916).
The Times, obituaries, notices of deaths and of wills.
Kelly's County Directories.
Streeter's Directories of Scotland.
Edward Walford (ed.), *The County Families of the United Kingdom*, 60 vol.
    (1860–1920).
Dictionary of Business Biography, 5 vol. (1984–6).
J. Mordaunt Crook, *The Rise of the Nouveaux Riches* (1999).

R. Britton, 'Wealthy Scots, 1876–1913', *Bulletin of the Institute of Historical Research*, 58 (1985), 78–94. Where Britton's description of an individual, for example, as 'thread manufacturer and landowner', is the only evidence of combination of business and non-hereditary landownership, the description is given as 'landowner (Britton)'.

Note

This list is not closely comparable with the list in Appendix 1 of millionaires, 1809–93, since after the introduction of the Harcourt death duties in 1894 there are no accessible public records equivalent to the Legacy and Succession Duty Registers. This means that evidence on estate and country house acquisition comes primarily from the self-descriptions of entries in *Who's Who*, supplemented by information from obituaries and details of wills recorded in *The Times*. In turn this means that some 3 per cent of the millionaires in the group have not been traced, chiefly because they did not rate entries in *Who's Who* or *The Times*; the probability is that they did not acquire estates or any country houses of note. Also these sources do not record cases in which heirs acquired estates under the terms of the wills under which they inherited, while the Appendix 1 list does include them.

SCOTTISH MILLIONAIRES DYING BETWEEN 1894 AND 1914 NOT IN
W. D. RUBINSTEIN'S LIST

Orr-Ewing, Sir Archibald, 1819–94, dyer, £1,077,234, dyer and landowner, son of William Ewing, landowner, d. 1853, worth £316.
Clark, Stewart, 1831–1908, sewing thread manufacturer, £1,947,281, thread manufacturer and landowner, of J. & P. Coats, son of John Clark, d. 1864, thread manufacturer.

3. MILLIONAIRES DYING BETWEEN 1915 AND 1940

Rothschild, Nathan M., 1st Lord Rothschild, 1840–1915, banker, purchased Tring Park, Herts., and 10,000 acres in all; 148 Piccadilly.
Eno, James C., 1828–1915, fruit salts, lived at Woodhall, Dulwich.
Keen, Arthur, 1835–1915, ironmaster, residence Sandyford, Edgbaston.
Cayzer, Sir Charles, 1843–1916, shipbuilder, purchased Gartmore House, Perth; Ralston, Paisley; Kinpurnie, Forfar, where 1 out of 3 principal landowners in parish of 5,197 acres; Lanfine, Ayr.
Harrison, Thomas F., 1852–1916, shipowner, purchased King's Walden Bury, Herts., where principal owner of parish of 4,392 acres.
Beecham, Sir Joseph, 1848–1916, patent medicines, lived at Ewansville, Huyton, Liverpool, and West Brow, Hampstead.

Holcroft, Sir Charles, 1843–1917, colliery owner, purchased The Shrubbery, Kingswinford, Staffs; died unmarried.

Rothschild, Leopold, 1845–1917, banker, acquired Ascott, Berks., where 1 of 2 principal owners of parish of 5,698 acres; Palace House, Newmarket.

Royden, Sir Thomas B., 1831–1917, shipowner, purchased Frankby, West Kirby, Cheshire; Brockwood Park, Alresford, Hants; Tillypronie, Aberdeen.

Vaughan Philip H., 1829–1917, brewer, residence Redland House, Bristol.

Taylor, Seth, 1827–1917, miller, lived at Granard, Putney Park Lane.

Cunliffe-Lister, 2nd Lord Masham, 1857–1917, wool comber, added to father's purchase of Jervaulx and Masham estates, York, WR, 34,000 acres in all.

Reckitt, Francis, 1827–1917, starch manufacturer, lived at Crag View, Hessle, Hull; and Highgate.

Coats, George, 1st Lord Glentanar, 1849–1918, sewing thread manufacturer, purchased Forest of Glen Tanar, Aberdeen; Belle Isle, Ayr; London town house, Hill Street, Berkeley Square. In all owned c.29,000 acres.

Rothschild, Alfred, 1842–1918, banker, purchased Halton, Bucks., where sole owner of parish of 1,444 acres.

Wertheimer, Asher, 1844–1918, art dealer, London town house, left his art collection, including 6 family portraits by Sargent, to the nation.

Crigoe-Colmore, William B., 1860–1918, urban property, not traced.

Worthington, Albert O., 1844–1918, brewer, purchased Maple Hayes, Lichfield, Staffs., where 1 of 3 principal landowners of parish of 4,360 acres.

Thomas, David A., 1st Lord Rhondda, 1856–1918, colliery owner, purchased Llanwern estate, Newport, Mon., where chief landowner of parish of 716 acres; house in Ashley Gardens, London SW.

Mackinnon, Duncan, 1844–1918, shipowner, purchased Balinakill estate, Argyll, where 1 of 3 principal landowners of parish of 28,403 acres; also London town house.

Schiff, Sir Ernest F., 1840–1918, stockbroker, London town house, Carlos Place.

Hutchinson, Thomas H., 1861–1918, shipowner, lived in Glasgow.

Burns, James C., 3rd Lord Inverclyde, 1864–1919, shipowner, purchased Castle Wemyss, Renfrew, where chief landowner of parish of £6,609 rateable value; Hartfield Cove, Dumbarton; London town house, Berkeley Square.

Stern, Herbert, 1st Lord Michelham, 1851–1919, banker, purchased Strawberry Hill, Twickenham; Imber Court, Thames Ditton, with a 'trotting course'; Rue Nitot, Paris.

Greenwell, Sir Walpole L., 1847–1919, stockbroker, purchased Woodcock Lodge, Little Berkhamsted, Herts.; Marden Park, Godstone, Surrey; Greenwell, Wolsingham, Co. Durham; London town house, Portman Square.

Barbour, George, 1841–1919, cotton exporter, purchased Bolesworth Castle, Cheshire.

Mills, Charles W., 2nd Lord Hillingdon, 1855–1919, banker, purchased The Wildernesse, Sevenoaks, Kent, estate of 1,500 acres; Hillingdon Court, Uxbridge, Middx., where 1 of 9 principal landowners of parish of 2,937 acres.

Courtauld, George, 1830–1920, silk manufacturer, purchased Gosfield, Essex, with park of 300 acres.

Morley, Howard, 1846–1920, hosiery manufacturer, purchased Hall Place, Leigh, Kent, where 1 of 4 principal landowners of parish of 3,975 acres.

Waddilove, Sir Joshua K., 1841–1920, credit agency, Town house, The Elms, Spaniards Row, Hampstead.

Cook, Sir Frederick L., 1844–1920, warehouseman, his father purchased Doughty House, Richmond, Surrey; Monserrate, Cintra, Portugal.

Combe, Charles, 1836–1920, brewer, purchased Cobham Park, Surrey, where 1 of 3 principal landowners of parish of 5,278 acres.

Cassel, Sir Ernest, 1852–1921, banker, London town house, Brook House, Park Lane; Grafton House, Moulton Paddocks, Newmarket; Brankstone Dene, Bournemouth.

Morrison, Walter, 1836–1921, warehouseman, purchased Malham Tarn, Longcliffe, Settle, York, WR, in all about 13,900 acres; house in Cromwell Road, London SW.

Tetley, Henry G., 1852–1921, silk manufacturer, London town house, Avenue Road, Regent's Park; Alderbrook, Cranleigh, Surrey.

Radcliffe, Henry, 1857–1921, shipowner, purchased for £250,000 estates in Glamorgan and Monmouthshire.

Chrystal, William J., 1855–1921, chemical manufacturer, purchased Auchendennan estate, Arden, Dumbartonshire, where principal landowner of parish of 8,373 acres.

Park, James S., 1854–1921, shipowner, purchased Auchenkyle, Monkton, Ayr.

Tate, Sir William H., 1842–1921, sugar refiner, purchased Highfield, Woolton, Lancs.; Bodrhyddan, Rhuddlan, Flint.

Harmsworth, Alfred, 1st Viscount Northcliffe, 1865–1922, newspaper owner, purchased Elmwood, Thanet; Buckthorn Hall, Crowborough, Sussex; Chapelizod, Co. Dublin; London town house, Carlton Gardens.

Wills, Henry H., 1856–1922, tobacco manufacturer, purchased St Vincent's, Clifton Park, Bristol.

Birkin, Sir Thomas I., 1831–1922, lace manufacturer, purchased country house, Ruddington Grange, Notts., and Park House, Nottingham.

Glen-Coats, Sir Thomas G., 1846–1922, sewing thread manufacturer, purchased Ferguslie Park, Paisley.

Constantine, Joseph, 1855–1922, shipowner, purchased Harsley Hall, Northallerton, Yorks, NR, with estate of 1,600 acres.

Milburn, Charles T., 1860–1922, shipowner, purchased Compton Manor, King's Somborne, Hants., where 1 of 7 principal landowners of parish of 6,766 acres; also Milburn House, Newcastle upon Tyne.

Brown, Sir Alexander H., 1844–1922, banker, purchased country houses, Broome Hall and Bearchurst, Holmwood, Surrey.

Coats, Daniel, 1844–1922, sewing thread manufacturer, purchased Brockwood Park, Alresford, Hants, where 1 of 3 principal landowners of parish of 1,237 acres.

Miller, Alexander, 1837–1922, W. Africa merchant, purchased country house, Stoatley Hall, Haslemere, Surrey.

Cohen, Louis S., 1846–1922, retail chain stores, former Lord Mayor of Liverpool, where he lived.

Smith, Sir Prince, 1840–1922, worsted machinery, purchased Southburn estate, Driffield, York, ER; estate in Kirkcudbright; Hillbrook, Keighley, York, WR.

Hartley, Sir William P., 1846–1922, jam manufacturer, lived at Sea View, Southport, Lancs.

Cadbury, George, 1839–1922, chocolate manufacturer, purchased Winds Point, Malvern, Worcs.; Manor House, Northfield, Birmingham.

Watson, Joseph, 1st Lord Manton, 1873–1922, soap manufacturer, purchased Compton Verney estate; in all 5 estates, 20,000 acres.

Rothschild, Nathaniel C., 1877–1923, banker, purchased Ashton Wold, Oundle; London town house, Arundel House, Kensington Palace Gardens; international authority on fleas.

Marcus, Maurice, 1844–1923, financier, purchased High Trees, Redhill, Surrey, where 1 of 4 principal landowners of parish, leaving legacies to his farm servants.

Bibby, Frank, 1857–1923, shipowner; father purchased Hardwicke Grange, Sansaw, Salop, where 1 of 2 principal landowners of parish of 1,493 acres.; The Avenue, Newmarket; London town house, Hill Street, Berkeley Square.

Beasley, Charles, 1842–1923, brewer, purchased The Cottage, Abbeywood, Middx.

Jackson, Sir Charles C., 1849–1923, builder, London town house, Ennismore, Gardens.

Mills, Joseph T., 1836–1924, silk manufacturer, purchased Langton Hall, West Langton, Leics., where principal landowner of parish of 829 acres; Stockgrove, Leighton Buzzard, Beds.

Ropner, Sir Robert, 1838–1924, shipowner, purchased Preston Hall, Stockton; Skutterkelf, Yarm, York, NR, where principal landowner of parish of 1,007 acres.

Reddihaugh, John, 1841–1924, woollen merchant, residence, Beachmount, Baildon, Bradford.

Cunliffe-Lister, John 3rd Lord Masham, 1867–1924, silk plush manufacturer, owned about 24,000 acres, Swinton, Masham, York, WR.

Clark, Sir John S., 1864–1924, sewing thread manufacturer, purchased Dundas Castle, West Lothian.

Larnach, Sydney, 1855–1924, banker, purchased Brambletye, Sussex.

Foster, William H., 1846–1924, ironmaster, purchased Spratton Grange, Northants; father purchased Apley Park, Bridgnorth, Salop.

Knowles, Robert M., 1843–1924, colliery owner, purchased Colston Bassett Hall, Bingham, Notts., in 50-acre park, where principal landowner of parish of 2,447 acres.

Cain, Sir William, 1864–1924, brewer, purchased Wargrave Manor, Berks., where 1 of 6 principal landowners of parish of 4,392 acres.

Winterbottom, William D., 1858–1924, book cloth manufacturer, purchased Aston Hall, Derbyshire, left legacies to his farm bailiff and his stud groom.

Hulton, Sir Edward, 1869–1925, newspaper owner, purchased Downside, Leatherhead, Surrey; London town house, Great Cumberland Place.

Hambro, Sir Everard A., 1842–1925, banker; father purchased Milton Abbey, Dorset, 5,000 acres (in 1925); Hayes Place, Kent.

Lever, William H., 1st Viscount Leverhulme, 1851–1925, soap manufacturer, purchased Thornton Manor, Cheshire; Isle of Harris; Stafford House, London (Lancaster House); Rivington, nr. Bolton, Lancs.

Pickering, Warley, 1868–1925, shipowner, purchased Hutton Hall, Guisborough, Yorks, NR.

Wheatley, Joshua H., 1854–1925, woollen manufacturer, purchased Berkswell Hall, nr. Coventry, where principal landowner of parish of 5,878 acres; left legacies to his gamekeepers, coachmen, and gardeners.

Shuttleworth, Alfred, 1843–1925, agricultural engineer, purchased Hartsholme, Lincs.; Eastgate House, Lincoln.

Coats, William A., 1853–1926, sewing thread manufacturer, residence Ferguslie House, Paisley; intestate, his 2 sons had estates at Levensholme, Ayrshire, and Dailskaith, Dumfries.

Guinness, Edward A., 1st Earl of Iveagh, 1847–1927, brewer, purchased Elveden Hall, Suffolk, 15,000 acres; Farmleigh, Castle Knock, Co. Dublin; Kenwood, Hampstead-Highgate, Middx.; London town house, Grosvenor Place.

Samuel, Marcus, 1st Viscount Bearsted, 1853–1927, Shell oil, purchased The Mote, Kent, about 2,000 acres; London town house, Hamilton Place.

Pearson, Weetman D., 1st Viscount Cowdray, 1856–1927 oil, civil engineering contractor, purchased Paddockhurst, Worth, Sussex, 6,000 acres; Cowdray Park, Sussex; Dunecht House, Aberdeen; in all 25,000 acres in England, 28,000 acres in Scotland; London town house, Carlton House Terrace.

Jardine, Sir Robert W., 1868–1927, China merchant, purchased Castlemilk, Lockerbie, Dumfries, where 1 of 2 principal landowners of parish of 10,231 acres, £13,775 p.a. rateable value; The Kremlin, Newmarket; London town house, St James's Place.

Tibbitts, William F., 1842–1927, urban property, the extreme antithesis of the gentrified businessman, he lived in Meadow Street, Sheffield, the slum district in which he was property owner.

Deuchar, James, 1851–1927, brewer, purchased Stichill, nr. Kelso; Middleton and Ilderton, Northumberland; in all 13,000 acres.

Haslam, Sir Alfred S., 1844–1927, refrigeration, purchased country house, Breadsall Priory, nr. Derby.

Wills, Sir George A., 1854–1928, tobacco manufacturer, purchased Coombe Lodge, Blagdon, nr. Bristol, where 1 of 2 principal landowners of parish of 3,135 acres; Burwells, Leigh Woods, nr. Bristol.

Wills, Frederick N. H., 1888–1928, tobacco manufacturer, purchased Miserden Park, Cirencester, where chief landowner of parish of 3,218 acres; Holme Lacy, Hereford; Invergarry, Inverness.

Smith, William F. D., 2nd Viscount Hambleden, 1868–1928, newsagent; father purchased Greenlands, Henley, and Moretonhampstead, Devon; he added North Bovey, Devon; owned about 6,000 acres in 1926.

Oxley, James W., 1834–1928, banker, residence, Spenfield, Weetwood, Leeds.

Dalziel, Davison, 1st Lord Dalziel, 1854–1928, pullman cars, purchased house at Wooler, Northumberland; London town house, Grosvenor Place.

Watney, Vernon J., 1860–1928, brewer, purchased Cornbury Park, Oxon., about 2,100 acres; Fannioch Loch Luichart, Ross; London town house, Berkeley Square.

Farquhar, Alfred, 1852–1928, banker, London town house, Belgrave Square.

Cohen, Rex D., 1876–1928, chain store owner, purchased Condover Hall, Salop, 1927; leased Pitchford Hall, Salop; kept racing stud.

Pope, Edwin, 1845–1928, brewer, residence, Mertone Lodge, Dorchester, Dorset.

Gretton, Frederick, 1869–1928, brewer, purchased Stapleford, Leics., 919 acres; Egginton Hall, Derby.

Nairn, John, 1853–1928, linoleum manufacturer, purchased house in Kirkcaldy.

Cliff, Stephen, 1852–1928, steel manufacturer, purchased Crayke Manor, Easingwold, Yorks, NR, where 1 of 2 principal landowners of parish of 2,876 acres; left legacy to his farm bailiff.

Coats, William H., 1866–1928, sewing thread manufacturer, purchased Woodside, Paisley.

Holt, Sir Edward, 1849–1928, brewer, purchased Woodthorpe, Prestwich, Lancs.; Holmacre, Alderley, Cheshire; Blackwall, Windermere.

Barbour, Robert, 1876–1928, cotton exporter; father purchased Bolenorth Castle, Cheshire, where 1 of 3 principal landowners of parish of 1,694 acres.

Berry, Henry S., 1877–1928, 1st Lord Buckland, steel manufacturer, purchased Buckland, Bwlch, Brecon, where 1 of 2 principal landowners of parish of 9,930 acres; London town house, Whitehall Court.

Strutt, George, 1854–1928, cottontot, purchased Bridge Hill, Belper, Derby.; Kingairloch, Argyll.

Baron, Bernhard, 1850–1929, tobacco manufacturer, lived at The Drive, Hove, Sussex.

Dewar, James A., 1856–1929, 1st Lord Forteviot, distiller, purchased Dupplin Castle, Perth, where sole owner of parish of 4,165 acres.

Baring, John, 2nd Lord Revelstoke, 1863–1929, banker, purchased Coombe Wood, Norbiton, Surrey; London town house, Carlton House Terrace; yacht 'Waterwitch'.

Evans-Bevan, Evan, 1853–1929, brewer, purchased country house, Cadoxton House, Cadoxton-juxta-Neath, Glam.

Craig-Sellar, Gerald H., 1871–1929, distiller, London town house, Prince's Gate; Ardtornish estate, Morvern, Argyll (probably inherited); left legacies to his factor, gamekeeper, and estate workers.

Morley, Samuel H., 1st Lord Hollenden, 1845–1929, hosiery manufacturer; father purchased Hall Place, Leigh, Kent; London town house, Grosvenor Square.

Harmsworth, Sir Hildebrand A., 1872–1929, newspaper owner, London town house.

Fyfe-Jamieson, James H., 1866–1929, colliery owner, purchased country house, Ruthven, Meigle, Forfar.

Bibby, Frank B. F., 1893–1929, shipowner; grandfather purchased Sansaw, Salop; London town house, Charles Street.

Mason, James F., 1861–1929, copper smelter, purchased Eynsham Hall, Witney, Oxon. park over 800 acres; London town house, Bruton Street; married only daughter of 26th Earl of Crawford.

Brocklehurst, William B., 1851–1929, silk manufacturer, purchased Butley Hall, Macclesfield; Lytherington House, Macclesfield, with 30-acre park.

Williamson, James, 1st Lord Ashton, 1842–1930, linoleum manufacturer, purchased Ashton Hall, Lancaster, 1,500 acres, from Duke of Hamilton in 1884; Ryelands, Lancaster; London town house, Alford House, Prince's Gate.

Dewar, Thomas R., 1st Lord Dewar, 1864–1930, distiller, purchased The Homestall, East Grinstead, Sussex; London town house, Savoy Court.

Coats, Andrew, 1862–1930, sewing thread manufacturer, purchased Castle Toward, Dunoon, Argyll; Burrough Hill, Melton Mowbray, Leics., 1,500 acres.

Watson, Sir William G., 1861–1930, dairy proprietor, purchased Sulhamstead House, nr. Reading, about 1,000 acres.

Brotherton, Edward A., 1st Lord Brotherton, 1856–1930, chemical manufacturer, purchased Roundhay Hall, Leeds; Kirkham Abbey, York, WR.

LeMarchant, Francis C., 1844–1930, insurance broker, London town house, West Eaton Place.

Findlay, Sir John R., 1866–1930, newspaper proprietor, purchased Aberlour House, Aberlour, Banff, where 1 of 4 principal landowners of parish of 14,781 acres, £13,462 p.a. rateable value; Edinburgh town house.

Carr, Ellis, 1852–1930, biscuit manufacturer, purchased country house, Yewbarrow, Broadwater Down, Tunbridge Wells; left legacies to his coachman, chauffeur, gardeners.

Mond, Alfred, 1st Lord Melchett, 1868–1930, chemical manufacturer, purchased Melchett Court, Romsey, Hants., about 1,800 acres; Landford Manor; London town house, Lowndes Square.

Ralli, Sir Lucius E., 1846–1931, banker, purchased Beaurepaire Park, Berks.; London town house, Park Street, Grosvenor Square.

Morrison, Hugh, 1868–1931, insurance broker, purchased Fonthill House, Wilts., where principal landowner of parish of 1,797 acres; Islay House, Islay; London town house, Halkin Street.

Boyd, Thomas L., 1850–1931, meat importer, house in San Remo, where he died.

Napier, Montague S., 1871–1931, motor manufacturer, house in Cannes, where he died.

Parsons, Sir Charles A., 1854–1931, turbine manufacturer, purchased Ray, Kirkwhelpington, Northumberland; Holeyn Hall, Wylam, Northumberland; London town house, Upper Brook Street.

Hood, Sir Joseph, 1863–1931, tobacco manufacturer, purchased Greycourt, Wimbledon; Ivanhoe, Finton on Sea, Essex.

Keene, John H., 1864–1931, insurance broker, purchased country house, Carlton House, Galleywood, Chelmsford, Essex.

Wills, Sir George V. P., 1887–1931, tobacco manufacturer, inherited Coombe Lodge, Blagdon, nr. Bristol.

Cook, Frank H., 1862–1931, travel agent, purchased Ashburnham House, Bennett Hill, Surrey

Mackay, James Lyle, 1st Earl of Inchcape, 1852–1932 [not in WDR], shipowner, purchased Glenapp Castle and estate, Ayr, where 1 of 4 principal landowners of parish of 33,584 acres, £10,471 p.a. rateable value; yacht 'Rover' on which he died at Monaco.

Ellerman, Sir John R., 1862–1933, shipowner, purchased Longhaven estate and Slains Castle, Cruden, Aberdeen, 1918; London town house, South Audley Street.

Mills, Henry T., 1861–1933, silk manufacturer, purchased Langton Hall, Leicester, where principal landowner of parish of 829 acres.

Fleming, Robert, 1845–1933, banker, purchased Joyce Grove, Nettlebed, Oxon., about 1,000 acres; London town house, Grosvenor Square.

Sutton, Thomas M., 1847–1933, pawnbroker, lived over the shop in Victoria Street, London SW.

Salvesen, Frederick G., 1870–1933, shipowner, lived in Glasgow; left most of his fortune to Church of Scotland missions.

Dunn, David G., 1907–33, tobacco manufacturer, purchased Knock Castle, Largs, Ayr, where 1 of 5 principal landowners of parish of 21,848 acres, £30,064 p.a. rateable value; well-known speedboat owner.

Garton, Charles H., 1860–1934, brewery sugar manufacturer, lived at Banstead, Surrey.

Garton, Sir Richard C., 1857–1934, brewery sugar manufacturer, purchased Lythe Hill, Haslemere, Surrey, where 1 of 2 principal landowners of parish of 2,253 acres; Loch Buie, Mull; London town house, Hamilton Place, Piccadilly.

Riddell, George A., 1st Lord Riddell, 1865–1934, newspaper owner, London town house, Queen Anne's Gate.

Kearley, Hudson E., 1st Viscount Devonport, 1856–1934, grocery chain owner, purchased Whittington Manor, Marlow, Bucks., about 1,500 acres; Kinloch, Dunkeld, Perth; London town house, Grosvenor Place.

Samuel, Samuel, 1855–1934, banker, London town house, Berkeley House, Hay Hill, Berkeley Square.

Henderson, Alexander, 1st Lord Faringdon, 1850–1934, stockbroker, purchased Buscot Park, Faringdon, Berks, about 2,800 acres; Glenalmond House, Perth; London town house, Arlington Street.

Singer, Washington M. G., 1866–1934, sewing machines, purchased country house, Norman Court, Salisbury, Wilts.; The Cottage, Newmarket.

Harrison, Sir Heath, 1857–1934, shipowner, purchased Le Court, Greatham Liss, Hants, where 1 of 4 principal landowners of parish of 2,030 acres.

Soames, Arthur G., 1854–1934, maltster, purchased Sheffield Park, Uckfield, Sussex, park 650 acres, plus about 4,000 acres estate.

Winterbottom, George H., 1861–1934, book cloth manufacturer, purchased Horton Hall, Northants, where principal landowner of parish of 1,930 acres; well-known breeder of Shire horses and Friesian cattle.

Buchanan, James, 1st Lord Woolavington, 1849–1935, distiller, purchased Lavington Park, Petworth, Sussex, where principal landowner of parish of 674 acres; Knockando, Speyside, Moray; Grove House, Newmarket; Northaw House, Middx.; London town house, Berkeley Square.

Wills, Arthur S., 1863–1935, tobacco manufacturer, leased country house, Eshton Hall, Gargrave, Yorks, WR.

Scribbans, John H., 1877–1935, cake manufacturer, purchased country house, Little Aston Park, Staffs.

Benyon, James H., 1849–1935, urban property, purchased Englefield House, Berks., where 1 of 2 principal landowners of parish of 1,400 acres; Sulhamstead, Berks; Lord Lieutenant of Berks.

Ralli, Peter, 1868–1935, banker, London town house, Hyde Park Gardens.

Colman, Geoffrey R., 1891–1935, mustard manufacturer, purchased Gatton Park, Surrey, where principal landowner of parish of 1,200 acres.

Crabtree, John A., 1886–1935, electrical manufacturer, leased country house, Little Aston Park, Staffs.

Clark, Sir George S., 1861–1935, shipbuilder, purchased Dunlambert, Fortwilliam Park, Belfast.

Wellcome, Sir Henry, 1854–1936, drug manufacturer, purchased London town house, Gloucester Gate, Regent's Park.

Joicey, James, 1st Lord Joicey, 1846–1936, colliery owner, purchased Ford Castle and Longhirst, Northumberland, where sole landowner; Gregynog, Montgomery (resold to David Davies); London town house, Cadogan Square.

Cohen, Harold L., 1873–1936, retail chain stores, purchased country house, Barwythe, Dunstable, Beds.

Charrington, Charles E., 1850–1936, brewer, residence, Broadoaks, West Byfleet, Kent.

Runciman, Walter, 1st Lord Runciman, 1847–1937, shipowner, purchased Shoreston Hall, Northumberland; Doxford Hall, Chathill, Northumberland, sole landowner; Fernwood House, Newcastle upon Tyne.

Scrutton, Frederick, 1860–1937, shipowner, leased country house, Woolpits, Nutfield, Surrey.

Harrison, Charles W., 1875–1937, shipowner, London town house, Cadogan Place.

Harrison, William E., 1875–1937, colliery owner, purchased Wychnor Park, Burton on Trent, and Orgreave Hall estate, Alrewas, Staffs.

Palmer, Charles H., 1860–1937, biscuit manufacturer, purchased Bozedown House, Whitchurch, Oxon.

Henderson, George E., 1844–1937, urban utilities, lived in Newcastle upon Tyne, left his art collection to the Laing Gallery, Newcastle.

Levy, Sir Albert, 1864–1937, tobacco manufacturer, purchased Elstead, Surrey; London town house, Devonshire House, Mayfair,

Butler, Hubert L., 1858–1937, insurance broker, country house, Warren Wood, Hatfield, Herts. In his youth was a captain in the West Indian Regiment, and, in the colonialist words of his obituary in *The Times*, 'introduced cricket to the negroes, who proved apt pupils'.

Grant, Sir Alexander, 1864–1937, biscuit manufacturer, purchased Glenmoriston, Edinburgh; Logie House, Dumphail, Moray; Dumphail House, Dumphail, Moray; Moray House, Hampstead: purchased nucleus of Scottish National Library.

Beckett, Sir William Gervase, 1866–1937, banker, purchased Kirkdale Manor, Nawton, York, NR about 1,000 acres; London town house, Green Street.

Fowler, Sir George J., 1858–1937, insurance broker, purchased London town house, The South House, Hyde Park Street.

Smith, John, 1868–1938, tobacco manufacturer, residence, Giffnook, Renfrew.

Greenall, Gilbert, 1st Lord Daresbury, 1867–1938, brewer, purchased Walton Hall, Warrington, Lancs.; Mount Coote, Kilmallock, Limerick; Waltham Hall estate, Melton Mowbray, Leics.

Wharton, William H., 1859–1938, urban utilities, inherited Skelton Castle, Cleveland, York, NR, about 4,000 acres; purchased London town house, Eaton Square.

Reddihaugh, Frank, 1871–1938, woollen merchant, not traced.

Molyneux-Cohan, William M., 1879–1938, shipowner, London town house, Buckingham Gate.

Sassoon, Sir Philip A., 1888–1939, foreign merchant, purchased Trent Park, Middx., 1,000-acre estate; built Port Lympne House, Kent; purchased London town house, Park Lane.

Tate, Sir Ernest W., 1867–1939, sugar refiner, purchased Gallfaenan, Trefnant, Denbigh.

Davey, Thomas R., 1871–1939, tobacco manufacturer, purchased Wraxall Court, Somerset, where 1 of 3 principal landowners of parish of 4,125 acres.

Cargill, David W. T., 1872–1939, oil company director, not traced.

Williams, Sir Howell J., 1859–1939, building contractor, lived at 263 Camden Road, N.7.

Greenwell, Sir Bernard E., 1874–1939, stockbroker, purchased Marden Park, Godstone, Surrey, where 1 of 3 principal landowners of parish of 6,791 acres; Butley Abbey, Woodbridge, Suffolk, where principal landowner of parish of 1,981 acres; London town house, Eaton Square.

Heath, Cuthbert E., 1859–1939, insurance broker, purchased country house, Anstie Grange, Holmwood, nr. Dorking, Surrey; Leith Hill estate, Surrey; Eze estate, Alpes-Maritime, France; London town house, Davies Street.

Furness, Marmaduke, 1st Viscount Furness, 1883–1940, shipbuilder, inherited Grantley Hall, York, WR, purchased London town house, St James's Street.,

Cooper, Sir George A., 1856–1940, foreign property, (inherited fortune from 'Chicago' Smith, d. 1900) purchased Hursley Park, Winchester, Hants., where 1 of 2 principal landowners of parish of 6,949 acres; The College, Elgin; London town house, Grosvenor Square.,

Courtauld, Sir William J., 1870–1940, rayon manufacturer, purchased Penny Pot, Halstead, Essex.

Fry, Conrad P. 1865–1940, chocolate manufacturer, residences in Clifton, Bristol, and Weston-super-Mare.

Crawford, Archibald J., 1870–1940, biscuit manufacturer, not traced.

A total of 185 'probate millionaires', who were not hereditary landowners, died between 1915 and 1940. Of these, 87 purchased estates, ranging from a few hundred acres up to 29,000 acres, or more where Scottish moors were acquired: the rateable values of the largest Scottish parishes have been noted, in order to indicate something of the general character and financial value of the land in question. Fifty purchased country houses without much land, 20 acquired London town houses but not estates or country houses, and 22 lived at other addresses in the UK and 2 in France; 4 have not been traced.

Source

All millionaires who were not hereditary landowners listed in W. D. Rubinstein, 'British Millionaires, 1809–1949', *Bulletin of the Institute of Historical Research*, 48 (1974), 206–10.

Source of information on estate, country house, and London town house purchases (and leases of latter)

As in Appendix 2: *Who Was Who, ii, iii* (1916–28, 1929–40), plus *Kelly's County Directories,* and Clive Aslet, *The Last Country Houses* (New Haven, Conn., and London, 1982).

Note

The listing in Appendix 3 is broadly, but not exactly, comparable to that in Appendix 2. The main difference lies in the method of distinguishing between acquisition of 'estates' and of 'country houses'. There was a large increase in the number of millionaires who did not obtain an entry in *Who's Who*, which possibly indicates that a declining percentage of millionaires engaged in the kind of public service, particularly in local government, which normally attracted an invitation to have an entry in *Who's Who*. All except 4 of those not in *Who's Who* were, however, noted at death in *The Times*. The custom of including in *Who's Who* entries statements of the number of acres owned, by those who had country estates, declined sharply after 1914, although a few of these self-descriptions continued to provide such information. Hence for this period the distinction between acquiring a 'country estate' and simply a 'country house' without much land attached relies more heavily on reference to a *Kelly's Directory* close to the date of death of those individuals with a known address in the country. Where *Kelly* (or, for Scotland, *Streeter*) states that the individual was 'the principal' or 'one of the principal' landowners of the parish in which the named house was situated, that person has been classified as acquiring a 'country estate'. Where there is no mention of the individual as a landowner in the parish in which the named house was situated that person has been credited with acquiring a 'country house'. This method classifies as country estates some properties which may have been no more than 500 acres or so; since it does not provide information on holdings in adjoining, or more distant, parishes it may also underestimate the size of estate acquired by some millionaires.

The exercise of pursuing the property acquisitions of millionaires has not been taken beyond 1940 for two main reasons. First, the goalposts for defining 'millionaire' were moved in 1925, when probate values for the first time included the value of settled real estate, previously excluded. Second, inflation, and especially movements in the values of both stocks and shares and land, became so substantial after 1940 that the concept of a 'millionaire' lost such stability and reasonable comparability over time as it had enjoyed since 1809.

4. BUSINESSMEN LEAVING LESS THAN £1 MILLION WHO PURCHASED COUNTRY ESTATES

(i) (A) THOSE WHO DIED BEFORE 1914

Before 1898 the figure in £s is the probate value of personalty left at death. After 1898 the figure in £s refers to the probate value of unsettled realty plus personalty left at death.

Adam, William, 1828–98, carpet manufacturer, £211,291, purchased 2,000 acre estate, Glos., in 1897.

Adamson, Daniel, 1820–90, engineer, £71,065, purchased hunting lodge, Flint.

Allcroft, John Derby, 1822–93, glove manufacturer, £492,063, purchased 8,500 acre Stokesay estate, Salop, built Stokesay Court, 1891.

Bagnall, John Nock, 1826–84, ironmaster, £5,671, purchased Shenstone Moss estate, Lichfield, Staffs., High Sheriff, Staffs., 1875.

Bainbridge, Emerson Muschamp, 1817–92, department store owner, £407,715, purchased country house, Eshott Hall, Northumberland.,

Bainbridge, Emerson Muschamp, 1845–1911, coal owner, £461,769, purchased 40,000-acre deer forest, Ross.

Baldwin, Alfred, 1841–1908, iron and steel manufacturer, £199,376, purchased country house, Bewdley, Worcs.

Balfour, Alexander, 1824–86, S. American merchant £132,148, purchased estate near Chester.

Barham, Sir George, 1836–1913, dairyman, £259,222, purchased ancestral estates, Snape and Tappington Grange, Wadhurst, Sussex.

Barker, Sir John, 1840–1914, department store owner, £247,706, purchased 300–acre estate, Bishop's Stortford, Essex, bred polo ponies and Syrian sheep.

Bell, Sir Isaac Lowthian, 1816–1904, ironmaster, £768,676, purchased Rounton Grange estate, Northallerton, York, NR and built house 1872–6; built Washington Hall, Co. Durham, 1854.

Bolckow, Henry William, 1806–78, ironmaster, £800,000, purchased Marton Hall estate, nr. Middlesbrough, built house 1854–7.

Brand, Henry Bouverie William, 1st Viscount Hampden, 1814–92, £54,752 (2nd son of 21st Lord Dacre) estate developer and Speaker of House of Commons, 1872–84, managed family estate of Glynde, Sussex, developing cement works, steam flour mill, and dairy, expanding from 3,300 acres to 4,500 acres; this estate given to his son when he inherited main Dacre estate 1890.

Broadwood, Henry Fowler, 1811–93, pianos, £84,550, purchased Lyne estate, 5,052 acres, Surrey.

Bryant, Wilberforce, 1837–1906, match manufacturer, £98,577, purchased Stoke Park estate, Bucks., High Sheriff, Bucks., 1892.

Cammell, Charles, 1810–79, steel manufacturer, £250,000, purchased Norton Hall estate; Ditchingham estate, Hants, 2,000 acres; Brookefield Hall estate, Hathersage, Derby; in all owned 6,563 acres.

Campbell, Colin Minton, 1827–85, £189,921, pottery manufacturer, purchased Woodseat estate, Uttoxeter, Staffs (534 acres worth £3,901 p.a. 1873).

Charlesworth, John Charlesworth, 1815–80, coal owner, £200,000 purchased Grinton Lodge estate, Swaledale, York, WR, in all owned 3,469 acres.

Cochrane, Sir Henry, 1836–1904, mineral water manufacturer, £47,358, purchased Woodbrook estate, Bray, Co. Wicklow, and Lisgar Castle, Co. Cavan.

Colman, Jeremiah James, 1830–98, mustard manufacturer, £883,380, purchased small estate at Carrow, Norwich, and holiday home at Corton, Suffolk (315 acres worth £1,512 p.a., Norfolk, and 49 acres worth £316 p.a. Suffolk, 1873).

Cook, John Mason, 1834–99, travel agent (son of Thomas Cook) £622,534; son, Thomas Albert Cook, 1867–1914, entered family business, purchased 8,000-acre Sennowe Park estate, Norfolk, built Sennowe Park mansion.

Cookson, Norman Charles, 1841–1909, lead manufacturer, £201,403, purchased Oakwood, Wylam and Nether Warden, Hexham, Northumberland.

Courtauld, Samuel III, 1793–1881, silk manufacturer, £700,000, purchased Gosfield Hall estate, Essex, 2,000 acres.

Crawshay, George, 1821–96, iron and heavy engineering, £25, purchased Haughton Castle estate, Northumberland, obliged to sell it in 1889.

Dale, Sir David, 1829–1906, iron and steel manufacturer, and railway manager, £122,504, purchased West Lodge, nr. Darlington.

Daw, William Adams, 1856–1908, builder, £189,774, purchased sporting lodge in Hampshire.

Dobson, Sir Benjamin Alfred, 1847–98, textile machinery manufacturer, £240,134, purchased country house, Doffcockers, Lancs.

Edwards, James Coster, 1828–96, Tile and brick manufacturer, £54,904, purchased West Tower estate and Trevor Hall, Llangollen, Denbigh, High Sheriff, Denbingh, 1892.

English, John, 1789–1878, needle manufacturer, £2,000, purchased estate nr. Feckenham, Worcs.

Evans, Sir John, 1823–1908, paper manufacturer, £147,347, purchased small estate nr. Hemel Hempstead, Herts. (117 acres worth £1,404 p.a., 1873).

Fairbairn, Sir Andrew, 1828–1901, textile machinery manufacturer, £349,612, purchased Askham Grange estate, nr. York, High Sheriff, Yorks., 1892.

Farley, Reuben, 1826–99, ironfounder, £167,735, art collection; 3 sons acquired estates in Hunts. and War.

Firth, Mark, 1819–80, steel manufacturer, £600,000, purchased Oakbrook estate, nr. Sheffield, 1860; gave 35 acres of Page Hall estate, Sheffield, to form Firth Park, 1875; purchased shooting estate at Moscar (not identified) (231 acres worth £1241, 1873).

Fowler, Sir John, 1817–98, civil engineer (Forth Bridge) £179,330, purchased Braemore Castle, 1865; Inverbroom, 1867; in all 57,000 acres, Ross.

Freake, Sir Charles James, 1814–84, speculative builder, £697,101, built Onslow Square, Onslow Gardens, Cranley Gardens, etc. on the Smith Charity estate, Kensington; purchased Copt Hall and Fulwell Park estates, Middx. (for residence and possible future development).

Gamble, Sir David, 1823–1907, chemical manufacturer, £388,265, purchased country house, Windlehurst, nr. St Helen's, and a steam yacht (36 acres worth £3,069 p.a., 1873).

Gibbs, Henry Hucks, 1st Lord Aldenham, 1819–1907, guano merchant, purchased Aldenham estate, Herts. (1,257 acres, worth £2,406 p.a., 1873).

Gooch, Sir Daniel, 1816–89, railway engineer, £669,658, purchased Clewer Park estate, nr. Windsor, and farm in Wilts.; will provided that eldest son lay out £400,000 in land purchase.

Gordon, Harry Panmure, 1837–1902, stockbroker, £86,714, houses in Brighton, Carlton House Terrace, and country house near Rickmansworth, Herts.; had best collection of carriages in the world; bred collies.

Greene, Edward, 1815–91, brewer, £356,945, purchased Nether Hall estate, Pakenham, Suffolk and leased Ixworth Abbey estate.

Hambro, Carl Joachim, 1807–77, banker, £500,000, purchased Milton Abbey estate, 8,500 acres, Dorset, 1852, worth £8,667 p.a. (1878).

Harben Sir Henry, 1823–1911, life assurance manager, £393,929, purchased Warnham estate, Sussex.

Heath, Robert, II, 1816–93, ironmaster, £320,045, purchased Biddulph Grange estate, Staffs., owned in all 3,300 acres.

Hedley, Thomas, 1809–90, soap manufacturer, £107,103, purchased Coxlodge Hall, Gosforth, Northumb. (331 acres worth £422 p.a., 1873).

Hermon, Edward, 1822–81, cottontot, £588,000, purchased Wyfold Court estate, Oxon. and built country house, 1872–6; 938 acres, worth £823 p.a. (1873); also Scottish shooting lodge.

Hick, John, 1815–94, steam engine manufacturer, £149,707, purchased Mytton Hall estate, Lancs.

Hingley, Sir Benjamin, 1830–1905, chain and anchor manufacturer, £158,696, High Sheriff, Worcs., 1900; purchased country house, Hatherton Lodge, Cradley, Worcs.; heir, nephew, Sir George Hingley, purchased substantial estate, Worcs.

Howard, James, 1821–89, agricultural machinery manufacturer, £82,703, purchased Clapham Park estate, Beds., 1,000 acres.

Houlder, Edwin Savory, 1828–1901, shipowner, £128,382, purchased country house, Ingress Abbey, Greenhithe, Kent, and land in Argentina.

Illingworth, Alfred, 1827–1907, worsted spinner, £172,470, purchased country house with shooting, Stanbury, nr. Howarth, York, WR.

Inman, William, 1825–81, shipowner, £121,359, purchased country house, Upton Court, Cheshire, and house on Windermere with steam launch.

Johnston, John Lawson, 1839–1900, Bovril manufacturer, £850,000, owned yacht, 'White Ladye', on which he died in Cannes harbour; heir, 2nd son, bought estate in Beds. (see App. 3).

Kynoch, George, 1834–91, gunpowder, £ negligible, purchased Hamstead Hall, Handsworth, Staffs. with 300-acre park; died in 'comparative poverty' in Johannesburg.

Laverton, Abraham, 1819–86, woollen manufacturer, £47,417, purchased large farm at Sutton Veny, Wilts., and castle at Farleigh, Hungerford, Berks. (288 acres worth £2,311 p.a., Wilts. (1873)).

Lewis, William Thomas, 1st Lord Merthyr, 1837–1914, coal owner, £615,522, purchased Heans Castle estate, Saundersfoot, Pembroke.

Lister, Samuel Cunliffe, 1st Lord Masham, 1815–1906, wool combing machine, £633,637, purchased Swinton estate, York, WR for £400,000, 1883; Jervaulx estate, York, WR for £310,000, 1887, High Sheriff, Yorks., 1887.

Lowood, John Grayson, 1835–1902, refractory materials manufacturer, £141,156, purchased Swinton Hall, nr. Rotherham.

Lubbock, John, 1st Lord Avebury, 1834–1913, banker, £315,137, purchased Kingsgate Castle estate, Kent, and High Elms, Downe, Kent.

Lysaght, John, 1832–95, galvanised sheet manufacturer, £424,214, purchased Hengrave Hall estate, Suffolk.

Matheson, Hugh Mackay, 1821–98, overseas trader and international mining director, £88,895, purchased Elswick House, Strathpeffer, Ross-shire, launched Rio Tinto Co.

Morley, Samuel, 1809–86, hosiery manufacturer, £484,291, purchased Hall Place, Leigh, Kent, 1,400 acres, built house, 1872–6.

Mulholland, John, 1st Lord Dunleath of Ballywater, 1819–95, linen manufacturer, purchased Southwell estate, Downpatrick, 1865, later expanded in Co. Down and Tyrone.

Nettlefold, Joseph Henry, 1827–81, screw manufacturer, £287,887, purchased Allean House, Pitlochry, Perth.

Owen, Owen, 1847–1910, department store owner, £477,800, purchased Penmaenmanor estate, 1896, and estate nr. Machynlleth, 1906.

Palmer, Sir Charles Mark, 1822–1907, coal and ironmaster, shipbuilder, £15,226, purchased Grinkle Park estate, York, NR in 1876, 2,664 acres, increased to 4,000 acres by 1907, built house 1882.

Palmer, George, 1818–97, biscuit manufacturer, £969,373, 'became important landowner in Berks and adjoining counties'.

Pender, Sir John, 1816–96, telegraph and cables, £337,180, purchased Middleton Hall estate, Linlithgow, Minard Castle, Argyll, and Footscray Place, Kent, London town house Arlington Street.

Peto, Sir Samuel Morton, 1809–89, contractor, £0 (bankrupt), purchased Somerleyton estate, Suffolk, and built country house, 1855, London town house, Kensington Palace Gardens, bankrupt 1867.

Platt, John, 1817–72, machinery manufacturer, £800,000, purchased country estate in Llanfairfechan, Carnarvon, High Sheriff, Carnarvon.

Quilter, William, 1808–88, accountant, £580,934, purchased Silwood estate, Suffolk, rebuilt Bawdsey Manor, Woodbridge, Suffolk, London town house, South Audley Street.

Rae, George, 1817–1902, banker, £192,000, puchased country house, Redcourt, Claughton, Cheshire; large collection of pre-Raphaelites (Ford Madox Brown, Burne Jones, and Rossetti).

Richardson, John Wigham, 1837–1908, shipbuilder, £92,001, purchased Hindley Hall estate, Stocksfield, Northumb., 1902.

Ruston, Joseph, 1835–97, agricultural machinery manufacturer, £929,348, purchased Monks Manor estate, Lincs., High Sheriff, Lincs.

Samuelson, Sir Bernhard, 1820–1905, agricultural engineering, £755,793, purchased Bodicote Grange, Oxon.

Salt, Sir Titus, 1803–76, worsted manufacturer, £400,000, purchased small estate, and country house, Lightcliffe, Yorks, WR (close to Saltaire; 282 acres worth £1,359 p.a., 1873).

Sanger, George, 1825–1911, circus owner, £33,805, purchased Park Farm estate, Finchley, Middx.

Short, John Young, 1844–1900, shipbuilder, £384,898, purchased Braweth Hall estate, nr. Thirsk, York, NR.

Shuttleworth, Joseph, 1819–83, agricultural engineering, £554,613, purchased Hartsholme estate, nr. Lincoln, 1861, Old Warden estate, Beds., 1871.

Siemens, Sir Charles William, 1823–83, electrical manufacturer, £393,858, purchased Sherwood estate, nr. Tunbridge Wells, Kent.

Singer, Isaac, 1811–75, sewing machine, £ c. 900,000 (in Britain), purchased Fernham estate, Paignton, nr. Torquay, and built country house The Wigwam. Eldest son, Paris, remodelled Wigwam in style of Versailles and Petit Trianon, and invented and developed Palm Beach, Florida; second son, Sir Mortimer, purchased Milton Hill estate, Berks., High Sheriff, Berks. 1921; third son, Washington, purchased Norman Court estate, Wilts., High Sheriff, Wilts., 1924.

Smith, George Samuel Fereday, 1812–91, canal and colliery manager, £174,127, purchased Grovehurst estate, nr. Tunbridge Wells, Kent, 1870, High Sheriff, Kent, 1884.

Street, George, 1827–93, advertising agent, £6,474, purchased country house, Heathmount, East Liss, Hants., 1876.

Thompson, Robert, 1850–1908, shipbuilder, £159,804, purchased Over Dimsdale Hall estate, nr. Darlington.

Walter, John, III, 1818–94, owner of *The Times,* £310,229, purchased Bearwood estate, Berks. and built country house; also owned land in Hants.

Wardle, Sir Thomas, 1831–1909, silk dyer, £50,277, purchased Swainsley Hall estate, nr. Butterton, Staffs.

Waterhouse, Alfred, 1830–1905, architect, £163,575, purchased Yattenden Court estate, 700 acres, Newbury, Berks., and built country house.

Whitworth, Sir Joseph, 1803–87, machine tool manufacturer, £462,928, purchased Stancliffe estate, nr. Matlock, Derby, built house 1872, notable for iron billiard table and Shorthorn herd.

Wilson, Arthur, 1836–1909, shipowner, £673,041, purchased Tranby Croft estate, 3,000 acres, York, ER, built house, 1874–6, scene of baccarat scandal, 1890, Master of Holderness Hounds.

Wilson, Charles Henry, 1st Lord Nunburnholme, 1833–1907, shipowner, £988,000, purchased Warter Priory estate, 8,000 acres, York, ER, London town house, Grosvenor Square.

Wostenholm, George, 1800–76, cutlery manufacturer, £250,000, purchased country house and 150 acres, Sharrow, nr. Sheffield.

Wright, Whitaker, 1845–1904, financier, company promoter, £148,200, purchased Lea Park estate, 1,400 acres, Godalming for £250,000, and spent £400,00 on house, renamed Witley Park, theatre under one lake, billiard room under another; 1903 prosecuted for swindling (Ponderevo in H. G. Wells's *Tono Bungay*), 1904 suicide.

Note

See Table 2, Chapter 3 (p. 71). Those listed above are all those businessmen in the *Dictionary of Business Biography* who died before 1914 and who acquired landed estates or country houses, except for the 30 millionaires in Table 2, who are listed in Appendices 1 and 2. Thus, there were 294 non-millionaire businessmen in Table 2, of whom 90 (31 per cent) are listed in Appendix 4 (i) (a); of these, 18 (6 per cent) acquired houses in the country, and 72 (25 per cent) purchased landed estates ranging between a few hundred acres and 34,000 acres. The 'set' of 294 non-millionaire businessmen includes many public servants, professional men, and salaried managers, as well as owner-manager businessmen: see discussion in Chapter 3 (pp. 69–70). The individuals in this listing are arranged in alphabetical order, following the arrangement in *DBB*, and this is repeated in Appendix 4 (ii).

(i) (B) SCOTTISH BUSINESSMEN LEAVING UNDER £1 MILLION AND DYING BEFORE 1914 WHO ACQUIRED LAND

Gunnis, George Ponton, 1824–79, merchant, £138,695, 'merchant and landowner'.

White, John, d. 1881, chemical manufacturer, £886,496, 'chemical manufacturer and landowner', son of John White, chemical manufacturer, d. 1860, worth £374.

Moffat, John, 1815–82, civil engineer, £194,143, 'civil engineer and landowner'. Father was 'land factor'.

Dunlop, Alexander, 1802–83, landowner, £324,800; father was foreign merchant.

Young, James, 1812–83, chemist, £165,660, 'chemist and landowner, of Young's Paraffin Light and Mineral Oil Co.'; father was a joiner.

Baxter, Mary Ann, 1802–85, landowner, £283,586, 'landowner'; father was linen merchant.

Campbell, Colin, 1820–86, rope manufacturer, £629,176, 'rope manufacturer, landowner, director N.Z. Australian Land Co.', son of Colin Campbell, West India merchant, d. 1863, worth £189,351.

Kirkpatrick, Alexander, 1818–87, stockbroker, £174,807, 'Glasgow stockbroker and landowner'.

Beveridge, James Adamson, 1833–88, manufacturer, £139,505, 'manufacturer and landowner', partner in Erskine, Beveridge & Co., Dunfermline.

Younger, William, d. 1889, brewer, £328,209, 'brewer and landowner', Dumfries.

Neilson, Walter Montgomerie, d. 1889, engineer, ironmaster, £282,383, 'engineer, ironmaster, and landowner, partner Lancefield Forge Co., Glasgow'.

Carnegie, David, 1814–90, merchant, £246,938, 'merchant and landowner, Aklie Colagel D. Carnegie & Co., Gothenburg'; father with East India Co.

Baxter, William Edward, 1825–90, merchant, £128,903, 'merchant and landowner, M.P.'; father was Dundee merchant.

Mackinnon, Sir William, 1823–93, merchant, £560,563, 'merchant and landowner, founded British East Africa Co.', son of Duncan Mackinnon, distiller, d. 1836, worth £536.

Findlay, John Ritchie, 1825–98, newspaper owner, £299,332, 'owner of *Scotsman* and landowner'.

Orr, James, 1825–99, publisher, £787,034, 'wholesale publisher and landowner', son of Francis Orr, publisher.

Cox, Robert, 1845–99, glue manufacturer, £543,503, 'glue manufacturer and landowner and M.P.', son of George Cox, glue manufacturer.

Cox, George Addison, 1821–99, textile manufacturer, £218,499, 'textile manufacturer, Dundee, and landowner'.

Johnston, George, 1823–1901, banker, £854,492, 'banker, Edinburgh and Cupar, and landowner', son of William Johnston, banker, d. 1868, worth £260,311.

Coats, George, 1847–1902, sewing thread manufacturer, £571,873, 'thread manufacturer and landowner', son of Sir Peter Coats, thread manufacturer, d. 1890, worth £214,000.

Burns, George Arbuthnot, 1st Lord Inverclyde, 1862–1906, shipowner, £295,456, 'shipowner, Greenock, and landowner'.

White, John Campbell, 1st Lord Overtoun, 1842–1908, chemical manufacturer, £689,022, 'chemical manufacturer and landowner', son of James White, chemical manufacturer, d. 1884.

Weir, James Alexander, 1846–1910, paper manufacturer, £691,392, 'paper manufacturer and landowner', son of James Weir, solicitor.

King, Robert, 1848–1910, manufacturing chemist, £337,015, 'manufacturing chemist and landowner, Hurlet & Campsie Alum Co.', son of John King, merchant.

Birkmyre, John, 1835–1910, rope manufacturer, £319,014, 'rope manufacturer and landowner (further £110,000 abroad).'

Smith, Finlay, 1830–1911, tobacco merchant, £552,414, 'tobacco merchant and landowner.'

Borthwick, Sir Thomas, 1835–1912, colonial merchant £320,569, 'colonial merchant and landowner.' Father was a farmer.

Younger, Henry Johnston, 1833–1913, brewer, £385,043, 'brewer, Dunoon, and landowner.'

Source

R. Britton, 'Wealthy Scots, 1876–1913', *Bulletin of the Institute of Historical Research*, 58 (1985), 78–94. The description of occupation, and identification as 'landowner', are as given by Britton.

(ii) THOSE BORN BEFORE 1870 WHO DIED AFTER 1914

Before 1926 the figure in £s refers to the probate value of personalty plus unsettled real estate left at death; after 1926 the figure in £s refers to the probate value of all realty plus personalty left at death.

* refers to purchasers noted in the *Estates Gazette* but not in the *DBB*: see note below.

Addis, Sir Charles Stewart, 1861–1945, banker, £114,299, purchased Woodside estate, Sussex.

Bain, Albert Wellesley, 1853–1937, insurance broker, £134,900, purchased country house, Harlow Grange, Essex.

Banbury, Frederick George, 1st Lord Banbury, stockbroker, 1850–1936, £290,209, purchased country house, Warneford Place, Wilts.

Barham, George Titus, 1860–1937, dairyman, £515,063, purchased Sudbury Park estate and mansion, Middx.; childless, left estate and art collection to the public.

Baxendale, Lloyd Henry, 1853–1937, road haulage, £309,042, purchased Greenham Lodge estate, Newbury, Berks., part sold 1905 to form Newbury racecourse.

Beale, George, 1864–1953, food retailer, £276,599, purchased Pottersbury Lodge, 1,000 acres, Northants; joint Master Grafton Foxhounds, 1934–6.

Bell, Sir Thomas, 1844–1931, industrialist (Dorman Long, steel), £260,000, purchased Red Barns, Coatham, and Arnclisse Hall, Northallerton, Yorks, NR.

Bird, Sir Alfred Frederick, 1849–1922, custard manufacturer, £653,656, purchased country house, The White House, Solihull, art collector.

Bolitho, Thomas Bedford, 1835–1915, tin mine adventurer, £550,038, purchased Tredwidden estate, Buryas Bridge, nr. Penzance; Greenway estate, Dittisham, Devon, Tregenna Castle, St Ives, Cornwall.

Bonsor, Sir Henry Cosmo Orme, 1848–1929, brewer, £717,528, purchased Liscobe Park estate, Leighton Buzzard, Bucks, and Kingswood, Epsom, Surrey.

Boot, Jesse, 1st Lord Trent, 1850–1931, Boots the Chemists, £222,317, purchased Glenborrodale estate, Ardnamurchan, Ross.

Broadhurst, Sir Edward Tootal, 1858–1922, cottontot, £149,903, purchased country house, Manor House, Congleton, Cheshire, and Scottish grouse moor.

Burbridge, Sir Richard, 1847–1917, Harrods, and Dickins & Jones, £186,262, purchased Littleton Park estate, 11,000 acres, Shepperton, Middx., a further 1,500 acres, Middx., and 52,000 acres in W. Australia, and land in Canada.

Chivers, John, 1857–1929, jam manufacturer, £54,450, purchased Impington Hall estate, Cambs., 1925.

*Clark, Kenneth Mackenzie, 1868–1932, sewing thread manufacturer, £100,780, purchased Sudbourne Hall estate, 13,800 acres, Suffolk, 'the largest shooting estate in England'; Acharacle estate, Ardnamurchan, 75,000 acres, Ross, 1919.

Cross, Herbert Shepherd, 1847–1916, textile bleacher, £374,639, purchased Hamel's Park estate, Herts, 1884.

D'Arcy, William Knox, 1849–1917, petroleum, £990,988, purchased Bylaugh Park estate, Norfolk, and mansion in Stanmore, Middx.

Davis, Sir Edmund Gabriel, 1862–1939, mining financier, £394,518, purchased Chilham Castle estate, nr. Canterbury, Kent, 1918, and villas in France and Italy.

*Devitt, Sir Thomas, 1839–1923, shipowner, £470,576, purchased Bear Wood estate, 1919; London town house, Buckingham Gate.

Dewrance, Sir John, 1858–1937, coal and engineering, £589,171, purchased Wretham Hall estate, Thetford, Norfolk, High Sheriff, Kent, 1925.

Dorman, Sir Arthur John, 1848–1931, steel manufacturer, £132,173, purchased Nunthorpe estate, nr. Middlesbrough.

Douglas, George, 1858–1947, woollen and worsted dyer, £391,248, purchased Farfield Hall estate, 500 acres, Addingham, York, WR.

Drewe, Julius Charles, 1856–1931, Home & Colonial Stores, £207,700, purchased Culverdon Castle, Tunbridge Wells, Kent, 1890, Wadhurst Hall estate, Sussex, Drewsteignton estate, 1,500 acres, Devon, and built Drogo Castle.

Fielding, Charles William Ewing, 1863–1941, mining executive, £73,170, purchased 1,200 acre estate, Billinghurst, Sussex.

Forwood, Sir William Bowyer, 1840–1928, Liverpool merchant, £357,358, purchased country house, Bromborough Hall, Cheshire.

Foster, Alfred James, 1869–1959, lead manufacturer, £2,625, purchased Hindley Hall estate, Stocksfield, Northumberland.

Fuller, George Pargiter, 1833–1927, rubber manufacturer, £431,011, inherited Neston Park, purchased Great Chalfield estate, Wilts.

Gamage, Albert Walter, 1855–1930, department store owner, £28,766, purchased country house, Grange Farm, Chartridge, Herts.

Garforth, Sir William Edward, 1845–1921, colliery manager, £108,747, purchased country house, Halesfield, nr. Altofts, York, WR and Snydale Hall estate, York, WR.

Goodenough, Frederick Cranford, 1866–1934, banker, £120,580, purchased Filkins estate, Oxon.

*Gray, Sir William Cresswell, 1867–1924, shipbuilder, £279,069, purchased Membland estate, Devon, 1900, Thorp Perrow estate, Bedale, York, WR, 1904, High Sheriff Co., Durham, 1909.

Greenway, Charles, 1st Lord Greenway, 1857–1934, petroleum, £298,953, purchased Stanbridge Earls estate, Hants.

Harmwood-Banner, Sir John Sutherland, 1846–1927, accountant and steel manufacturer, £449,279, purchased country house, Ingmire Hall, Sedbergh, York, WR.

Heath, Sir James, 1852–1942, ironmaster, colliery owner, £61,514, purchased country seat, War.

Hewlett, Alfred, 1830–1918, coal owner, £286,509, purchased Haseley Manor estate, War., and country house, The Grange, Coppull, nr. Wigan, Lancs.

*Hill, Sir James, 1849–1936, Bradford wool merchant, £450,817, purchased Hexton Manor estate, Herts.

Hirst, Hugo, 1st Lord Hirst, 1863–1943, electrical engineering, £498,651, purchased Berks. estate with racing stables.

Hollins, Henry Ernest, 1842–1920, cottontot, £198,999, purchased country house and estate, Westmorland.

Hooley, Ernest Terah, 1859–1947, company promoter £nil, purchased Papworth Hall estate, Cambs., Risley Hall, Derby, owned land in six counties, High Sheriff, Cambs.; bankrupt 1898.

Horlick, Sir James, 1844–1921, malted milk manufacturer, £450,481, purchased large Sussex estate, exhibited Shorthorns, and Oxford Down sheep; Cowley Manor, Glos., rebuilt 1890; London town house Carlton House Terrace.

Houldsworth, Sir William Henry, 1834–1917, cotton and iron manufacturer, £467,489, purchased Coodham estate, Ayr.

Jackson, William Lawies, 1840–1917, tanner, currier, leather merchant, £91,014, purchased country house, Allerton Hall, Leeds, Park Hill estate, nr. Doncaster.

Johnston, George, 1st Lord Luke, 1873–1943, Bovril manufacturer, £356,020, purchased Stowell Park estate, Northleach, Glos. (sold to 1st Lord Vestey, 1923), Odell Castle estate, Beds., 1934.

Lancaster, Arthur Henry, 1841–1928, lead manufacturer, £527,731, purchased Sendholme estate, Send, Surrey.

Lawrence, Sir Joseph, 1848–1919, industrialist, £26,600, became 'a country squire' in Surrey.

Lawson, Edward Levy, 1st Lord Burnham, 1833–1916, newspaper owner, £267,871, purchased Hall Barn and 4,000-acre estate, Bucks.

Lee, Lennox Bertram, 1864–1949, calico printer, £282,556, purchased How Caple Court estate, Hereford, High Sheriff, Hereford, 1915.

*Leon, Sir Herbert, 1850–1926, stockbroker, £660,620, purchased Bletchley Park estate, Fenny Stratford, before 1904, and Denbigh Hall estate, in 1918, High Sheriff, Bucks., 1900. 1 of 2 principal landowners in parish of 3,714 acres.

Liberty, Sir Arthur Lasenby, 1843–1917, store owner, £343,505, purchased Lee Manor estate, Chesham, Bucks., over 3,000 acres, High Sheriff, Bucks.

Livesey, James, 1833–1925, civil engineer, £304,308, purchased Rotherfield estate, Sussex, villas in France and Norway.

Lysaght, William Royse, 1858–1945, steel manufacturer, £277,368, purchased country house, Castleford, Chepstow, Monmouth.

McKenna, Reginald, 1863–1943, banker, £89,448, purchased Halnaker Park estate, Sussex, built house 1936, owned 3 houses designed by Lutyens.

McLaren, Charles Benjamin Bright, 1st Lord Aberconway, 1850–1934, shipbuilder, iron and coal, £15,043, married Laura Pochin sole heiress of Henry Pochin, chemical manufacturer, owner of Bodnant estate, Denbigh, created Bodnant garden, built London town house, Aberconway House, South Street, 1920–2.

Mallerby-Deeley, Sir Harry C., 1863–1937, property speculator, £488,863, purchased Ravensbury estate, Biggin in Derby, Tamworth. 1919 loaned Lord Edward Fitzgerald £60,000 on his reversionary interest in Duke of Leinster's estates, which Fitzgerald inherited 1923, Mallerby-Deeley and his heir enjoying income of £80,000 p.a., from which he gave bankrupt Duke £1,000 p.a., until Duke committed suicide in 1976.

Markham, Charles Paxton, 1865–1926, coal, iron, engineering, £632,139, purchased Haslam Hall, nr. Chesterfield, and Scottish grouse moor.

Nelson, Sir Amos, 1860–1947, textile manufacturer, £444,246, purchased Gledstone estate, nr. Skipton, York, WR., 6,000 acres, 40 farms, Lutyens designed 'one of most magnificent houses in Yorkshire', 1925–7, Gledstone Hall.

*Norman, Sir Henry, 1858–1939, coal owner, £5,594, purchased Chiddingford estate, Surrey, 1922. 1 of 8 principal landowners in parish of 7,036 acres.

Oliver, Frederick Scott, 1864–1934, draper, c.£750,000, purchased Checkendon Court, Oxon, 1905, sold 1928; Edgerston estate, Roxburgh. Store merged with Marshall & Snelgrove, 1919, and acquired Harvey Nichols; bought out by Debenham Group for £750,000, 1926.

*Palmer, Alfred, 1852–1936, biscuits, £28,795, purchased Wokefield Park estate, Stratfield Mortimer, Berks.

Pease, John William Beaumont, 1st Lord Wardington, 1869–1950, banker, £83,264, purchased Wardington Manor estate, nr. Banbury, Oxon.

Pease, Joseph Albert, 1st Lord Gainford, 1860–1943, industrialist, £26,878, purchased Headlam Hall estate, Co. Durham.

Philips, Sir Ivor, 1861–1940, industrialist, £26,563, 2nd son of Sir James Erasmus Philips, 12th bart, vicar of Warminster, Wilts.; purchased Cosheton Hall estate, Pembroke, and Amroth Castle, Pembroke; knighted 1900.

Pirrie, William James, 1st Vicount Pirrie, 1847–1924, shipbuilder, £175,841, purchased Witley Park estate, Godalming, Surrey, formerly owned by Whitaker Wright, 1911.

Richardson, James Nicholson, 1846–1921, linen manufacturer, £75,000; father, linen manufacturer, purchased Mount Canfield estate, Armagh, 1846, from Lord Charlemont.

Salomons, Sir David Lionel Goldsmid-Stern, 1851–1925, electrical engineer, £388,412, inherited baronetcy and Broomhill estate, Tunbridge Wells, from uncle, banker David Salomons (1873), and expanded estate (305 acres worth £1,043 p.a. 1873); London town house, Grosvenor Street.

Sears, John George, 1870–1916, shoe manufacturer, £400,719, purchased Collingtree Grange estate, nr. Northampton, built up prize Shorthorn herd.

Smith, Vivian Hugh, 1st Lord Bicester, 1867–1956, banker, £212,277, purchased Tismor Park estate, nr. Bicester, Oxon. Chairman, Bicester Hunt committee, Lord Lieutenant, Oxfordshire, 1934–54.

Steel, Henry, 1863–1920, steel manufacturer, £558,472, purchased Skellow Grange estate, nr. Doncaster.

Stern, Sir Edward David, 1854–1933, banker, £66,414, purchased Fan Court estate, Chertsey, Surrey, High Sheriff, Surrey, 1904, (first cousin, James Julius Stern, d. 1901 leaving £1.1 million; first cousin, Herbert Stern, 1st Lord Michelham cr. 1905, d. 1919 leaving £2 million).

Vestey, William, 1st Lord Vestey, 1859–1940, meat retailer, £261,515 (but said to be worth £2.15 million), purchased Stowell Park estate, Glos., 1923, from Sir George Lawson Johnston, Bovril manufacturer; Warter Priory estate, York, ER, 8,000 acres (previously bought by 1st Lord Nunburnholme), built Stowell Hill, Somerset, 1927.

Vickers, Albert, 1838–1919, steel and arms manufacturer, £774,686, purchased Meallmore estate, Daviot, Inverness.

Waring, Samuel James, 1st Lord Waring, 1850–1940, furniture, £ nil, purchased Gopsall estate, Twycross, Leics., 1918.

Williamson, Archibald, 1st Lord Forres, 1860–1931, S. American merchant £187,590, purchased Glenogil estate, Forfar, Angus.

Wright, Sir John Roper, 1843–1926 steel manufacturer, £150,487, purchased Widcombe Manor estate, nr. Bath.

Note

See Table 3, Chapter 3 (p. 72). Those listed above are all those businessmen in *DBB* who were born before 1870 and who died after 1914, and who acquired landed estates or country houses, except for the 47 millionaires in Table 3, who are listed in Appendix 3. Thus, there were 332 non-millionaire businessmen in Table 3, of whom 67 (21 per cent) are listed in Appendix 4 (ii); of these, 8 (3 per cent) acquired houses in the country, and 59 (18 per cent) purchased landed estates ranging between a few hundred acres and 13,800 acres (88,000 acres if Scottish moors are included). The 'set' of 332 non-millionaire businessmen includes many public servants, professional men, and salaried managers, as well as owner-manager businessmen: see discussion in Chapter 3 (pp. 69–70). In Appendix 4(ii) there are also 7 non-millionaire business-purchasers, marked by an asterisk, who are not in *DBB*, included by way of illustrating the type of such information recorded in the *Estates Gazette*.

Sources

Dictionary of Business Biography, 5 vols. (1984–6), all those entries which note that the businessman in question acquired a country estate or a country house. The distinction between 'country estate' and 'country house' is mainly derived from the descriptive terms used by the contributors to the entries, supplemented in some instances by information from *The Times* and the *Estates Gazette*. A 'country estate' being acquired not as an income-producing asset, or as an asset which could support a country house, but for reasons of pleasure, display, recreation, or status, might be small in extent and annual value, but larger than a simple paddock and hay field, probably 500 acres upwards.

Clive Aslet, *The Last Country Houses* (New Haven, Conn. and London, 1982).
J. Mordaunt Crook, *The Rise of the Nouveaux Riches* (1999).
Mark Girouard, *The Victorian Country House* (New Haven, Conn. and London, 1979).

Index